4 $2.50 N

D1329966

HAVELOCK ELLIS

BY THE SAME AUTHOR

Novels

TWO OF A KIND
ABOUT LEVY
AT SEA
DEAD CENTRE
PIE IN THE SKY
THE WAY TO SANTIAGO
A MAN REPRIEVED
OCCASION OF GLORY

Short Stories

A DATE WITH A DUCHESS

Autobiography

THE MAGIC OF MY YOUTH

Biography

NO EARTHLY COMMAND

Travel

GLORY DEAD
THE WATERSHED

For Children

THE MAN FROM DEVIL'S ISLAND

HAVELOCK ELLIS IN OLD AGE

Havelock Ellis

A BIOGRAPHY BY

Arthur Calder-Marshall

RUPERT HART-DAVIS
SOHO SQUARE LONDON
1959

© Arthur Calder-Marshall 1959

Hum
PR
6009
L8
Z62

LIBRARY
FLORIDA STATE UNIVERSITY
TALLAHASSEE, FLORIDA

Printed in Great Britain by Richard Clay and Company, Ltd.
Bungay, Suffolk

To Françoise Delisle

To describe the products of a single man's activity, whenever it is worth doing at all, is to write prolegomena to history. To describe the birth and growth of a great man as he was in his real nature, physical and psychical—as a grape-cluster on the tree of life and not as a drop of alcohol in the vat of civilisation—that is biography.

I have it against you, then, that you who are charged with this high task are perpetually seeking to merge it in a lower or at all events a different task. But I would content myself if, after all, you really enabled me to gain a picture of the man.

Havelock Ellis, *An Open Letter to Biographers*

Whenever a great literary personality comes before us with these imperative claims, it is our business to discover or divine its fundamental instincts; we ought to do this with the same austerity and keen-eyed penetration as, if we were wise, we should exercise in choosing the comrades of our daily life. He poses well in public; he has said those brave words on the platform; he has written those rows of eloquent books—but what (one asks oneself) is all that to me? I want to get at the motive forces at work in the man; to know what his intimate companions thought of him; how he acted in the affairs of every day, and in the great crises of his life; the fashion of his face and form, the tones of his voice. How he desired to appear is of little importance; I can perhaps learn all that it imports me to know from a single involuntary gesture, or one glance into his eyes.

Preface to *The New Spirit*, 4th ed., 1926

ILLUSTRATIONS

Havelock Ellis in old age *frontispiece*
James Hinton *facing page* 78
Olive Schreiner 90
Havelock Ellis as a medical student 106
Edith Ellis about the time of her marriage 128
Amy 142
Lily 176
Margaret Sanger 198
Edith Ellis in 1914 206
Hugh de Selincourt 250
Françoise Delisle 254

A Note

HAVELOCK ELLIS dwelt in a world of emotions, ideas and spiritual intuitions. What he did is less important than how he did, why he did, and the contrast between what he thought he was doing and what he was actually doing.

Among his published works, which are voluminous even for a man who lived for eighty years and published books for half a century, there is an abundance of autobiographical material. There is scarcely anything that he wrote which did not spring directly from his personal life, however objectively scientific it may appear at first sight.

The major sources of his life are his own autobiography, *My Life*, which in fact covered in detail only the first fifty-seven years of his life and might, at least as regards the last half, have better been called My Marriage; and the autobiography of Françoise Delisle,[1] *Friendship's Odyssey*, the last half of which covers the final twenty-three years of Ellis's life with her.

My Life is a strange, tantalising and ultimately disappointing book. Ellis spent forty years writing it and adding to it in order to correct what he felt he had expressed crudely or inaccurately. He demanded that it should be published exactly as he had left it. He was afraid that some Mrs Grundy of a publisher would cut out those passages of intimate revelation which he felt, rightly, were at the very centre of his bewildering story. But he did not succeed, as he had hoped, in explaining the strange mystery of his life or of his tempestuous marriage.

Friendship's Odyssey is in a way a far more successful book, and the last half reveals in a most moving way what Havelock Ellis meant in the life of a woman young enough to be his daughter,

[1] Delisle (an anagram of de Ellis) is the pseudonym employed by Mme Françoise Lafitte-Cyon.

who was lifted to a pinnacle of happiness and self-sacrifice and self-fulfilment by her love for him.

With *My Life*, as a biographer, I found it necessary to analyse at what period of the forty years of its composition different passages were written and to check all of them, where possible, against contemporary documents, letters, journals and published work.

In doing this I was helped most generously by Madame Françoise Delisle, who allowed me to see Ellis's unpublished *Australian Journal* and voluminous correspondence to and from Edward Carpenter, Olive Schreiner, John Addington Symonds, F. H. Perrycoste, Radclyffe Hall and others. I was also helped by Gilbert Beith, Edward Carpenter's literary executor, who made available to me Havelock Ellis's, Edith Ellis's and Olive Schreiner's letters to Carpenter. I am also indebted to Mrs Helga S. Hacker for her elucidation of certain references to her father, Professor Karl Pearson, in the Olive Schreiner period. If I have been guilty of inaccuracies with regard to Professor Pearson, it is because I was not allowed to consult the original letters.

I have not tried to supersede *My Life*, which must always command its own authority as Ellis's long meditation on his childhood and marriage. My aim has been to supplement. Where Ellis expressed the significance of an event to himself, I have tried to estimate its significance to Olive Schreiner, shall we say? or to Edith Ellis. This is a deliberate redressing of balances which any biographer must do who is seeking to find not merely how his hero viewed himself but also how others viewed his hero.

With *Friendship's Odyssey* a different problem arose. Françoise Delisle gave her view of her life with Havelock. I have had to give my view of Havelock's life with Françoise. Once again I have tried not to supersede but rather to supplement.

An Open Letter to Biographers has been published in several collections, of which the Everyman's Library *Selected Essays* is the most readily available.

I would like to pay the warmest tribute to Madame Delisle, for whom my admiration and friendship have steadily grown. After some three months of fumbling, I had almost driven her to the verge of despair, when I suddenly understood what the clue to Havelock Ellis's life was. The next day I received a desperate letter from her to say that she felt she could not go on. When would I find wings of my own?

It was wonderful to be able to reply that I had found the wings. I had achieved at last a *rapport* with Havelock Ellis himself which did not depend upon her. Thenceforward we were able to write and talk of him as a person we both knew.

But it produced for Madame Delisle, as I became painfully aware with the deepening of my affection, a spiritual trial very seldom laid upon a woman in her middle seventies. I, young enough to be her son, was exploring the whole life of the man with whom she had spent the last twenty-three years of his life in the completest happiness she had ever known. It was inevitable that my view of the whole life would be different from her view of the part, because mine was more extensive and at the same time more detached.

At times I despaired of the possibility of writing the book, because I feared that we should never reconcile our two visions of the same man. My only bases of faith were that I was convinced, and she was convinced, that we were writing about the same person; and she was such an intrepid person that she had never flinched from facing the facts of a situation.

I frequently found myself going wrong, but was encouraged because I more frequently found myself going right. Mme Delisle in letters and conversations tirelessly led me on.

We had, and still have, a disagreement about religion. I am a Christian and think that Christianity contains all the mystical truths which Havelock Ellis and she discovered, as well as others even more important. She considers that though I have come some little way along the mystic path I am still a prey to superstition, idolatry and adherence to sacramental cannibalism. "One thing I will not tolerate," she said, "is that you should try to pretend that Havelock was a Christian." "I don't want to," I answered, "but you mustn't try to force me to pretend that I am not."

There we have amicably left it. We respect one another's religion and abominate one another's beliefs, but have agreed to postpone the argument until we meet in the Ellisian Fields.

So in recording my debt of gratitude to Françoise Delisle I must state that, though the indulgence to see and quote is hers, the views are mine. I may very well have been wrong in many respects, though I have tried to be as truthful as I am capable of being.

I should like to record that Madame Delisle considers I have not paid enough attention to Havelock Ellis's pacifism. I consider that he was a man of peace, who abhorred violence in all forms and abominated war and evil. I think he considered pacifism as one of many means of preserving peace, but himself laid even more stress on the positive means of solving problems that may issue in violence, through love, good-will, intelligence.

Madame Delisle wishes me to state that she is now, as she has always been, a believer in voluntary euthanasia.

I have been very grateful to Mr J. S. Collis for producing at the same time a study of Ellis's work and life from the more orthodox Ellisian point of view. If he had not been doing so, I would have felt it necessary to expatiate at much greater length on Ellis's influence on his contemporaries and on the content of his writing.

This is a biography of Havelock Ellis and not a literary appreciation or criticism. I realise that I have done scant justice to his literary and scientific work. But I have intentionally concentrated on the psychological aspects of his way of writing.

I must thank Françoise Delisle for permission to quote extracts from Havelock Ellis's unpublished and published work; Messrs Constable for allowing me to view their letters from Ellis to the firm and to quote from the books under their imprint; Messrs Heinemann for permission to quote from *Friendship's Odyssey*, *My Life* and other works by Ellis, including the Essays on Love and Virtue, now published under the title *On Love and Sex*, by Heinemann Medical Books Ltd.

I wish to thank Clifford Bax, Mr and Mrs Dennis-Earle, Dr

Winifred de Kok, E. S. Sachs, Mrs Hacker, Una, Lady Troubridge, Gilbert Beith, Dr Joseph Wortis, Herr Picton-Sommers, the literary executor of Olive Schreiner, Mr Smith, Dr Stanley Jones, Senhor A. H. Bizarro, Mrs Margaret Sanger, Mrs Gregg and Vincent Brome for their stimulating assistance.

Apart from the books mentioned in the Bibliography at the end of this volume, I have been indebted to *Ideas and Beliefs of the Victorians* (Sylvan Press), for its conspect of the intellectual climate of Havelock Ellis's childhood and early manhood, to Houston Peterson's *Havelock Ellis, Philosopher of Love*, for its Appendices on the Commonplace Books and the compendious bibliography up to 1928, and most notably the verbatim report of the Bedborough Trial. Edward Carpenter's autobiography *My Days and Dreams* (George Allen & Unwin Ltd), rather light-weight as autobiographies go, but important as a self-portrait of Ellis's friend and fellow-worker, and the essays collected by Gilbert Beith entitled *Edward Carpenter, In Appreciation* are very useful, showing rather similar ideas to Ellis's working in the temperament of a very dissimilar man.

Apart from unpublished biographical sources, I have used for details of Olive Schreiner's life *The Life of Olive Schreiner* by S. C. Cronwright-Schreiner, *The Letters of Olive Schreiner*, edited by S. C. Cronwright-Schreiner (both published by T. Fisher Unwin), *Not without Honour*, a most unreliable biography by Vera Buchanan-Gould (Hutchinson), *Mrs John Brown* edited by Angela James and Nina Hills (John Murray), *Autobiographies* by W. B. Yeats (Macmillan), which also contains some interesting material on Arthur Symons, and *Memories of Olive Schreiner* by Lyndall Gregg (Chambers). None of these works is wholly satisfactory and the definitive biography of this remarkable woman still remains to be written.

I have consulted *Margaret Sanger, An Autobiography* (Norton), and *The Margaret Sanger Story* by Lawrence Lader (Doubleday), the second of which contains a number of minor inaccuracies with regard to Ellis.

I am indebted to François Lafitte for his brilliant study of

'Homosexuality and the Law', published in the *Journal* of the British Institute for the Study of Delinquency, August, 1958, and to certain articles on homosexuality to which he drew my attention.

I read with profit *Fragments of an analysis with Freud* by Joseph Wortis, M.D. (Simon & Shuster) in which there are very interesting letters from Ellis, clarifying his position in relation to psychoanalysis.

Having made these acknowledgements, I must stress once more that the views expressed in the book are my own and not those of any of the people who have given their assistance so generously. I am aware that in the depiction of certain emotional situations of an imprecise nature I may have been guilty of falsification by putting into words what was never stated or perhaps even thought in words. It will be for the reader to judge whether this course has been wise. But I have been careful to make clear the boundary between evidence and speculation.

In conclusion I wish to thank my wife for her sympathy, her criticism and forbearance over the many months spent in exploring and reliving this long and puzzling life.

A. C.-M.

Cranleigh, Surrey
1957–59

I

I will gladly recognise that now-a-days you generally tell me of the hero's ancestors; formerly you told me nothing of the mothers of great men, seldom even the name, and that is one of the most helpless *lacunae* in the right understanding of genius. . . . And yet while race and family are certainly an enormous factor in the making of every man, I would wish to point out to you that they are not omnipotent—for then the hero's brothers and sisters would always be heroes too.

An Open Letter to Biographers

AT 1 Saint John's Grove, a small semi-detached flint house in Old Croydon, Susannah Wheatley Ellis gave birth to a son and heir at 8.15 on the morning of 2 February 1859, after a night so stormy that the family doctor, Alfred Carpenter, never forgot it.

Susannah Wheatley had married her cousin Edward Peppen Ellis four years before, just after he had been given command, at the age of twenty-eight, of his first merchant ship. It was her only major act of disobedience to her father, who as he lay dying had warned his daughter never to marry a sailor.

He gave the warning perhaps because he himself had been a merchant sea-captain, and love for his ardent clinging wife had forced him to abandon the sea.

Susannah followed neither her father's warning nor her mother's example. She behaved to Captain Ellis as perhaps she would have liked her mother to have behaved to her father. She put no pressure on him to give up his career. During his long voyages, which kept him away some nine months in every year, she carried on very well without him. She combined in herself the qualities of mother and father; and when Captain Ellis came home, he was accepted by her more as a lover than a husband, and by her children more as a visitor than a parent.

The example of married life which the Ellis children had placed before them was, in consequence, less ordinary than they imagined.

Parental life was less continuous than it is in most families, and also more harmonious. There was no conflict between mother and father; married life appeared to be an annual honeymoon, broken by long periods of tranquil separation. It was an arrangement which worked well because Edward Ellis accepted the fact that, while he was captain of his ship, Susannah was captain of his home.

It was thus natural that the naming of their son and heir should fall to Mrs Ellis. She chose Henry Havelock after the hero of the Indian Mutiny, who was a second cousin on her mother's side. He had been given a posthumous baronetcy fifteen months earlier and the fame of his relief of Lucknow was undimmed. But it was not his courage or military ability which led Susannah to name her son after him. What she admired was the fervour of his Baptist faith.

Captain Ellis was no fanatical Christian. He conformed because not to conform would have implied contrary convictions which he did not have. In him the Greek ideal of *μηδὲν ἄγαν* or Nothing Too Much had degenerated into Nothing Very Much. His mediocrity was not golden. Yet he respected in his wife the religious ardour which left him cold.

General Havelock had been converted to the Baptist faith at the age of thirty-four. Susannah Ellis had found hers at half that age, "almost a kind of Quakerism without the Quaker's eccentricities." She was in fact Church of England, with strict evangelical principles, a fundamentalist belief in the literal inspiration of the Bible, the avoidance of all "worldliness" and was a constant attender of church services.

Her conversion had given her an emotional serenity and joy. She was a complete and integrated person, unshaken by doubt because intellectually incurious, unconscious of her narrowness because religion and marriage fully satisfied her emotional needs. Shortly after her conversion a rich aunt offered to take her to Paris, but she refused because she preferred not to go to "that wicked city." Yet she was not a bigot. She did not try to impose her own principles on others. Each person must act according to conscience.

In later life Ellis came to look on her conversion as a misfortune. "Essentially a Suffolk or at all events East Anglian woman—a type in which vitality and character and fine emotional impulse are sometimes happily combined—her full development was arrested. The 'volatility' of the young girl never found its natural matured expression in the woman's life. Grave, though with no formal solemnity, reserved if not exactly repressed, shy and nervous beneath the imposing presence she had inherited from both her parents, she was yet a woman of unmistakable force of character."

It was the force of character, her "great and unconscious power", which impressed itself permanently on her son. But in childhood force of character, religious fervour, shyness and gravity were not qualities which he could analyse; they were aspects of Mother, the source of his being, the fount of all good things. She was even to him many of the things that a father is to most children.

And Harry, as Henry Havelock was known in the family, was to his mother many of the things that a husband is to a wife. He was the only male permanently in the house, the father being away so often and when at home so unobtrusive. Havelock gave his mother a male companionship; and when four more children were born to her, all girls, Havelock, being four years older than the eldest, Louie, came to be elder brother and father rolled up in one.

In such circumstances one might have expected that Havelock's mother would have lavished on him rather more of those caresses which it is the delight of motherhood to give and of childhood to receive. But "her love for her children was not of the petting kind" and "there was no physical intimacy." This was not due to lack of love on either side; they were devoted to each other. I suspect that the true reason was that Susannah Ellis felt so deeply towards her son that she could not give him even the physical tenderness normal from a mother to her son for fear that this maternal love might become entangled with feelings that had to be repressed except when her husband was home on honeymoon.

That this was so is suggested by an incident which Havelock Ellis recalled in *My Life*.[1]

"Once at the age of twelve she took me to spend the day at the London Zoological Gardens. In the afternoon as we were walking side by side along a gravelled path in a solitary part of the Gardens, she stood still, and soon I heard a very audible stream falling to the ground. When she moved on I instinctively glanced behind at the pool on the path, and my mother, having evidently watched my movements, remarked shyly: 'I didn't mean you to see that.' I accepted the incident simply and naturally. Much later in life, recalling the episode—I remembered it clearly so it must have made an impression on my mind—I realised that my very truthful mother's remark could not be taken at its face value. Nothing could have been easier than to step on the grass, where detection might possibly have been avoided, or to find a pretext for sending me a few yards off, or to enter a Ladies Room. Her action said clearly: 'I meant you to see that.' To-day I probably understand it better than she herself could. No doubt there was a shy alarm as to what her now tall serious boy would think of this new experience with his mother, but there was also the impulse to heighten a pleasurable experience by blending with it the excitement of sharing it with her son. There was evidently a little touch of exhibitionism, the added pleasure of mixing a private and slightly improper enjoyment with the presence of a beloved male person, for a mother is always a little in love with her firstborn and only son. Every woman who has a streak of what I have called Undinism will understand the fascination of this emotion on the threshold of intimacy. Her real feeling would have been better stated as: 'I loved you to see but I didn't want you to see if you would have been disgusted.' On the next occasion, some time later, there was no longer any shyness and she confided in me

[1] *My Life*, Eng. ed., pp. 69–70, Am. ed., pp. 85–6. The passage in brackets occurs only in the English edition. There are many minor discrepancies between the English and American editions (most notably the absence of any description of the death of Ellis's mother in the American edition). In each case the publishers observed Ellis's request to print the typescript as they received it; but the American typescript was parcelled some time before his death, and lacked the additions he made to the English script.

beforehand. We had just had dinner at an exhibition and, as there were people strolling about, this time she really took some precautions. She stood on the grass, and before she had finished walked on a few paces and copiously recommenced, while I spontaneously played a protective part and watched to see that no one was approaching. When in much later life I mentioned this experience to Louie, my sister, she assured me that our mother had always been extremely reserved with the girls in regard to this function, and remarked, after consideration: 'She was flirting with you.'

"I could add various significant details which confirm the presence in my mother of this trait, such as the habit of urinating on her hand, which, she confided to me, was good for the skin, but, I doubt not, found pleasurable (I remember, too, that, earlier, when I was about nine or ten, she once thrust suddenly in my face the hot wet diaper she had just removed from the baby, a mischievous little trick played on her serious son, but also, I now think, with latently in it the challenge to accept this function as natural and sweet. I turned my face away in disgust but I perhaps understand her better now)."

I have given this passage at length in Ellis's own words because it cannot be condensed or paraphrased without the injection of alien ideas; and it is essential to understand the significance of this situation. A man is a very complex organism, but it is possible to detect, in even the most complex of us, certain primary situations, just as we can find at the centre of a pearl the speck of grit on which it grew.

Ellis confessed to the "germ of a perversion" in what he called urolagnia, an interest and pleasure in the act of urination, which continued throughout his life, instead of dying away at puberty. Whether he received it as he thought hereditarily from his mother or acquired it from contact with her does not greatly matter. It was the one form of sexual activity which his beloved and revered mother blessed. If she had been able to give him a normal mother-love as well, this oddity of hers might have passed off as something trivial. As it was, the simple act of making water or rather watching his mother, and later other women, make water became invested with the emotions normally expressed and dissipated by a myriad acts of love and tenderness. His reverence for his mother sanctified the act, which became for him one of quite singular beauty.

The reader may be inclined to smile at the endowment of this simple natural act with such qualities of beauty. But consider your own feelings if you had been deprived as a child of all the manifold caresses which are the testimony of love with a mother as wonderful as God and almost as distant-seeming, then suddenly to be given in this oblique way a message of love, a caress so to speak in code betraying an intimacy even deeper than you had hoped for; then the code becomes precious in itself, as a token of love, like half a broken ring or any of the faded mementoes that lovers treasure.

It was a mildly immodest act in a woman normally reserved, and he may have had his mother in mind when, forty-two years after that visit to the Zoological Gardens, he wrote "Men have rhapsodised much on the modesty of women, but a woman who was always modest would be as insipid as a woman who was always courageous would be repellent. An incalculable and dynamic combination of Shyness and Daring is at the core of a woman's fascination."

Whereas some men seek in the women they love qualities they admired in their mothers, either physical, moral or emotional, Havelock Ellis was always drawn to women very different from his mother. She was tall, imposing, reserved, in her quiet way "a tower of strength;" whereas the chief women in his life were very short, ebullient, vital and yet in need of help.

The reason for this, I think, lay in his hereditary resemblance to his mother. The qualities she possessed in a positive developed in him to a superlative degree, because he deliberately modelled his character upon hers. From his father he took only the preference for a middle way between extremes, turning the nothing too much back to a golden mediocrity.

Unlike Lord Fisher, who claimed to remember arguing with his mother whether he should be weaned, Ellis remembered little of his early years. He relied upon scrutiny of early photographs, in the first of which he "looked out into the world from his mother's lap in all the robust and fearless self-satisfaction of babyhood." It was, however, the only portrait in which he ever manifested that attitude. "In the next, dating from a year or so later, one sees a rather sad, puzzled and forlorn little child placed on a large chair and carefully dressed in a frock and an ornamental hat with rosettes coming down over the ears." [1]

As Ellis was imprecise about dates it is hard to decide whether this picture was taken while he was still the only child or after Louie appeared. His first reaction to her arrival was a normal outburst of childish jealousy. "Take away that piece of dirt and rubbish," he shouted.

The main fact, whichever the date may be, is that after his mother weaned him, she was unable to give him the love he needed, in terms which a child of his age could understand. It was a period, it must be remembered, when the favourite precept of child education was "children should be seen and not heard."

Havelock attributed to that time, what was to become his lifelong attitude. "Of Nature I have never been afraid. But the world has always seemed to me to be full of strange human beings, so unknown, mysterious and awe-inspiring, so apt to give joy or pain, so apt also to receive either. I have always felt a mixed reverence and fear of human creatures, so that I have sometimes even been afraid to look into the eyes of strangers; they seemed to me gates into chambers where intimate and terrible secrets lie bare." [1]

Since his mother was at that time the most important person in his life, this was in fact a devastating criticism of her failure to establish what to-day we call a mother–son relationship but in those days was something unknown except to rarely intuitive women. The same thing was going on in countless middle-class Victorian homes, and only here and there did it produce any strong reactions, like those of Samuel Butler in *The Way of All Flesh* and Edmund Gosse in *Father and Son.* Most late-Victorian

[1] *My Life,* Eng. ed., p. 42, Am. ed., p. 54.

children accepted the vagaries of their parents as Alice accepted the Ugly Duchess, the Mad Hatter and The White Queen. Where Ellis's childhood differed from most was that his mother was also the father in the house, and that he did not revolt from her but determined to love her in whatever way she allowed. Perhaps it would be better to say, that however unknown, mysterious and awe-inspiring his mother was, he knew that she loved him, and she knew that he loved her, though they had no language in which to declare their love.

We all of us at times have the feeling of being prisoners within the cells of our own consciousness, and that the best that we can do is to tap out a code with which to communicate with the prisoner in the cell next door. But usually that separating wall is a difference in character, which can be broken through only by imperfect communication. Life would be intolerable, Baudelaire said, if each of us really understood what the other said. But with Havelock Ellis and his mother, it was not that they did not understand, but that they did not dare to say to each other all the things which they might have been able to say, if Captain Ellis had been at home.

When I say this, I hope that no reader will go off and glibly say that Havelock Ellis suffered from an "Oedipus complex." In formulating the concept of an Oedipus complex to symbolise certain mother–son relationships, Freud himself oversimplified the very complex relationships which may exist between mother and son. As a working hypothesis, the concept had a certain limited value. But it very soon became a cramping and vulgarising idea in the minds of his disciples and readers.

At the time when Ellis was a boy of seven, Freud was a boy of ten with his own puzzling problems, such as an uncle younger than he was. For neither Freud nor Ellis were there problems which could be reduced to scientific formulae—or jargon. There was no Oedipus complex, no Undinism, no Urolagnia. Mother liked weeing on her hand and to young Ellis that was marvellous. It showed that despite her distance and godlike power and strength this woman was a human being. He loved her for it as a man may adore a woman, in other respects utterly perfect, for a mole, protrusive ears, large feet or a downy moustache.

Externally the first six years of Ellis's life were of rather more than usual uneventfulness. He learned to read easily by the age of five. He was fairly active, above the average in physical development and below the average in stamina. There was no strong impulse to play games, though he would join in when he couldn't decently refuse. There was a degree of muscular awkwardness, perhaps caused by his being naturally left-handed. He could not throw a ball with his right hand, and though he never wrote with his left, his handwriting was the despair of his teachers. All his energy was in his brain which was "rather of the massive and receptive than the impulsive and active sort." He liked reading more than anything else, because books opened up worlds beyond home.

When Havelock was seven, Captain Ellis took him on a voyage round the world. It was, Havelock Ellis wrote in *My Life*, doubtless for the benefit of his health. There were perhaps other considerations, Captain Ellis feeling that he had never got to know his son and hoping that on the voyage he might do so, a certain anxiety on his and his wife's part that in an exclusively feminine household the boy was becoming too bookish, a hope perhaps that aboard ship Harry might form the ambition to follow in his father's footsteps.

Captain Ellis's ship was the *Empress*, an American-built wooden sailing-ship belonging to Holder Brothers. His first commission was to take a large company of Irish passengers from Queenstown to New South Wales. It included several bishops, numerous priests and many nuns. Havelock, the captain's little boy, was petted and spoilt and thoroughly enjoyed the trip to Sydney, even singing solos to the accompaniment of the piano at the ship's concert without any feeling of shyness. Sister Agnes, a gentle quiet nun, supervised his studies on board; a kind-hearted old Mother Superior was always making him little presents, some of which he still had at the time of starting his autobiography more than thirty years later; and a mischievous priest called Father Doyle egged him on to pull the whiskers of a solemn gentleman called Mr Walsh, who promptly boxed Havelock's ears. A German steward, considering that the seven-year-old was spending too much time on frivolities like Hans Andersen and *Masterman Ready*, lent him some beautifully illustrated natural history books. "I like travelling," Havelock wrote his mother from Sydney, "though I should not wish to be a sailor."

At no time in his long life, either before or after, did Havelock mix with other people so freely and unselfconsciously as during that voyage to Sydney. Soon after, at no precise point, there descended between him and the outside world a sort of safety curtain, behind which he was utterly at liberty but through which he found himself incapable of communicating his feelings, however strong they were, to those outside.

It is impossible to determine what produced this "undemonstrative impassibility" as Havelock Ellis called it. But there were certain episodes on the voyage home via Callao and the Chincha Islands, round Cape Horn to Antwerp, which stood out in Ellis's memory and were obviously of emotional importance.

The voyage out had been with a large company of adults to a country culturally the same as that which he had left. The first truly foreign country he saw was Peru, a totally different and more graceful civilisation, with which he fell in love. In manhood he would escape whenever possible to Spain, finding there the dignity and colour which he had first glimpsed at Callao.

It may sound fanciful to imagine a way of life as rival to a person. But I think that in Callao and the Chincha Islands Havelock Ellis found in the external world a correspondence to the richness and colour and beauty of his interior life. It showed that what he dreamed could be true; it was the alternative to his family world, his mother so strong but so narrow, so good but incurious, so safe but unadventurous. "It was on this coast of Peru," Ellis wrote, "at the age of seven, that I first gained full self-consciousness; I was beginning to become a person."

They sailed back round Cape Horn and during that voyage two things happened which aroused in Havelock a curiosity about the world inside himself, which appeared as strange as the world outside in Peru, compared with South London and his mother.

At Callao a young Englishman came aboard as a passenger. He was kind, gentle and well-bred, and seeing that Havelock was fond of reading he gave him a novel by Mrs Craik, called *A Noble Life*. For some reason which he could not analyse even in maturity, Havelock could not bring himself to thank the Englishman and for a long time would not touch the book, though eventually he read it.

He was not the sort of boy to be put off by the title. Nobility of life did not seem boring. It seems to me possible that the kind, gentle, well-bred stranger may have been a paederast, whose gesture of friendship Havelock rejected because he intuitively apprehended something ulterior in the gift. Most people can remember premonitions of imperfectly understood danger in childhood.

But the reason for the ingratitude is unimportant. Ellis remembered the incident because he had behaved in a way contrary to reason and good conduct. It made him conscious that he had a self which did not conform to the accepted social self. In such a consciousness lay the seed of Psychology.

The second incident was one which Ellis kept to himself as a guilty secret until he confided it to his autobiography.

On board the *Empress* was a large cat, the favourite of the sailors, who hung little trinkets round its neck. One day Havelock was watching the cat walking between the rails at the ship's stern. The cat was sure-footed, but its position was precarious. The merest touch and it would fall overboard.

Moved by a sudden impulse, Havelock leant forward and gave it the merest touch.

Immediately filled with remorse, he ran to his father and told him that the cat had fallen overboard. A rope was thrown overboard but the cat had disappeared.

"No one suspected me of any part of the cat's death, and I never revealed to anyone—I believe unto this day—that I was guilty in the matter. I have always, however, regarded it as a criminal act."[1]

Ellis mentions another memory of this voyage, which he does not connect with the drowning of the cat, though it follows it in his narrative. "As the ship sailed swiftly past, I observed the floating body as it seemed to me of a negro in a red shirt, though the negro effect may possibly have been due to discoloration; I alone saw it and with my characteristic reticence said nothing about it."[2]

Havelock's behaviour in the case of the drowned negro appears to me inexplicable unless the corpse was associated with his guilt over the drowned cat. Though the reticence was characteristic of him from that time forward, he had not been too reticent to sing before a large audience of strangers on the voyage out to Sydney. I do not want to labour a point which can never be determined certainly one way or the other. Only a deep analysis would have determined who or what the ship's cat stood for in his unconscious. But there seems to me the possibility that the separation of his interior and exterior worlds occurred at this time; and the probability that they were caused by the discrepancy between his mother in South London and himself, the imaginative girdler of the globe.

[1] It is interesting that Ellis's first scientific work should have been on *The Criminal* and that he frequently stresses the close relationship between the criminal and the genius in their deviation from the norm.

[2] *My Life*, Eng. ed., p. 50, Am. ed., p. 63.

2

In every man of genius a new strange force is brought into the world. The biographer is the biologist of this new life. I come to you to learn the origins of this tremendous energy, the forces that gave it impetus and that drove it into one channel rather than another.

An Open Letter to Biographers

At about the age of seven a change takes place in the personality of all boys. Hitherto a boy may have expressed himself freely, showing off by singing, dancing, drawing or telling stories. Then, sometimes in a few weeks, he becomes self-conscious. He enters the Cowboys and Indians period, in which he acts a role to express his emotions. The simple exhibitionism of infancy is too crude. He sheers away into energetic war-games, the hunter and the hunted, or into the more violent sports. The pattern is very similar all over the world, whether it is repeated in the jungles of Africa, where it is useful, or on the backlots of city suburbs, where it is the survival of a primitive and no longer useful education.

Even if Havelock Ellis had not sailed round the world at the age of seven, some change would have taken place in him at that age. The expression of emotion would have been inhibited or diverted. He might perhaps have made friendships with other boys going through the same phase, which would have helped to preserve the contact with the outside world. It is impossible to say; or yet to judge whether he would have done his lifework better if he had grown like other boys. He himself would have thanked God that he was as he was, so that he could do as he did.

On his return to England, his life was outwardly the same as it had been when he went away. He returned to the same school he had attended before he sailed for Sydney and he re-entered the home life, dominated by his mother, once more the solitary male in a household of women after his father sailed again.

Memories of this period are scanty. A boy named Smith, seeing how rotten Havelock was at cricket, gave him a serious lecture about the need to be good at games. But Havelock took no notice, thinking that the advantage of not being good at games was that you didn't have to play them. The headmistress, misunderstanding one of the games played in the school, asked Mrs Ellis whether Havelock was "quite right in the head." Mrs Ellis was indignant. The suggestion "was never made by anyone else at that time, however 'odd', at a later period, some people may have considered me." Ellis added with sweet reasonableness, "Still it is possible that this shrewd and intelligent old lady ought to have the credit of first detecting in me whatever strain of mental anomaly I possess."[1]

At home he had a little garden, for which he bought flowers such as polyanthus. He refused to plant eschscholtzias, because "its virulent-orange flowers and its strange glabrous stalks with their thin milky juice inspired me with ineffaceable repulsion." Language so forceful shows they stood for something the thought of which repelled him. Perhaps the milky juice was an image of lactation. It is impossible to say.

One day—about a year after his return—he was in the garden. His mother was away. She had gone to stay with his father, whose ship was at Hamburg. He was swinging in the swing, when he heard his mother call him. "Harry!" and then a second time "Harry!" He ran into the house, thinking that for some reason his mother had come home again. He saw the maid and asked her if she had called him, knowing that it was not her voice but his mother's he had heard.

"No," she said. "Why?"

He did not tell her.

When Havelock was nine, the Ellises moved to a smaller house in the low-lying district between Wimbledon and Merton. He left the dame school and for the next three years went as a day-boy to what was called the French and German College opposite Merton Old Church.

[1] *My Life*, Eng. ed., p. 53, Am. ed., p. 66.

Havelock did not like the new house or district, but the school and Merton Old Church quickened his sense of beauty. Other churches he had seen were modern and uninteresting. Though of no great architectural merit, Merton Church had the charm and beauty of age, with its ancient monuments, the old helmet hung above the reading desk, the row of blazoned escutcheons with mottoes such as *In Coelo Quies*.

The school was Elizabethan in its oldest part, with later additions, including a small eighteenth-century theatre which had been converted into a swimming-bath and gymnasium. The headmaster, de Chastelain, was a pale, compact little mannequin, English in everything except name and descent. He was competent and energetic, but like so many pedagogues used sarcasm to maintain authority. "Do you write with a poker?" he asked young Ellis, "or perhaps you have a tame spider which runs across the page with inky feet?" Havelock disliked him, because he bullied his wife, a rather pretty American woman of thirty, with a low voice and a faded, crushed air. It was the first time he felt what he came to know later as "the need to champion woman's rights."

Mrs de Chastelain was unaware of young Ellis's chivalry, and when he passed her in the street without raising his cap, she reported him to her husband. His next termly report read "Manners passable."

Havelock's lapse was due not to bad manners but to absorption in his dreams. Wrapt in his personal world, he would not see or, if he saw, recognise those he met in the street. "I have even passed my own sweetheart who had come to seek me, and who let me pass, not revealing that incident to me until years afterwards. De Chastelain seems to have found *le mot juste* in the word 'passable'."

The three years at the French and German College were uneventful. He learnt a little Latin and more French. He played games dutifully but without skill or zest. He made no intimate friends or enemies. There was no bullying or schoolboy vice that he knew of, and the nearest approach to impropriety was a master asking him to take a note to the house of a pretty dressmaker, whom Havelock had admired in church. Havelock refused, but the master bore him no grudge.

On his voyage round the world, the son of another captain had tried to show him how to masturbate and one of the apprentices had slipped Harry's hand into his trousers so that he could hold his member. The first had told Harry that rubbing would make it grow, which he thought was a good idea but it did not when *he* tried; and Havelock told the second that it was jolly big. But neither incident had produced in him any emotion except naive wonder. But one day he saw the schoolmaster whose note he had refused to carry naked in the swimming-bath, and his sexual organs struck Havelock as ugly—almost repulsive.

Far more important than what he learnt during these three years at school was the emergence of his "real self" through reading at home, the enlargement of the universe of the imagination. His appetite was omnivorous. He read everything he could beg, borrow, buy or swop.

It was at this stage that Ellis evolved what was to become his lifelong method of composition. He began by copying out any passage from a book which impressed him. A little later he started to co-ordinate different passages under headings and build up a system of indexing and cross-reference. He could not recall when he first began this habit, but by the age of ten he had developed the main outline of his literary and scientific method.

At the age of twelve he compiled his first book. It was called *The Precious Stones of the Bible* and it contained not one word of original material. It was an orderly arrangement of all the facts he could find about precious stones mentioned in the Bible from the books on which he could lay his hands. These were not many, but he augmented his supplies of books by combing the penny boxes outside second-hand bookshops and by using the columns of the *Exchange and Mart* for the sale, purchase or exchange of books.

Less modest than later, he longed to see his book in print and encouraged by his mother he enquired the cost of having it printed. Twelve copies he thought would be enough and he was dismayed to find that such an edition would cost as many pounds. Though later on he came to learn more about publishing, he remained all his life the least business-like of writers and would never have said with Evelyn Waugh, "I do not write for money, but when I have written, I get as much as I can for it."

Havelock abandoned thought of publishing *Precious Stones*, but he worked on other compilations, planning a book on flowers and another on trees. He did not collect flowers or study trees. His books were made from other books. Though he maintained later that this puzzled him, because he had little interest in anything with which he could not come in close contact, it remained true throughout his life that, for his scientific and literary work, most of his research material was derived from others and not from first-hand investigation. His wife was to quote with relish a remark of one of their Cornish neighbours that Mr Ellis wrote books about books and Mrs Ellis wrote books about people. It was truer than Ellis admitted, because to him from a very early age his experience of the outside world was derived more through the printed page than from personal observation; and because this was so, he never became very highly critical of what he read. If A's book contradicted B's, he would find a means of reconciling the contradiction, but he lacked the personal experience against which he could measure the reliability of either of them. Or perhaps it would be truer to say that he was less concerned with the reliability of their evidence than with the use to which he could put them both. He selected his authorities, as a joiner might the planks of wood from which he would make an entirely new article of furniture to adorn his speculative world.

The original productions of his juvenilia started as glosses on passages which he had lifted from other authors. The next stage was the linking of similar or contradictory passages with Havelock acting as a sort of literary referee; and the final stage consisted of Havelock taking over command and using quotations from other writers to reinforce his arguments with the authority of former masters or to embellish his page with felicities he admired.

This method of composition was to impress his contemporaries with his erudition and scholarship; but in view of its early origin, the more significant element in it must be found in his personal loneliness. With no intimate friends, he sought the companionship of the literary great, receiving their confidences without having to give anything in exchange, except into the safekeeping of his notebooks. And when quoting from other writers, he had—at least in his early years—the image of his unintellectual family in the back of his mind. It was as good as saying "You may think these ideas are very strange coming from your Havelock, but in fact lots of other people have thought in a very similar way."

It was a habit which once formed was to carry him through a literary and scientific career with the sense that however estranged he might be from the public opinion of his day he belonged in the select company of the great.

He had no sense that he was training himself to be a writer. Authors were unknown in the Ellis family circle and never mentioned. No one he knew would have dreamed of holding up an author as worthy of his imitation.

On the other hand, Havelock had met and conceived great admiration for John Erck, the vicar of Merton. Until then Havelock had taken his religious instruction from his mother. She had made him read and learn passages from the Bible and the Prayer Book; had seen that he was regular in church attendance, had sown in fact the seed of Christianity in him. But it needed the warmth of someone like Erck to make it germinate.

John Erck was a remarkable man to find in a small village close to London. He was an Irishman, short of stature, straight of bearing, with black hair, sallow skin and dark eyes which glowed. In daily life a shy, silent man who walked straight ahead with his forearm carried at his back, looking neither to left nor right, he was transformed when he climbed into the pulpit. Ellis was later to hear the famous preachers of his day, men to whom the congregations flocked, like Liddon, Stanley, Spurgeon and Parker, "but never one who possessed so fine a natural eloquence, in which passionate sincerity blended with poetic imagination, wholly guided, it seemed, by the inspiration of the moment and yet always the instinct of the artist. . . . He had a beautiful voice with a wide range between the high and the low tones, and he would modulate this voice with a skill and effect which in a popular preacher must soon have become a conscious affectation, but in this unappreciated country parson of a quiet village seemed altogether natural. There come back to me the summer evenings in the dim church—it was only in the evening that his eloquence was fully revealed and when dusk came on and the lights were not lit—and the stream of Irish eloquence that rose and fell over the heads of those prim and stolid Anglo-Saxon villagers. I well remember, on the sudden death by a fall from his horse of Bishop Wilberforce—a diocesan whose exceeding charm had won the heart of the Low Church vicar—with what impassioned eloquence Erck preached on Elijah who had suddenly been swept to the clouds in a chariot of fire; and how again, in a very different mood, having apparently found that the tradesmen of his parish were not above the trick of giving false measure, he preached a fierce sermon on this subject: 'People of Merton, repent!' Perhaps more than by his sermons I was moved by Erck's exquisite way of reading the lessons and especially the prayers. He would sometimes subtly graduate and deepen his voice through the various collects of evensong, and the low and grave tones with which at length he reached 'Lighten our darkness' still lingers in memory. These influences enabled me to understand something of the reality of the Bible and the beauty of the English Prayer Book, and so to some extent counteracted the dulling effect of familiarity with these things when imposed as a task in early life." [1]

All Havelock's emotional life became directed towards religion.

[1] *My Life*, Eng. ed., pp. 63–4, Am. ed., pp. 78–80. In *The Task of Social Hygiene* Ellis argued that children should not be taught religion till the age of twelve, because childish misapprehension so frequently prevents adult comprehension. He quotes Rousseau's *La Nouvelle Héloïse*, where "Saint-Preux writes that Julie had explained to him how she sought to surround her children with good influences without forcing any religious instruction on them: 'As to the Catechism, they don't so much know what it is.' . . . 'So pious a mother!' I exclaimed; 'I can't understand. And why don't your children learn their Catechism?' 'In order that they may one day believe it. I wish to make Christians of them.' "

He wrote essays which he preached as sermons to the congregation of his sisters, using the head of the sofa as a pulpit. He began to carry with him a pocket New Testament, which he studied devoutly, though with the narrow understanding of a boy. He began the self-conscious pursuit of righteousness. He found among the old neglected books in the house a small manual on self-education, which presented a list of Faults in tabular form with the suggestion that the self-improver should enter a mark against each fault every time it was committed. The table was dutifully copied and Havelock started to enter up his delinquencies.

He soon found that it was impossible to define faults accurately; and anyway it was a waste of time. He did not dispose of his table of faults by tearing it up, burning it or dumping it on the rubbish heap. He folded it up and slipped it down between the boards of his bedroom floor, symbolically burying the past in which he had thought it possible to become better by ticking off faults.

Though he admired John Erck so much, he never talked to him about religion or his own spiritual difficulties. "I had then in a high degree, as I have always had more or less since—though as one grows old and detached from the world it grows less rather than more—an instinctive secretiveness in intimate emotional matters, an almost inconquerable impulse to keep my own personal life to myself." [1] If he had done so, it is likely that Erck would have been able to unite his mother's very simple religious training to a mature Christian faith, even though Ellis's mysticism, love of beauty and interest in sex might have brought him in the end to Catholicism.

But our concern is not with hypothetical lives. The actual is, God knows, quite complicated enough. Ellis himself was puzzled by it. "In recent years," he wrote in *My Life*, "I have sometimes looked back at my childhood to observe how it appears in the light of modern views of the more subtle mechanism of sex and its manifestations and repressions in childhood. That much may thus be revealed I am now well aware by my own investigations on others. . . . In childhood I was not sexually excitable. It seems to

[1] *My Life*, Eng. ed., p. 65, Am. ed. p. 81.

me that, however numerous the exceptions, this complete sexual latency in the pre-pubertal period is probably the rule. But I am not here concerned to generalise, nor am I prepared to assert that I was myself either as child or adult completely normal; on the contrary, I was from the first—beneath a reserved and impassive surface—a highly nervous and sensitive person. I was in some degree perhaps, what may be called an 'introverted' child; my timidity, my self-consciousness, my self criticism perhaps drove me in on myself, not, however, towards day-dreaming, which only began at puberty, but to books. . . . There were no sexual emotions and not even any sexual curiosities at this period. . . . I was affectionately devoted to my mother, but quite calmly and undemonstratively, without at any time the slightest touch of excess or any cravings for the manifestation of love in her, or any curiosities, and without, also, the slightest hostile feeling towards my father. Moreover, I shared the curious reserved critical aloofness which most children feel towards their parents. I am at the same time able to believe that my mother exerted some moulding influence on my later sexual life, and that this would have been much greater if, as never happened, she had allowed her love for me to become unduly tender; but as it was, her chief influence lay in unconsciously moulding my ideal of womanhood generally." [1]

It is very difficult to know exactly when Ellis wrote any particular passage of his autobiography. We know he did not start it until he was forty, and that he advanced roughly at the pace of a year a year for the first seventeen years. But after that he kept interpolating material, of which this passage may be part. I think that it probably is, and I am sure that he was looking back to see whether his childhood fitted in to the rather crude popular idea of the Oedipus situation. And he was right in saying that it didn't.

On the other hand he was viewing his childhood from the point of view of at least thirty-five years later, thirty-five years in which his main preoccupation had been to come to terms with his childhood situation. To the extent to which he had been successful, his view of his childhood is liable to be inaccurate.

[1] *My Life*, Eng. ed., pp. 66–7, Am. ed., pp. 82–3.

As I see it, his mother could not trust herself to be "duly tender" and what drove the young Havelock back into himself was the lack of educational maternal love.

Ellis did not see this because he was defending himself against the Freudians on an issue from which he had already found his way out.

Freud in his *Three Essays on Sexuality* had already published the Little Hans papers, revealing, at least in the case of Little Hans, an infantile sexual awareness, which Havelock Ellis could not detect in his own childhood. He did not feel that he had ever been the victim of repression or suppression. So the quotation goes on: "The question arises whether this seeming absence of sexual phenomena in childhood may not be due to a deliberate repression or automatic suppression of the phenomena into the unconscious. If so, they ought when thus repressed or suppressed to give some sign in disorder of the conscious life; but there seem no signs. (Something more, however, I now see, remains to be said. There was no need for it, not entirely because there was nothing to be put away, but because the veil of impassive reserve with which I concealed the whole of my intimate personal life rendered repression or suppression completely superfluous. Beneath the veil I was free to think or to feel what I liked; there was no one to say me nay and I saw no reason to say nay to myself.)" [1]

After this, though printed as the same paragraph, there is yet another note, an afterthought written in towards the end of his life. "This fact now seems to me of immense significance for the whole of my life; it is, from one point of view, the key to all my work and my whole attitude towards the world. I have never repressed anything. What others have driven out of consciousness or pushed into the background, as being improper or obscene, I have maintained and held in honour. It has become wrought into the texture of my whole work."

This is true and important for the understanding of Ellis's work and his attitude to it. But it does not take us any further towards

[1] *My Life*, Eng. ed., p. 67, Am. ed., p. 83. The passage between brackets is obviously a later gloss.

understanding young Ellis's liberty beneath the veil, accompanied by an inability to communicate intimately with anyone outside himself.

The truth is that intimacy is a habit which a child acquires, usually from its mother; and from Susannah Wheatley, who suffered from something of a Jocasta complex, the only gesture of intimacy which Harry received was a warm, wet diaper thrust playfully in his face. He turned away in disgust at first, but later recognised it as an act of love. Hence the germ, not merely of perversion, but of maintaining and holding in honour what others have driven out of consciousness or pushed into the background as improper or obscene.

The diversion of the sex instinct into urolagnic channels produced a preoccupation with the act of micturition, which Ellis regarded as his "earliest scientific interest." He observed how far he and his schoolfellows made water—or to use his graver language, he "observed the differences in vesical energy among his schoolfellows, his own being below the average." [1] The psychological significance of Havelock's below-average performance becomes apparent from the *Studies in the Psychology of Sex*, where he pointed out "the remarkable relationship—sometimes of transference and sometimes of compensation—which exists between genital tension and vesical tension, both in men and women. . . . Vesical power is also commonly believed to be in relation with sexual potency, and the inability to project the urinary stream in a normal manner is one of the accepted signs of sexual impotency." [2]

Of course at the time when Havelock Ellis was making his first study of vesical energy, he knew nothing about sexual impotency. "There were no sexual emotions and not even sexual curiosities at this period. I remember that at some time—I cannot remember when—I considered the question of the origin of babies and decided that they emerged from their mothers' navels, but this

[1] Many years later he continued these observations and published the results in the *American Journal of Dermatology* under the title, "The Bladder as a Dynamometer."

[2] *Studies in the Psychology of Sex*, Vol. V, F. A. Davis Co., 1906, p. 55.

was to me a purely scientific question which involved no morbid feelings nor undue attention." [1]

But it seems clear that, at the stage when he began to equate vesical and genital tension, he accepted the idea that if a man lacked vesical energy, he lacked sexual potency. I do not mean that he was right in so thinking—the psychology of sexual potency is far more complicated than that—but if he had that conviction, much of his later conduct is understandable, which would otherwise be most puzzling.

One can see how the young Ellis evolved a fairly satisfactory adjustment to his pre-pubertal situation. He accepted life as he found it with a resignation which his religion sanctioned. If things were the way they were, it was because God willed it so. There was no use in kicking against the pricks. Misfortunes were sent to teach a lesson. Weakness embraced became strength. Enclosed in his private world, he could be as happy as a monk. It was only if he tried to get out that he would find he was a prisoner.

[1] *My Life*, Eng. ed., p. 66, Am. ed., p. 82.

3

> Next in importance comes the curve of life that has its summit at puberty and ends with the completion of adolescence; whatever else there is to make is made then. The machine has been created; during these years it is wound up to perform its work in the world.
>
> *An Open Letter to Biographers*

THOUGH MRS ELLIS would occasionally have people in to meals, she did not like strangers staying in the house. Sometimes a boy or girl cousin came for a week, but it was not until Havelock was twelve that a stranger not of his own kin came to stay.

Her name was Agnes, her age sixteen, and she was the only daughter of Mrs Ellis's step-brother. Dark, pretty, vivacious, with long black ringlets, she was old enough to be a young woman in Havelock's eyes, and young enough to be a playmate and an equal. He lost his heart to her immediately.

In house or garden she played and romped with him without reserve, but when they went for walks together—as they often did without Havelock once regretting the time taken from his beloved books—she would sometimes make him offer her his arm as if they were both grown up, and at others would treat him like a little boy, buying him lemonade at the best shops she could find.

One day as they were strolling arm in arm through the poppied cornfields which lay between Merton station and the French and German College, they came suddenly on Mr de Chastelain. Havelock felt sudden embarrassment at being caught by his headmaster with his arm in a girl's. But he had the courage to keep it there and just raise his cap as he passed. "I have ever since prided myself on that early little act of moral courage."

The headmaster asked Captain Ellis who the girl was, without, Havelock believed, mentioning that he had seen them arm in arm.

There can have been no need to tell Mrs Ellis, who could see by the change in her son that he was head over ears in love.

At the end of two weeks Agnes went back to her home. Havelock had not kissed her or felt any desire to. But she held his heart in thrall. When she left, he lent her the poems of Keats and she lent him *The Wide, Wide World* and they both swore they would write to one another, which they did once or twice.

Then a trivial quarrel developed between Mrs Ellis and the mother of Agnes. During her stay, Agnes had asked if she could help in any way and Mrs Ellis gave her some peas to shuck. Agnes's mother protested that this menial task was degrading to her daughter, a coldness ensued and Agnes was never invited to the house again. At least that was the story as Havelock had it. It seems to me that Mrs Ellis was either a very unobservant woman not to notice what had happened between her son and Agnes; or that she did notice and that was why Agnes was invited no more.

Havelock said nothing to anyone about Agnes. He made no effort to see her and never mentioned her name. He was sure that no one knew that he gave her another thought. "But for four years her image moved and lived within me, revealing myself to myself. I had no physical desires and no voluptuous emotions; I never pictured to myself any joy of bodily contact with her or cherished any sensuous dreams. Yet I was devoured by a boy's pure passion. That she should become my wife—though I never tried to imagine what that meant—was a wild and constant aspiration. I would lie awake in bed with streaming eyes praying to God to grant that this might some day be. I have often felt thankful since that our prayers are not heard." [1]

For a fortnight the monk had left his cell and then happily returned, not with a girl he loved but with the image of a girl who revealed himself to himself. Once she left, she ceased to matter. What he loved was not her but loving her. It made him a person, a poet. The world became beautiful. Emotions flowered in his spirit such as he had never dreamed of. He began to enjoy art. His writing became more personal and imaginative. Love, ideal

[1] *My Life*, Eng. ed., p. 72, Am. ed., p. 89.

and pure, untrammelled by contact with an actual person, revealed not the glory of the beloved but the luxuriance of loving.

These four years in which he dreamed and wrote poetry to Agnes were important in other ways. He left the French and German College and went as a weekly boarder to a school called The Poplars, between Tooting and Mitcham.

Ellis did not think highly of the academic standards of the school. He learned little Latin and no Greek. His formal studies were in no way outstanding and he did not master the discipline of tackling subjects which he did not like. He was however fortunate in his French and English masters, both as teachers and friends.

De Chastelain had given him a good grounding in the French language, and shortly after Ellis went to The Poplars, there arrived a Douai man, called Joseph Stevens, who loved his language and its literature. Havelock saw a lot of him outside the classroom and Stevens introduced him to French books, which he read for their own sake. He also helped Ellis to master the elements of German and Italian, which with the Spanish he picked up later gave him the equipment to read all the main literary and scientific works he later needed to consult in their original language.

More profound even than the influence of Stevens was that of Angus Mackay, the English master. Mackay was very young for a schoolmaster, scarcely turned twenty. But he had already seen more of life than most pedagogues. He came of poor parents, had left school at an early age and worked first as an office boy, then as a city clerk, continuing in the evenings that search for betterment and higher education which was so characteristic and admirable a feature of Victorian England. He had now reached the stage of teaching, while he studied for a degree at London University. After that he proposed to take Holy Orders.

In religion he was a Broad Churchman, a follower of Carlyle, Ruskin, Charles Kingsley and Frederick Denison Maurice. He was less concerned with the mystery of the Holy Sacrament or the literal inspiration of the Bible than with the application of Christian teaching to the social and economic problems of nineteenth-century Britain. Mackay was Liberal, not to say Radical, in politics and he opened up prospects intellectually and morally far more exciting than Mrs Ellis's religious Fundamentalism and Conservative politics.

Mackay's first love was literature, especially poetry. He had already published two small books of verse. They were strongly influenced by Wordsworth and Tennyson, but one of them had been successful enough to go into a second edition. He was strongly grounded in the poetry of the first half of the century and had some knowledge of contemporary poetry and prose. He was a great admirer of Thomas Hardy, whose *Far From the Madding Crowd* he lent Havelock as it appeared instalment by instalment in the *Cornhill.*

Angus appeared "a God-given revelation" to Havelock, as perhaps he was. Havelock might have travelled round the world, but he had never before talked to an intellectual and imaginative man to whom books were not a refuge from life but an aid to fuller living. "Our relationship was soon that of friends rather than of master and pupil. It was scarcely possible for him to speak a sentence that did not strike across the beliefs and conventions that I had grown up in, that I had accepted without ever thinking about them. For the first time I realised that there were great questions and problems in life, great aspirations beyond one's personal longings, great ideals to be passionately fought for. A touch had awakened my soul and my intellect; they were now to work at no man's bidding, not even Mackay's—who indeed never consciously sought to influence me—but in accordance with the laws of their own inborn nature. For years, however, Mackay was a banner that waved before me on the road to fresh spiritual conquests." [1]

The only friends he made at The Poplars were these two masters. Intellectually precocious, athletically undistinguished, abnormally shy, he had little in common with his schoolfellows. For a time, when he was thirteen, he was cruelly bullied by an elder boy who rode him like a horse round the bedroom, pricking him with pins for spurs. His mother found out what was happen-

[1] *My Life*, Eng. ed., p. 77, Am. ed., p. 98.

ing and complained to the headmaster, who moved him to another room with a boy who was congenial. "But I am inclined to think that the suffering I had silently endured was not without evil influence on my nervous system. I was just then at the critical period of puberty. While subjected to this treatment, at about the age of thirteen, copious seminal emissions began to take place during sleep, once or twice a week, always without dreams or any sensations, and continued, whenever I was alone, for some thirty years." [1]

At the age of sixteen Ellis left school. He had taken no public examination such as the Oxford Locals or London Matriculation, and the only career he had ever contemplated was that of the two men whom he admired most, John Erck and Angus Mackay. The Church of England was very accommodating, but the views he was developing would strain the most tolerant of Churches. Like the youthful Diderot, he wanted to be nothing, absolutely nothing. But for Ellis, as for Diderot, "nothing" meant something not far from "everything." For a time he stayed at home, teaching his two elder sisters and continuing the broad undirected studies which had always been more absorbing than anything he learnt in class.

His parents were mildly concerned about his uncertainty but they did not try to force him to make up his mind. "Do not worry about Harry," Mrs Ellis told her husband. She had faith and God would show the way. Captain Ellis did not worry. He had faith also, not so much in God as in his wife.

Havelock's health provided an excuse for a postponement of a decision about his career. At school he had suffered from bouts of dull, continuous abdominal pain, and though there was nothing definitely wrong with him, he was not robust. The voyage round

[1] *My Life*, Eng. ed., p. 79, Am. ed., pp. 100–1. The word "copious" is used in *My Life* only of seminal emissions and examples of Undinism. His mother, as already quoted, "copiously recommenced." When years later he took his wife's maid on a tour of London, they climbed to the deserted dome of St Paul's and she released on the stones "a copious stream." It argues an identification of the two acts.

the world had set him up at the age of seven. Why not repeat it at the age of sixteen?

That was the way it was put to Havelock and accepted by him. I can imagine that there was more behind it in his parents' discussions, Mrs Ellis feeling that on the wings of his everlasting books her only son was flying away from her, and her husband wondering whether at sixteen the boy would revise his seven-year-old decision not to be a sailor. The voyage anyway would do him good. Look how well he had got on with the other passengers on that early voyage to Sydney. It would take him out of himself, make him meet people. A house full of women was all right for a boy, but Harry was a young man now, or almost. Do him good to meet some pretty young girls who weren't his sisters. Remember the way, when Agnes came to stay, he forgot his books for a fortnight. And if nothing else, the father might at least be able to make a friend of his son—not that Harry was ever rebellious, or rude or jealous. But he was his mother's son, and in that house of women Captain Ellis must often have longed for an ally.

So Havelock was given some money to buy books for the voyage—Swinburne's *Songs before Sunrise*, the notorious *Elements of Social Science* by George Drysdale and other works, the tendency of which was to take him away from the various sorts of Christian belief he had known, his mother's narrow evangelicalism, John Erck's prophetic eloquence and Mackay's broad Christian radicalism. He took a few textbooks so that he could prepare himself for the London Matriculation; but for the most part he chose literary classics in English or French with a few in German, a Shelley, a Spenser, a Rabelais, a *Faust*.

To these Captain Ellis added a harmonium, perhaps remembering Harry's singing at the concerts nine years earlier on the *Empress*. Anyway he liked singing himself and Harry had learned to play the piano from an old friend of his mother's, a Miss Johnston. Harry could play and he could sing—and that at least would be something they could do together.

As it happened, it was something they could not do together long. One morning after they had been at sea only a few weeks, a great wave struck the ship, the *Surrey*, astern, and carried in the middle window with the frame and deadlight of the cabin they shared together. It happened luckily while they were at breakfast, but when they came down to see the havoc, the broken chronometers, the Waverley novels reduced to pulp, the harmonium ruined, all Havelock said was "Does this happen often?" The old man never forgot it. His son might do things which appeared to him jolly odd, but when he remembered that question, he felt that everything was all right deep down. Except of course the harmonium.

The *Surrey* sailed from London on 19 April 1875 and proceeded to Plymouth to take on 325 Government-sponsored emigrants to Australia. Havelock and his father stayed at Lucey's Hotel and Captain Ellis took his son to the first theatre he had ever visited. There was no mention of Mrs Ellis, but it was a symbol of the liberty which as men they could enjoy together away from home. The show made less impression on him than a visit to a lady in Devonport, who had "a charming daughter and a buxom girl friend," both a little older than Havelock. Next day they visited the *Surrey*, and his father's friend, perhaps noticing Havelock's shyness as he thought, or briefed by Captain Ellis, told him that he needed "some jolly girl friends." Havelock heartily agreed, though he said nothing. His sisters were still children, Louie the eldest being only twelve. Apart from that fortnight with Agnes, who anyway was four years older than he, he had never known a girl outside his own family.

But when his father tried to jolly him along about flirting with the girl emigrants, he froze up. What the old man intended to be an invitation to a little fun of the most harmless type merely drove him further in on himself. He was not that sort of person; oh no! he was not.

What sort of person he was, during this voyage and the next four years, which he regarded as the most formative years of his life, we can luckily check from the journal which he started to keep the day they left London. Ellis never referred to this bulky notebook when he wrote his autobiography, perhaps because it is hard to decipher, perhaps also because his memory had ordered things better than they appeared at the time. For example, in *My Life* he wrote of the time before he sailed on the *Surrey*, "It was in the course of my reading that I slid almost imperceptibly off the foundation of Christian belief." It sounds like a new-built ship being gently launched on the high tide of doubt with scarcely a splash as the chocks are drawn away.

If one reads the journal one sees that it wasn't in the least like that. There was a gradual erosion of faith under the ebb and flow of doubt, with Ellis for years undecided and uncommitted. On the one side was his mother, with her undoubted faith, her strength of character, her simple trust in God (diluted and humanised, thank God, by Undinism) and there was John Erck who could make even a Low Church service so beautiful that one could accept it (thank God again) not as a religious service but as a work of art. Somewhere in the middle was Angus Mackay, the modern man who wanted to enter the Church (but *who* knew when the time came whether he would, and, if he did, whether this was merely because his intellectual development had stopped?). On the other hand, there were Ernest Renan, Charles Darwin, George Drysdale, Herbert Spencer—dozens of them, who were disproving the revealed truth of Christianity and supplanting it by a materialistic science which seemed intellectually true and yet was, he felt, false, because so mechanistic.

When John Erck told him he ought to become a minister in the Church of England rather than a Nonconformist Church as Mackay intended, because it would give him "greater liberty for prophesying," he agreed, at least about the need for greater liberty and the prophesying, but what Church would accept what he had to say when they knew what it was?

He was right in lamenting the fact that there had been no science master at The Poplars who could help him in that sphere as Stevens and Mackay had helped him in French and English. He was lost for years in the wasteland, longing for the beauty and security of his childish faith and yet led on by the *ignis fatuus* of materialist science. A religious young man without a valid faith, he groped his way towards science, for which he had no adequate training.

And there was his father, as normal as they come and when they do come how normal that is, trying to get Harry through the difficult period with all the love and sympathy at his command. But it did not begin to touch the problems with which his son was wrestling. He was still writing about Agnes, beginning at last to recognise that the image of a girl is no substitute for the girl herself, as in this passage written on the voyage:

> There was
> Close hidden in the corner of my soul,
> —As a dove a maiden fondles in her bosom
> And presses to her heart,—one spot of love
> Jealously guarded from the sight of all,
> Yes, even from its cherished object; but
> 'tis not enough to love, we must be loved;
> We must know all, know all, be all that life
> Can offer us; the kernel must be ours,
> Even though the shell be broken,
> And even then perchance 'tis rotten.

He had experienced the subjective joy of loving. But that was only one element of a two-way relationship, which he longed, but seemed forbidden, to establish. Shyness was his censor; or was it his protector, shutting him off from the public exposure of inadequacy?

That was the psycho-sexual problem, one which, had he known it, faces most sensitive adolescents around the age of sixteen, but which for him was complicated by the sexual and the urolagnic.

There remained the problem of belief, the reconciliation of the bleak truths of scientific materialism with the apparently fallacious yet undoubted comforts of faith, the false yet fine ecstasy of communion with God.

In the solution of either of these problems Captain Ellis could be of little direct aid to his son. Yet what he did was, without his realising it, exactly what was needed.

On their arrival at Sydney, Captain Ellis was instructed to

proceed to Calcutta, where the climate, thought the ship's doctor, might prove injurious to Havelock's health. The only thing to do was to leave him in Australia and pick him up later. Captain Ellis was probably not unwilling to do this because the voyage out had been long enough to show him that he was not the person to help his son out of his difficulties. It might do the boy a world of good to strike out on his own. He had been teaching his sisters well enough at home. Why couldn't he do what his friend, young Mackay, had done, teach in the day and study for his Matriculation in the evening?

Captain Ellis went to see his old friend Alfred Morris, who had been first mate on one of his earlier ships. On the voyage out he had fallen in love with one of the girl emigrants, had married her on board and on reaching Sydney had thrown up his job and settled in Australia. "Settled" perhaps is the wrong word. Morris was clever, versatile, well-spoken and attractive in personality. But he was restless and unable to persevere. He was very good at getting jobs and very bad at keeping them. After years of gathering no moss, this rolling stone had landed up in a little office between Pitt and George Street, Sydney, behind a door on which was painted EDUCATIONAL REGISTRATION SOCIETY. Here he sat with a Mr Frederick Bevill, the son of a baronet, an equally mossless stone that had rolled, still young but prodigiously fat, to Australia via Japan. "As Manager," said the brochure, "the Educational Registration Society has secured the services of a late Professor in a leading University." If pressed to name the University, Mr Bevill hinted that it was in Japan.

These two amiable adventurers greeted Captain Ellis and Havelock with enthusiasm. Of course a berth could be secured for Havelock. Australia was crying out for schoolmasters. With his qualifications, he should command a salary of at least £120 a year.

Havelock modestly pointed out that though of course he could teach, he could not be said to have any "qualifications," nor had he any testimonial.

"Don't worry about the testimonial," said Mr Morris. "I'll write you one." And taking from a drawer a sheet of the notepaper he had thoughtfully brought with him after being sacked from the headmastership of a small school in Melbourne, he wrote out then and there a glowing testimonial to the teaching abilities of Mr Henry Havelock Ellis. "Of course," he said, "no one knows *me.* But there happens to be another headmaster in Melbourne called Alfred Morris and he's jolly well known."

Armed with this testimonial, Havelock obtained a post as assistant master to Mr Hole of Fontlands, the Collegiate School, Burwood, a few miles outside Sydney, at a salary of £100 a year—a small fortune for a boy of sixteen in the year 1875.

4

Even the detailed account of the games and amusements devised by the young hero are welcome when obtainable; for the after-life of the man is often little more than the same games played more tragically on a larger field.

An Open Letter to Biographers

By the end of the year his elation had gone. Finding that Ellis was unqualified to take boys in the higher classics and uninterested in their outdoor sports, Mr Hole immediately reduced his salary to £40 a year; and soon after gave him notice to leave at the end of the term because he wanted a more highly qualified man. He realised that the blame did not rest on Ellis himself but on Morris and Bevill; and he gave him a pleasant testimonial, referring especially to his success in teaching French.

"The apparent blow to my vanity—if I had any—seems to have made no deep wound," Ellis wrote years later in *My Life*. But the entry in his Journal for 31 December 1875 shows that it produced deep physical and mental depression at the time. He did not feel very well. He was troubled frequently with bleeding at the nose. He felt very weak and "altogether incapable of any great exertion or fatigue, either physical or mental," which was "perhaps incident upon the anxiety and suspense I have lately undergone naturally working upon my very poor nerves and frame. . . . The scarlet fever too has been very much about; and though I should have been, I am afraid, but a too promising subject, I escaped with the rose-rash. I can only hope that my present feelings are not the prelude to something worse."

He decided to try if possible for a post as private tutor. It would give him more time for study; it would increase his age and capabilities; and perhaps, he added, his "real motive"—we generally have a real motive underlying all the rest, unknown almost to ourselves—was "inability of gaining a mastery over the boys as great as was desirable."

(In this fragment of self-analysis, one sees Havelock Ellis fumbling his way towards an understanding of unconscious motivation, which Sigmund Freud, at that moment a second-year medical student studying physiology under Brücke and Aristotle's logic under Brentano, had not yet dreamed of. But it was not the line he was destined to pursue; his was to the more difficult path of psycho-synthesis.)

His health improved as soon as Messrs Morris and Bevill found him a job. It was as private tutor to the family of an ex-government official called Platt, who had retired from Sydney to a station called Goongerwarrie, a few miles from Carcoar beyond Bathurst. Platt and his wife were quiet, kindly people, who so appreciated the reclusiveness of the young tutor that when he left they gave him a testimonial to say that he "gave no trouble in the house" as if he was a domestic animal. The children, boys and girls ranging from five to fourteen, were easy to manage, neither tiresomely stupid nor exactingly clever. One of them, a girl of ten named Minnie, became the object of Havelock's affection and he felt sad to leave her at the end of a year.

"Not that she is very superior to other children," he confided to his journal, "or that she shows great affection for me. I love her because she is a child and a girl. Not that she is beautiful—with that pretty little turned-up nose of hers, that—as it were creamy—Australian paleness of complexion, the deliciously red little lips, with the slight pout of health, her features are too undefined and slightly-made ever to approach beauty. She is a light graceful little thing—light even for her age—considering she is Australian—too big for her clothes though, round shouldered too, and wearing a strap; and with a constant habit of pulling up her stockings at all moments, which she does with such delightful naiveté that I have never found it in my heart to suggest any impropriety in so doing, if indeed there is any. She is quick, affectionate, thoroughly childish, no *arrière-pensée* in her little mind, over which the varying emotions shed the showers and sunshine of an English April; yet there is a sweet womanly thoughtfulness and considerateness mingled with the bubbling playfulness which will not be repressed even at lessons—which appears at all moments although the sunshine turns to showers at the most annoyingly trifling causes. I think it is these two characteristics of womanly considerateness and childish playfulness which chiefly endear her to me. One other feature may be depicted, the tendency to luxurious languid laziness which the Australian climate engenders even in children. I know there is much of sensuousness in her attraction for me. But does that sensuousness render my love less pure? That question I will leave unanswered; it is best left alone. I fear I have not yet mastered my tendency to morbid self-analysis."

This entry was written on 6 August 1876, four months before he left Carcoar. In many respects the child–adult love he felt for Minnie was a repetition of his relation which Agnes, with the roles reversed. But there was this difference: Agnes had sent him joyously to poetry; Minnie made him aware of the dangers of seeking from literature the proper satisfactions of life. "I fear my love of poetry and Beauty is becoming too strong, too intense. I am too much alone; too much with myself and my books in this quiet place. I want the world; I want human sympathies; human love; I love and sympathise too much; I want to be loved and sympathised with. I want to be shaken up with the rest of mankind; then perhaps I could throw off my reserve and physical nervousness which are now so hateful to me because I am so conscious of them."

On November 28th, the same mood was running, but sadder and more desperate. He quoted from a sonnet by Henry Kirke White, the butcher's son who died at twenty-one from overwork studying for Holy Orders:

> Though young yet sorrowful . . .
> Deep thought and dismal, verging to despair . . .
> I shrink dismayed before life's upland toil . . .
> And I do ponder with most strange delight,
> On the calm slumbers of the dead man's night.

He added a first tentative diagnosis of his trouble. "Poor Kirke White, I sympathise with you; and I pity myself. Such thoughts are not the thoughts of health but of disease—physical disease—for all disease is physical when one comes to think of it. A young, bright, happy, perchance noble life stained or broken or crushed altogether; and by the sin of someone—seldom by its own sin—the sin of someone turning round on it; or reaching down perhaps through generations and coming to it—it alone—and touching it and blasting it."

One must remember the date. In 1876 the idea of physical illness being psychological in origin was unfamiliar—it is to Ellis himself and Freud and others that we owe this knowledge. To Havelock at that time there were only four possibilities: physical disease contracted by the body, or passed on hereditarily; or punishment for sins committed by oneself, or by one's fathers. He was still floundering for lack of the right equipment, like a surgeon trying to operate with a meat-axe.

The explanation of punishment for the sin of another is nearest the mark, if my explanation is right that Ellis's sexual difficulties arose from his mother's expressing her love only in Undinist terms. Havelock used the word "sin" and not "fault," "error" or "mistake" because he had not slipped from his Christian beliefs as completely as he said he had in his autobiography. He was still debating with himself whether he should take Holy Orders.

"The Church? Well, yes, the Church would suit me in many respects. In her, I believe, I could display what ability I have; there I could do the most good; there, amongst men somewhat inclined to narrow and prejudiced views, my own broad and catholic opinions would attract attention they could excite nowhere else. But my opinions? They have undergone a revolution of the most awful and complete kind. To teach what I don't believe? From Sunday to Sunday? To be a hypocrite—nothing less? Is it to be thought of? Even from the best and highest ends, is it to be thought of? That is the question. I have thought a good deal over it; the two sides seem pretty evenly balanced. I wrote a short time ago to Mr Erck, stating my disagreements with the Church; and I shall like to know how he treats my scruples. His treatment of my letter may have a great effect on my course in life."

He was tormented by "a vast chaos of doubts, negations, denials —a seething mass which the deep love of truth can neither direct nor penetrate." If Christianity was destroyed, what was to be put in its place? "Sad when a mind has come to think that the false and the superstitious must be retained solely to save from what is worse than either; that it is better man should be made good by falsehood than evil by truth?"

Angus Mackay, his other friend and monitor, had fallen into a gloom almost as deep as his own. He wrote that he had lost all appetite for poetry and even for his work. He had left the school where he was teaching, and his departure had been made bitter by his love for a little boy there.

Havelock's own departure from Carcoar, which he left after he had succeeded in passing the Matriculation examination for Sydney University, was made bitter by the parting from Minnie with her "childish coquetry, the struggle between the free romping nature of the child and the thoughtful consideration and reserve of the woman." But he consoled himself with the thought that when the charm of these had vanished, the result might possibly be a plain commonplace girl.

With his certificate of Matriculation, Havelock felt more capable of coping with a classroom; and through the good offices of Mr Morris he soon obtained a post as the only assistant master at the "Grammar School" at Grafton on the Clarence.

The headmaster called on Havelock at his boarding house in Castlereagh Street, when Havelock was in the middle of a bout of stomach pains. He felt so ill, he had to ask the headmaster to leave. The headmaster left, wondering whether Havelock would be fit enough to take up the post.

As it happened, Havelock recovered quickly and almost as quickly the headmaster died. Before term started, he found himself promoted to a headmastership for the good will of which he did not have to pay a penny. It was a splendid opening for an educational career, supposing Havelock had possessed the qualities and ambition of a born schoolmaster.

But he was too young, too poorly qualified, bored by games and ineffectual in maintaining discipline. He commanded respect from neither the pupils nor their parents, some of whom just grumbled while others removed their sons. As a headmaster Ellis was a miserable failure.

But outside school he was not miserable. He lodged with a Mr Chapman in whose grounds the school building stood. In the Chapman home were half a dozen boarders, professional men working in Grafton, and a large brood of Chapman children, mostly female, ranging from a baby to a young lady of twenty-five. It was the first time since he had landed in Australia that he was really part of a family group—at Goongerwarrie he had been the adolescent filling in a sandwich of the younger and the older generation. As headmaster of the Grammar School he had a status among the boarders. He was a person in his own right and yet part of a large and happy family. Need it be said, he soon fell in love.

His fancy fell on the twenty-year-old May Chapman. "She was tall and well-made, dignified and reserved. I had not been in love since my boyish misplaced passion for my cousin seven years previously,[1] and my adoration—it was not passion this time—went out to the graciously imposing May. I worshipped in silence; I would have denied—indeed, I did deny when chaffed by a discerning fellow-boarder—that I worshipped at all. After I left Grafton I made no attempt to see or communicate with her, but merely wrote some verses to which I prefaced the words of Goethe: '*Wenn ich dich liebe, was geht's dich an?*' I am fairly certain that if I had desired to make any advances they would have been rejected. She was friendly to me, but scarcely sympathetic, cool, perhaps rather quizzical. She seemed, indeed, to be cool to men generally. . . . To me nothing tangible remains of my adoration

[1] In his journal Ellis counted the child Minnie as his "second love."

but a hairpin, once fallen from her hair, which I picked up and devoutly preserved." [1]

May Chapman was the one love in his life who bore a physical resemblance to his mother in stature and dignity. Her younger sister Berta, or Bertie, as she was nicknamed, was short like the women who were to mean most to him, Olive Schreiner, Edith Lees and Françoise Lafitte-Cyon (Delisle). His love for May Chapman was not sexual. He had no "honourable designs concerning her, most assuredly none dishonourable." It was far more like the deep, near-holy love a son might have for his mother; and for Berta his affection was more that of a brother towards his sister.

To neither was he able to express his feelings openly. He went for a picnic on the river with the Chapman family. Everyone was very jolly and Havelock wanted to join in but something forced him to draw aside and read a silly novel by Ouida, which bored him. "It is a great pleasure to think one gives pleasure; very pleasant to feel that one is a pleasant companion—a feeling unfortunately which is denied to me."

So, though the objective conditions existed for a sort of happiness, Havelock found himself no nearer being loved and sympathised with than he had at Carcoar; only this was worse, because he was forced to acknowledge that what held him back was not lack of opportunity but something inside himself. Berta would have liked him to confide in her, if nothing more, but he could bring himself to confide only in his journal, in the hope that one day he would meet a girl to whom he might show it.

"I have never yet uttered my heart in words to any living being; I cannot help writing it, though only for my own eye. And yet beyond all our outward motives, even beneath the reasons with which we deceive ourselves, there is generally some deeper cause lying. I feel that what prompts me to write in this book is not

[1] *My Life*, Eng. ed., pp. 109–10, Am. ed., p. 139. Whether Ellis kept this hairpin all his life I do not know. He certainly still had it in 1884. One must remember that the Victorians were great keepers of things, and that Ellis kept many of the little gifts from the Mother Superior on the *Empress* when he was only seven.

alone the mere relief of expression, but the chance that it may some day pass into the hands of someone by whom I shall in some measure perhaps be understood, perhaps even loved."

How far this entry on the night of Monday, 10 September 1877, was a recognition of something which he had been doing unconsciously all along it is impossible to say. But thenceforward one can take it that it was written to present to the woman, if he ever met her, whom he hoped would reciprocate his love. It was, in a rather bulky form, a letter of proposal with the words "perhaps be understood" as an escape clause, if perhaps he was not loved.

When it became clear that Grafton Grammar School was heading for disaster, the resourceful Messrs Morris and Bevill came forward with the suggestion that for the customary fee they should help him to realise this valuable asset. It would never have occurred to Havelock that he might sell something which he had been given for nothing; but once given the idea, he found a purchaser off his own bat, a gentleman called Mackintosh from South Australia.

When Mr Mackintosh looked the school over, he revised his ideas of price, pointing out that there was no good will—as far as will went it was bad—and the only pupils left were those whose parents were too lazy to take them away. He offered a fraction of the selling price, which Havelock gratefully accepted, paying over commission to Morris and Bevill, and to seal the bargain lending Mr Mackintosh a "curious book on sex" which he never returned.

Havelock was glad to be rid of the school, but he was sorry to see the last of the Chapmans. "I wished them all goodbye in the evening; and was sorry to say so to old Mr Chapman whom I like extremely. The two girls May and Bertie, who were up early, I wished farewell to the next morning. I am greatly wanting in self-possession. I shook May's hand, not with a squeeze; I don't think a squeeze is always the natural accompaniment of warmth of feeling; I then stumbled (though the sentence had been previously thought over) over a few words of kindly well-wishing which might be addressed, at parting, perhaps for ever, to a girl known, liked, lived in the same house with for nine months; then I shook hands again and—never once looked into her face—her eyes.

"It is to me astonishing how I should never have had an impulse to perform such a simple natural action. I cannot think of it without a pang of shame and regret. It might have revealed a pure warm look of regard which I should have felt as of no little price. I then turned to her sister Bertie, shook hands warmly, and as I remarked with a half-smile that her mamma said that she was to write and tell me how things went at Grafton, I looked into her eyes for an instant. That instant revealed the kind sympathetic brown eyes (I won't swear to them being brown; they simply gave me that impression) all suffused with moisture. I am perfectly aware that this indicated no very great depth of emotion, but it pleased me all the same. It is pleasant to feel we occupy even a very small corner in a human breast. She shall never know how much pleasure, lasting pleasure, that kind, sympathetic, foolish little mind of hers gave in filling those tender eyes of hers with tears. And she wouldn't understand it, if she did know. Although I never met May's gaze, I do not think there were tears in her eyes. Not that her feelings have less warmth, but she does not show them so much, a certain reticence she has, what I may call a certain *proud pudency*, modesty is hardly the word."

Berta with the insight which love gives might very well have understood more than Havelock gave her credit for. But he was not in love with Berta, and these words were written for the woman to whom he hoped eventually to give the book and who by implication would understand.

It was now twenty-six months since Havelock had landed in Sydney. During that time he had failed as an assistant master, been no trouble in the house as a tutor, and failed as a headmaster. On the credit side he had passed his matriculation examination, further widened his reading and improved his languages. Emotionally he had made no apparent progress in establishing contact with other people, he had reached no decision about his vocation, and the conflict between science and religion seemed as irreconcilable as ever. And yet there had been a certain advance. "Somehow I have the faculty of looking on myself *ab extra*," he wrote, "taking the position of an inquisitive unprejudiced onlooker, '*spectator et particeps*'." Some years ago this faculty assumed a morbid form; I have cleared myself from most of what is morbid; but the faculty still remains. And by this habit of looking on myself as a vast problem, and in the constant effort to understand it, I have reached many valuable conclusions—gone far in elucidating my own nature, though I am yet far, very far from understanding it. I find that one of my most marked characteristics is the large development which quite opposite sides of my nature have attained—the constructive and the destructive, the religious and the irreligious, the moral and the immoral, the conservative and the innovating. And I have a large development of strength and a large development of weakness." His strength he considered was to resist, to suffer, to be silent and to be misunderstood; and his weakness was to be self-conscious, hesitating, timid, dependent, yearning "to express itself, to be understood, to be *loved*—that yearning to express a something which is not expressible, or comprehensible, not perhaps lovable."

The advance which he had made was not towards a closer contact with the outside world, but towards the acceptance of the impossibility of that. The yearning to be *loved* he now regarded as a weakness, something to the impossibility of which he had to be reconciled. And this was not a passing emotion, because in 1884 he made a note in the journal, "I think this true—even now." That note was made just before passing the journal to the woman he had hoped would read it, and his underlining of the word "loved" was tantamount to saying to her, "Don't worry if you don't love me, because you can see for yourself that I regard my yearning to be understood and loved as a weakness, not a strength." It was a cripple code, the rule of maximal resignation and minimal happiness.

Yet it would be a mistake to think that he was not a very busy and occupied youth, as one can see from the outline of one of the days he spent after his return to Sydney from the Grafton fiasco.

At 9 a.m. he went into town with Mr Morris. He stopped at Lindsay's, the secondhand bookshop in Castlereagh Street, and read the passages in Furnival's Introduction to the Leopold Shakespeare relating to the Sonnets and *Measure for Measure.* Then he went to the Public Library for an hour, read J. S. Mill's *Essay on Nature*, from which he made brief extracts; and also a scene from Swinburne's *Bothwell.*

From there he went to the Council of Education to ask the secretary why he had had no answer to his request to be accepted as a pupil-teacher in a government school. He was sent on to the Examiner, who told him that the answer had been sent, but to the wrong address. He stayed till 12.30 filling in forms and was told to come back in the afternoon for an examination.

Lunch, for a treat, two twopenny bath buns instead of two penny buns with currants, or four ha'pennies without.

Back to the public library to look through a book on Michelangelo with good reproductions. Felt the muscular development of many of his creations exceeded the bounds of beauty as well as of nature. Glanced through Vol. 1 of Morley's *Rousseau* to get *ab extra* view of the man whose *Confessions* he was reading.

Back to Examiner's for a couple of hours. Stumbled through a passage from Caesar. Did a few sums, but stumped on one in interest which he could have done a few months before but had forgotten because mathematics bored him.

Returned to the Public Library, at the Lending Branch of which he exchanged Taine's *English Literature*, which he had been reading nearly all day, for Ruskin's *Lectures on Art*. Then he began to walk home. On the way he saw a horse dying in the street. He looked at it for a minute, thinking it would be a good time to observe veins and muscles. Then he walked on, meditating on horses and men, life and death, dying in harness, etc.

The outline of a day's activity such as this appears curiously dissipated, until one realises that it is like walking round the base of what after years of labour is to become a monumental pyramid; or alternatively collecting the material for a number of different mosaics, the arrangement of which would take a lifetime. This manifold and dispersed activity, going on in one form or another day after day, reading, extraction, meditation, observation, was really the single-minded pursuit of a treble purpose, the erection of a trophy to celebrate his victory over his limitations, his gift to humanity, and at the same time the realisation of himself.

And in his stride he took the next stage of his career. Despite the stumbling over Caesar, the mistake with the interest sum, fortified by two bath buns, he was accepted as a pupil-teacher for the model Fort School in Sydney and at the end of a month he did well in the examination for classification as a teacher. At the end of January 1878 he received his first government appointment as teacher in two part-time schools, one at Sparkes Creek and the other at Junction Creek, not very far from Scone, in the eastern section of New South Wales.

Havelock received the posting with stoical resignation. He didn't expect to like it, but there was no alternative. And at any rate it would give him a chance of visiting the Chapmans, the people in Australia for whom he most deeply cared.

5

My self was one with the Not-Self, my will one with the universal will. I seemed to walk in light; my feet scarcely touched the ground; I had entered a new world.

The Dance of Life

HE MADE the first stage of his journey, the hundred miles to Scone, comfortably by train. There, he was told, Mr Shaw at the Vicarage would tell him all about his job.

Mr Shaw was large and placid and kind and said he was pleased to give him a bed for the night. But though he was officially connected with the schools, there was so much to do in Scone and they were so far away that perhaps it would be better to have a chat with Mr Roberts, the schoolmaster of Scone.

Mr Roberts was a Welshman and he knew very little about the schools except the schoolmasters, who came to Scone before going to Sparkes Creek and back there when they left, which was often. There was one still in Scone, to whom Mr Roberts introduced him, a lanky defeated Australian without any qualifications. Even with his qualifications, Havelock felt depressed.

But his spirits rose when Mr Roberts promised to lend him a horse and his son as a guide to take him to Sparkes Creek next day; and the bed he slept in at the parsonage that night was so comfortable that it became in memory the symbol of luxury. It was to be long before he slept so soft again.

They set out next morning immediately after breakfast, going slowly because Ellis was no horseman, and in the late afternoon they came to the farmhouse of Mr Ashford, who lived closest to the Sparkes Creek schoolhouse. Back in Sydney they had told Ellis it would be easy to find lodging near the school. But Mr Ashford had a small house and a big family. He said Havelock could doss down on the settee in the living-room if he liked.

Next morning Havelock put on his black silk hat and walked down the hill to look at his schoolhouse. It was on the other side of the valley about a hundred yards up the slope from where the path from Ashford's place crossed the creek. It was built of rough-hewn planks which had warped, and let in the draught. He could see the sky through the roof-shingles too.

The schoolhouse consisted of two rooms, each of which had a bit at the back partitioned off and a door leading on to the verandah at the front. The room on the right was the schoolroom. It had a large open fireplace with a broad chimney and it was furnished with a table and rough school forms and desks; behind the partition at the back was a little kitchen. The room on the left was the teacher's bedroom. There was no furniture in it except a bed made from two sacks nailed to a wooden frame which stood on four rickety legs—which were liable to come off. There were no chairs, but behind the partition was a little bench on which there was a tin washing-bowl. Out at the back there was a privy in a little shed. The water for washing came from the creek. For drinking-water he had to go to the farm kept by a man called Barwick a few minutes away on the school side of the creek.

The school population of Sparkes Creek consisted of the children of Ashford's farm, Barwick's farm and Barwick's brother's farm a little further off.

Black silk hat and all, Havelock called on both the brothers Barwick and found that their farms were as small and their families as large as Ashford's. One of the Barwicks said that as Havelock would be living in the schoolhouse, he'd need to buy stuff to eat and all, and if he'd make a list Barwick would ride in to Scone and get it from Charles Trogg, the Chinaman. Charles Trogg, the Chinaman, had pretty nigh everything the schoolteacher would need, except bread and milk, which he could get from the Ashford place.

What with schoolmasters coming and going, the Ashfords and the Barwicks had worked out a routine. Ellis was just another master in the educational line. None of them lasted more than a year, but you had to let them down lightly or they wouldn't last that long. Ashford let Ellis sleep a second night on the settee and then told him it was time to move.

Havelock felt "like a lost child" as he staggered with his bag in his hand and the black silk hat on his head over the bridge and up the creek to his school. He had dreamed of being close to the Chapmans and instead he was miles away from anywhere.

Sparkes Creek was very beautiful, and arranging the stores which Barwick had brought from Scone was fun. But when night fell, it was different. He lay down on his bed of sacks and tried to sleep. But in the chimney there were wild beasts which scampered up and down, and when he woke from his troubled sleep in the morning, he found that a bandicoot "or some such small marsupial had evidently made a comfortable nest" in his silk hat, leaving some of its hairs behind.

For the first time in his life Havelock Ellis was roughing it. Mollycoddled by his mother, flannelled at Fontlands, house-trained at Goongerwarrie, ministered to at Grafton, he had come at last to a primitive community where they expected a teacher to teach, three days at Sparkes Creek and two at Junction one week, three at Junction and two at Sparkes the next. And the less fuss he made about it the better.

It wasn't a treatment that Captain Ellis could ever have given his son. But it was what Captain Ellis had hoped for and what Havelock, when it was forced on him, suddenly realised was what he had wanted all the time.

The bandicoots left after the first night. He didn't jump on his black silk hat. But he did realise that the advantage of the holes in the roof was that he could see the stars at night; and looking after himself, he found that he liked the simplest sort of food, involving the least amount of cooking. If someone had been cooking for him he might never have made that discovery.

Sparkes Creek put him in perspective. He had hitherto been emotionally younger than his age and intellectually more precocious. Sparkes Creek made him look after himself like a pioneer, and he loved it: except that a pioneer would have tidied the place up and improved it, whereas Ellis took it just as it was, taking delight in its absolute simplicity. He did not even mend the shingles on the roof, because it was so lovely to see the stars as he lay in bed. The only complaint he had was that when he lit the lamp at night, huge moths came hurtling through the broken transom above the door; but he did not repair the transom.

The school in Junction Creek was over the hill in the next valley, and twice or three times a week he would walk across and teach another group of farmers' children like the ones at Sparkes Creek, well-behaved, incurious, easy-to-teach little boys and girls, who left him free with his books and his dreams and his thoughts. His walks to work and back were a joy, to see huge jew-lizards lying along the branches of trees, native bears moving slowly, very slowly, away as he approached, and kangaroos bounding gracefully down the slopes. He loved to sit at his table on stormy evenings following with his nerves the rhythm of the great winds rolling and tumbling and crashing through the trees among the hills like the ocean let loose. And once, coming back from Junction Creek as dusk fell, he saw the roses climbing the verandah posts, the great crimson splashes on the green, and with a thrill he saw roses as never before or after, like a new flower made at that moment.

The loneliness that had haunted him at Grafton and Goongerwarrie, where there were people to yearn to be loved by, passed now there was no one. He wanted an ideal woman, a totally impossible she, who made all actual women pale and uninteresting. And as he hoisted the water in the bucket from the Barwicks' well, he murmured Swinburne:

> "Nothing is better, I well think,
> Than love; the hidden well-water
> Is not so delicate to drink."

But it was the delicacy of ideal love that he wanted. Sex was a matter of nocturnal emission unaccompanied by dreams, which had at first worried him because of the mess, but which he was by now noting, each time they occurred, by putting a tick in his diary.

Perhaps they would show that there was a rhythm of male periodicity.[1]

"At Sparkes Creek for the first time in my life I experienced the orgasm when awake. I was lying down on my simple bed, one warm pleasant day, reading something which evidently had in it for me some touch of erotic stimulation—I believe it was the *Dames Galantes* of Brantôme—and I suddenly became aware that the agreeable emotion aroused by the book, without any will or action of my own, was becoming physically translated and fulfilled. I realised what had happened and felt no alarm; evidently there was nothing in the occurrence that was not natural and beautiful, though it was of course easy to imagine circumstances under which it would have been yet more natural and beautiful. It was not until after this event that I ever became definitely conscious of any stirring of physical excitement at the thought or the proximity of an attractive woman." [2]

The occasion of the first orgasm plays a comparatively unimportant role in the lives of most people, however privately wonderful it may be. But with Ellis it had a special significance. He "felt no alarm"—so he clearly must have expected that he would feel alarm, and he realised with delight that it was "natural and beautiful," which implies that up to that time he had imagined it would be unnatural and ugly.

Though Ellis did not himself connect this revelation of the beauty and naturalness of sex with what followed, I believe that was the first phase of what made the year at Sparkes Creek "the most fateful, the most decisive" of all his years; it spiritually prepared him for what he called his "conversion."

There are several versions of this experience. He alluded to it in *Impressions and Comments* and he wrote about it at length in the third section of the chapter on the Art of Religion in *The Dance of Life*, and again in his autobiography. In each of these accounts he was writing from memory without consulting his journal. I

[1] He used them in the first volume of the *Studies*; but they proved nothing except his industry.

[2] *My Life*, Eng. ed., p. 125, Am. ed., pp. 157–8.

have chosen to print the entries from his journal, so that those who wish can compare them with the already printed accounts. They were not written at the time. Havelock Ellis did not think on paper. He thought, if one can use that word of a process that was largely intuitive, and then he wrote down later. So that the journal gives us not the detailed argument in his soul, but rather the conclusions which he reached.

Immediately preceding the conversion there were two entries; the first, dated 22 February 1878, is a long extract from George Eliot analysing the state of Daniel Deronda's mind, which Ellis thought magnificently described his own state of mind at the time, especially in passages which he underlined. The two most significant of these are:

"His early awakened sensibility and reflectiveness had developed into a many-sided sympathy, which threatened to hinder any persistent course of action; as soon as he took up any antagonism, though only in thought, he seemed to himself like the Sabine warriors in the memorable story—with nothing to meet his spear but flesh of his flesh, and objects that he loved." And later, "A too reflective and diffusive sympathy was in danger of paralysing in him that indignation and that selectness of fellowship which are the conditions of moral force . . . what he most longed for was either some external event, or some inward light, that would urge him into a definite line of action."

There were two quite separate external events. The first was news of the death of his mother's old friend Miss Johnston, who had taught him to play the piano. Though his journal is full of his feelings *towards* people, very tender feelings, the entry for March 17 is the only example of empathy, of an imaginative projection into the personality of a living person in its pages. "She was one of the very few friends who bear me affection," wrote Havelock, showing in his change of tense that though dead he felt her love as present, "and she was by far my earliest friend, out of my own family. I have always had affection for her; recently it had increased, as my sympathy grasped the fact of one of the unloved—of whom in our present baneful social state there must needs be many—passing through life with all the great capacities for love undeveloped or wasted on little objects, and finally lost in the grave never having found its fellow. I remember, as a child—I do not know how young I was—being allowed to look over the treasures in Johnny's desk. I came upon a little piece of twisted paper; I was about to untwist it, when she prevented me saying that a young gentleman had been playing with that, when talking to her many years ago. Doubtless she thought I was too young to take any notice of what she said; and it is only of recent years that this little piece of paper has had for me its true significance. I fancy that touching little incident in Wendell Holmes' *Professor* first showed it to me. I think of the whole treasures of affection of a human heart hung on that little scrap of paper twisted by a youth—more loved than loving, probably—kept sacred for a lifetime. Probably one or other of Johnny's treasures may come into my possession as a remembrance; rather than anything I would long to preserve sacredly that scrap of twisted paper."

The second external event was news from home that at long last the Rev. John Erck was writing to him. His mind turned once again to religion and whether he ought to take Holy Orders. He re-read Matthew Arnold's essay on Joubert and was struck by a remark of Joubert's, which he had not noticed before. "It is not hard to know God, provided one will not force oneself to define him." He felt there might be a profound truth in that. He had been going along all the time with the conviction that the intellect only must be appealed to in matters of belief. It never occurred to him that he ought to have proved that first. Notwithstanding the clearness with which he thought he was looking on the subject, it was a most monstrous assumption (whether true or not) that the intellect was the only appeal in matters of religion, he realised.

"The first glimmering of this truth I owe to Hinton, and the results of it on my religious beliefs I am unable to calculate," he wrote on May 16. "Already I begin to see a meaning in what had before had for me no meaning."

Hinton had started his career as a doctor and made a reputation as an ear specialist. He had then turned to writing about scientific, political, social and religious matters. The book which had fallen into Ellis's hands was called *Life in Nature*, an attempt to reconcile the apparent conflicts between scientific materialism and the Christian religion.

Ellis had read it through six months previously and been interested but not particularly impressed. Now with the words of Joubert in his mind, that first glimmer of the "inward light," he began to read it again, and the effect, not so much of what James Hinton said as of the vision behind his words, was electrical. He seemed to walk in light. He had entered a new world. Like all religious illuminations, it was describable only in metaphor. "In an instant the universe was changed for me. I trod on air."

When he began to write of it some two months later, he called it conversion. "It was not a change that could be formulated in precise rational terms, or that involved an act of faith in any creed; it was a profound change that yet had no intellectual content."

At the same time it was not a vision that is seen one moment and then passes, leaving nothing but the memory of a moment of glory. This illumination in an instant altered Havelock Ellis's attitude to the universe and his relation to that universe for the rest of his life. "It acted with the swiftness of an electric contact; the dull aching tension was removed; the two opposing psychic tendencies were fused in delicious harmony, and my whole attitude to the universe was changed. It was no longer an attitude of hostility and dread, but of confidence and love."

As well as this change of heart, there was the familiar experience of new-found certainty. Looking back in his first entry after the conversion, he wrote in his journal.

"For the last three years I have known nothing but doubt, or when I felt no doubt I felt misery. I was living in a vacant universe which I felt to be a machine. I was a living thing groping my way amid dead, blind relentless laws, ready at every moment to crush me. For the last three years, I said. It was not always so, as a boy I was religious (for I was always religious). Church of England and of rather Broad Church tendencies.

"There came a time when vast questions crowded one after

another, threatening to overwhelm me. For I would not shirk them—rather I could not. And so one by one I met them and was conquered, and they left me alone with my sorrow.

"I always sought for Truth—for Truth, even if it were Truth crucified. And I believe that even then I was following Truth; it was at the command of Truth and not of any phantom that I gave up my beliefs. For I had no right to them. I had found them and adopted them; they were not mine.

"But if Truth takes away, she also gives. And so for all she had taken away, she poured a thousandfold into my bosom. She took away my beliefs because they were not mine, not born in me—now I possess the beliefs that are mine, that were conceived in me not without anguish, and so which are mine. And thus for me there is no more doubt. I met the waves of that sea of doubt and battled with them and never looked back at the lowlands I had left. And I have reached shore now. I have reached a height I had not dreamed of before."

This passage is intellectually confused; but there is no doubt at all of the feeling of harmony, of the at-onement with—with what? With Christianity? With God? That was what was so puzzling. "What most strikes me about all this is the fact that I have actually acquired no actual, definite dogmas or beliefs at all—that is to say beliefs which would be recognised as religious by any ordinary Christian. I have no sense of the personality of God, or a future life, or any similar dogmas; indeed I think that the learning that these are not the highest spiritual beliefs was an essential part of the struggle I have gone through."

The long gap in the journal after the conversion was due perhaps in part of Ellis's hesitation to commit himself to the certainty that there really had been a change in spirit; and then when that became certain, he needed more time to discover its significance; that is to say, firstly what it meant to himself and secondly what had actually happened.

It seems to be a universal experience that immediately after an illumination of God, there is a self-dedication, the natural consequence of this sudden wonderful communion. The way that

Ellis put it in his journal was, "I feel that self-sacrifice, the merging of the self in the Not-Self, is the very essential part of all true spirituality . . . and I can see now how self-sacrifice is the keynote of Christianity. I have been helped in this a great deal by James Hinton." His reference here to Hinton was prompted by Hinton's idea that the resignation of the selfless man included a resignation of what he called "self-goodness," rather than self-righteousness, the attempt to be better through the effort of will than one was naturally according to one's spiritual development.

Like all Hinton's ideas, it was very muddled. Each person could get from it what he needed. What Havelock Ellis got from it was the belief that it was no longer necessary to worry whether he was this sort of person or that sort of person. He had to accept himself as he was and dedicate himself to what Christians called God but what he preferred with Hinton to call the Not-Self. Then the problems which had so absorbed him would fade. This pre-occupation with personal happiness—happiness might come, but if it didn't, it did not matter because one's life was dedicated to the service of others. The harmony which came from dedication and self-sacrifice was more important than anything else, and weakness, if accepted completely, became a source of strength. It was a sort of spiritual Judo.

This formed a rational explanation of the message contained in his illumination, the reason why he felt such calm. But where did the message come from?

He found his explanation in a book called *Natural Law, an Essay on Ethics* by Edith J. Simcox, who wrote that conversion was "seldom or never produced by any one rational consideration; a mass of, as it were, accumulative evidence of cognate impressions result at a particular moment in producing the conviction which is complete and effectual as soon as it exists at all. All previously received impressions and beliefs remain the same, but coloured and intensified by the sense of their connection and all-sufficiency. Religious writers insist that there has been a fundamental transformation of the will and character. . . .

"In practice the change is from a hostile to a friendly disposition towards the real order of the universe. It is the birth of love, the spontaneous opening of the heart to a new affection of loyal devotion, and *the affection is as real and irresistible as the personality of its object may be dubious.*"

The italics are mine, to emphasise what must have stood out from this description of what he recognised as his experience. Here was an explanation of what he recognised in his heart and soul as a valid experience, without having to admit of the personality of God. But what of the saints, who had had these experiences? Edith J. Simcox had the answer.

"The change of heart by which the saints themselves felt released at once from the bondage of natural iniquity and the law of the natural morality may be described as the recovery by a soul that has been out of harmony with its surroundings of the realisation that harmony, though not happiness, is possible—at a price; that though the self cannot remodel the universe in conformity to its best impulses, all its own best impulses can find scope and satisfaction in conformity with the true tendencies in the Not-Self."

The phrase "harmony, though not happiness, is possible—at a price" was very close to Havelock's feelings. "This is accurately expressed," he remarked, "only she scarcely insists enough on self-sacrifice."

The positive element in Ellis's conversion was his receiving the "inward light" for which he longed. If he followed that inward light, he would at the same time realise the fullness of his nature and do the maximum of good. It involved the sanctification of the total man, the acceptance of what in the world's eyes were weaknesses as gifts the possession of which was a potential source of strength; just as someone crippled at birth or by disease may by the acceptance of the limitation turn a physical defeat into a spiritual victory. Ellis followed this inward light during the rest of his life with a profound belief in harmony, which was a strong support, and a sad distrust in the possibility of happiness that sometimes betrayed him into error.

Theoretically he remained uncommitted as to the source of

that inward light, as Edith J. Simcox did. "The personality of its object" semantically may mean "It is not possible to be certain whether the personality of its object exists or not." But it is very hard to accept a spiritual experience without trying to produce an intellectual explanation of what has happened; and in rejecting the Christian explanation of his experience, Havelock Ellis found himself offering alternatives such as the union of the self with the Not-Self, or subjective explanations in terms of "the diastole of the soul," as analysed in the passage later devoted to *The New Spirit*.

These rationalisations were the negative element of his conversion, which may be criticised without impugning the experience itself or the grace it conferred.

His conversion had been precipitated by renewed meditation on whether he should take Holy Orders. The illumination gave him no guidance on his vocation. This did not come until September 1. Just as the illumination had been triggered off by reading Hinton's *Life in Nature*, this fresh revelation came from reading *The Life and Letters of James Hinton* by Ellice Hopkins. "I was reading how, at the age of nineteen by advice of the family medical man, who was of the opinion that the boy wanted something to engage the force of his mind, James Hinton was entered as a medical student at St Bartholomew's Hospital," Ellis noted in his journal on September 1: "When I got so far a flash of thought as it were passed through my brain. I laid the book down and jumped up. I may not be for a doctor, but I shall never make anything else. And then I wondered how ever it was that this had never occurred to me before."

He went on to discuss the oddity of this sudden vocational revelation, and ended with a vision of the career which lay ahead of him that was truly prophetic. "I can see so well how it was that my thoughts never turned in that direction until now; that *culture* has been my aim, that I have striven, in so far as may be, to put myself in sympathy with literature, religion, science, art and thought in their different forms, and that my tastes have never been more for one than another. For I know now that such culture, little though it may have been, was not wasted, and that I can never become a *mere* medical practitioner."

He seems to have had no doubt that the money would be forthcoming for his medical training, though his father and mother had no capital and four daughters to be launched in the world. It might need a miracle to provide the money, but his conviction of his destiny was so strong that he was sure the miracle would happen.

And so, as all the parents in Sparkes and Junction Creeks expected, Havelock Ellis handed in his notice at the end of the year, just like all the other schoolmasters. But unlike the others, he had found what he had come for.

6

After the age of twenty your task becomes easier and more obvious.

An Open Letter to Biographers

HAVELOCK ELLIS arrived home in the spring of 1880 and put to his family the idea that he should become a doctor. His mother approved and volunteered a hundred pounds, half of a small legacy which she had received from Miss Johnston; not enough to carry him through medical school, but at least a contribution more substantial than the scrap of twisted paper that Havelock had longed sacredly to preserve.

Where the rest of the money would come from Ellis did not worry. He had saved something in Australia and he settled down to take a holiday and get to know the family which he had not seen for four years. He had left his sisters children but in the meantime two of them had become young ladies whom he found sympathetic and attractive. The eldest, Louie, became very close to him and remained so for the rest of her life. In fact for a time he felt sexually attracted to her. He attributed this to the fact that he had been away so long that she appeared to him as a stranger; and he found in this experience material which enabled him "in later years to give clear precision to" his "conception of the psychological foundation of exogamy." If he had grown up with her, it would not have happened.

Like many of his generalisations from personal experience, it was challengeable. I have known many brothers who have grown up with their sisters and been attracted to them.

Louie was a devout young Christian and to please her Havelock resumed church attendance. He was anxious to free her from the desire to conform to an exterior pattern of Christianity and bring her the vision which he had been given at Sparkes Creek. He put it in Christian terms to make it easier for her to accept. "I believe that the essence of Christianity is self-sacrifice, but I feel now intensely the 'sweet-reasonableness' of that self-sacrifice; how right and natural and lovely it is that we should give ourselves to him who gave himself to us—who gave his *life*—not so much his death—to humanity." He wrote her a long letter blending Christian and Hintonian ideas and urging on her the need for total forgetfulness of self, self-goodness as well as self-badness.

Hinton at this time and for many years dominated his thinking to a far greater extent than he admitted when he came to write his autobiography. In Miss Ellice Hopkins's *Life and Letters of James Hinton* there had been a reference to a mass of unpublished material and he wrote to her for further details.

Miss Hopkins forwarded the letter to Hinton's widow—Hinton had died just over four years previously—and there followed in due course an invitation to call.

Though "the Wizard," as he was known to his familiars, had departed, there remained a faithful band of followers devoted to his memory and his ideas. They were mostly women; for had not Hinton said "Christ was the Saviour of men, but I am the saviour of women, and I don't envy him a bit." In addition to Mrs Hinton, who did not regard her late husband with quite such profound awe as the other devotees did, there was her sister, Miss Caroline Haddon, Miss Agnes Jones, a spinster of uncertain age and health, and Mrs Booley who was the wife of a well-known mathematician and whose daughter had married James Hinton's son, Howard, science master at Uppingham.

Faith in the Wizard was faltering at the time of Havelock Ellis's introduction to the Hinton circle. James had died suddenly in middle age of a cerebral tumour. His ideas, especially on the relations of the sexes, were original but startlingly confused. The muddleheadedness could be explained in terms of that mortal illness, but there was the uneasy doubt, not to be encouraged but sometimes hard to dismiss; were the ideas themselves the product of a diseased brain?

And what to do with all his papers? Howard had collected the

JAMES HINTON

various published essays and edited them into a posthumous volume, but there were two great piles of stuff, consisting of four large volumes which Hinton had had printed in his lifetime but never published, and bundle after bundle of manuscript notes and jottings made in the later years, after Hinton abandoned aural surgery, religion, science and philosophy for sexual morality. There was so much of them: and yet they didn't add up; they didn't, however loyal one was to the Wizard, make sense.

Then there appeared this young man from Australia, so bearded and handsome and intelligent (though his voice was disconcertingly high and thin, after a time one did not notice it) and the story he had to tell was so strangely linked to the Wizard's. He compared his sojourn in Australia to the three years which St Paul spent in Arabia; could it be that he was destined to play the role of the Apostle to the Gentiles for the Saviour of Woman?

Though almost embarrassingly shy, this young man was in no doubt as to what he had come for. He took away the privately printed papers, read them through and reported that a selection rearranged in a more logical order would make an interesting and useful book. It might be a task after the heart of Miss Caroline Haddon? That it was after her heart Miss Haddon agreed, but it was unfortunately too much for her intellect. The young man said that if he could be of any assistance, he would be only too pleased; and his offer was gratefully accepted.

Ellis then bore off the later manuscripts to see whether they could possibly be pieced together to make a pattern. What attracted him in Hinton's thought was the emphasis on motive rather than behaviour, that goodness does not reside in *what* is done but in the *spirit* in which it is done. "A chastity maintained by fear is as unchaste as harlotry . . . a feeling as if some physical relations of things were in themselves pure and others impure, which seems to me the most intense and profound of all possible impurities." Hinton was a stimulating thinker in young Ellis's view, rhetorical, confused and contradictory, but provocatively paradoxical. "Man is condemned to pleasure; but that does not mean to selfishness. It means the very contrary; that he must be free. Let him look at those pleasures which are service and take them." "Service consists in doing pleasant things." "This is the proclamation: Good has nothing to do with putting away pleasure. Come in, therefore, you pleasure-led people, and claim goodness as your reward. If there is any reason in a man for his putting away pleasure in order to be good, let him repent. Let him repent and become a new creature."

Havelock Ellis read and returned with the report that in the later papers there was material for another interesting and useful book. It might be a task after the heart of Mrs Hinton?

Mrs Hinton allowed her name to be used as editor of this second volume, which was called *The Law-Breaker*, but in fact all the editing was done by Ellis, who also contributed an introduction.

Havelock Ellis was a most valuable accession to the Hinton circle, because he restored to it some of its innocence. He did not see that women had been drawn towards Hinton either because their marriages had failed or because they had not succeeded in securing husbands; or that underlying Hinton's high-flown theory of polygyny was a promiscuous sexual urge which demanded the justification of a sexual philosophy. Theoretically Havelock believed in unlimited sexual freedom as he had no practical experience of any sort. He took Miss Agnes Jones on one side to question her about the Wizard and was embarrassed to find that this, to him, elderly lady had her own interpretation of Hinton's doctrine of selfless service. It was the limitation of the Hintonian system, as any other, that those longing to be selflessly serviced could not find those selfless enough to render the service. Miss Jones could only stand and yearn.

But as editor and director of operations for spreading the gospel according to James Hinton, the main dogma of which was that there was no dogma, Havelock Ellis so won the hearts of Mrs Hinton and her sister that they considered it a tragedy when through lack of money Ellis was forced to take a post as teacher in a school at Smethwick, a suburb of Birmingham. Even from there he showed his flair as a propagandist. A rather conventional article on Purity appearing in a magazine called *Modern Thought*,

Ellis replied with a Hintonian rejoinder "What is Pureness?", with a pungency which showed his value as a publicist.

Shortly after it appeared, Miss Haddon made the suggestion that she should advance Ellis £200 towards his medical training. The offer was made through Howard Hinton, with the suggestion that he should take out a life insurance policy to cover repayment in case he died before qualifying. Ellis hesitated because he did not like being indebted to anyone, but Angus Mackay, when consulted, told him that he should accept the offer gratefully. The last barrier to his career was down.

"It happened thus, as it happened before, as it has happened since, throughout my whole life, that, at the right moment, the gift of Heaven, without any effort of mine, fell miraculously upon me. I suppose it is so also for others." [1] So Ellis wrote years later, his heart warmed at the recollection of the goodness of God. And then remembering that he did not believe in God, but only in the Not-Self, he hastened to add, "And that is why we speak of 'Heaven' and 'miracles.' That is why we try to account for the unaccountable by picturing a fairytale God in the skies, who watches over his children and gives them all they need."

Returning to London in the autumn of 1881, Havelock enlarged his circle of friends. The total of £300 which he had to carry him through medical school was exiguous even for a student living at home. He would have to eke it out with some sort of literary work and he sought out John Foulger, the editor of the magazine *Modern Thought*. Foulger had an office in the city at 13 Paternoster Row. There he edited, printed and published two small progressive magazines—the other was called *To-day*; and there foregathered a group of thinkers united in agreement that Victorian society was all wrong, but at loggerheads about what was wrong and how to cure it. In Foulger's office, Ellis met H. M. Hyndman the Marxist politician, John Burns the working-class leader, Belford Bax who was a lion in the jungle of theory but too frightened of the working class to walk through the slum of Lisson

[1] *My Life*, Eng. ed., p. 144, Am. ed., p. 182.

Grove. He met two ardent advocates of land-nationalisation, one of whom married a washerwoman's daughter masquerading as a great lady and was shipped off by his family to America, while the other died in Australia of venereal disease.

Foulger was a man after Ellis's heart, a middle-of-the-road man, daring among the cautious and cautionary to the daring. He favoured a progressive educated democracy in the radical tradition, a dynamic democracy in which men and women earned their rights rather than having rights thrust upon them.

Ellis obtained a little work from Foulger, but it would be unfair to say that he was ever consciously job-hunting—though in his position there was every justification for doing so. He was fascinated by life in all its aspects. The world was opening out like a rose, every petal of which was beautiful. He was enrolled as a student of St Thomas's Hospital. He was studying to become a doctor. Agreed. But music and art and politics and ideas and social science and sex and psychology and religion were all parts of the life which he wanted to live, and with that curious certainty which he had had long before its confirmation at Sparkes Creek, he intended to go on the way he had started, even though it might take him rather longer to qualify as a doctor.

It was wonderful after all those years of loneliness in Australia to meet people with whom it was possible to talk, to find that he had read more than almost anybody of his own age and in more languages; and with these new people to try out his own ideas and those he had taken or was developing from Hinton, using people's minds as a child uses a wall to learn to play tennis.

The Hinton home was his base. There he was more at home than he was at his mother's because they valued him higher. Mrs Hinton said he was like James, but added, "Not that that is necessarily a compliment."

From this base he sallied forth, if not confident at least ardent. He was uncertain yet what was his line of country. Foulger proposed a "Progressive Association." Start with Sunday-evening meetings. Lectures and discussion-groups on the burning questions of the day. Havelock became a founder-member, thinking perhaps that if he was ever to meet the girl who might read his journal, it would be in such a company.

Foulger dressed his committee with good-sounding names, meaning much in the 1880s and little now. Havelock by virtue of youth and enthusiasm was given the post of Secretary. At committee meetings he was fertile with ideas for lectures or suggestions for speakers. He wrote persuasive letters which induced men and women of note to address rather smaller audiences than they were accustomed to, because they thought the audience was select. But the more public the activity became, the more reclusive grew young Ellis. Before the meetings Foulger shamed Havelock into going into the streets with him and handing out bills advertising the lectures. At the meetings Havelock refused to speak or even sit on the platform. His position was at the table placed at the entrance of the hall in a howling draught, receiving subscriptions, selling literature and catching colds which made him susceptible to throat and chest infections long after his enthusiasm for associations to advocate causes had withered away.

At the Progressive Association he met no girl to whom he could show his journal, but he met a clerk in the Local Government Board in Whitehall, called Percival Chubb. He was a sociable optimist who believed that the way to make people better was to organise a society to discuss how this could be done, with a well-planned agenda and good minutes. He became joint secretary of the Progessive Association and because he worked just north and Havelock just south of Westminster Bridge, they frequently met for lunch. They were both very poor and were usually driven to a pastrycook's in Westminster, whose sausage rolls developed in Havelock a lifelong aversion.

At these meetings, while Havelock discoursed on the wisdom and paradoxes of James Hinton, Chubb countered with eulogies of his own pet philosopher and sage, Thomas Davidson, who, if his sayings were less gnomic than Hinton's, had the advantage of being still alive. Davidson, said Chubb, was a great ethical leader who sought to renew the life of society on a higher plane. Ellis had met Davidson's brother at Foulger's office where *he* had tried to renew the life of society with beer, and he was not impressed.

"You must meet Thomas Davidson," Chubb said, "when he is next in London." He was an itinerant prophet, seeking disciples over Europe and the United States.

Ellis was impressed when he met Davidson. "He was alive, intensely and warmly alive, as even his complexion and colouring seemed to show; here was the perfervid emotional Scottish temperament carried almost or quite to the point of genius." Davidson had travelled widely. He had read equally widely in literature and philosophy. He had gained the experience of age without losing the ardour of youth. "I came away feeling that this was the most remarkable man, the most intensely alive man, I had ever met," Ellis wrote in *My Life*. "I am not sure that I should not say so still."

Ellis made friends with Thomas Davidson and expounded to him his own version of the gospel according to James Hinton. Davidson would listen to him patiently, the teacher in him drawing out the confused ideas of his pupil without interrupting. Then he patiently explained to the young man the flaws in all his arguments. If only he could get some discipline into young Ellis's unruly brain, Davidson saw in him a valuable disciple; and he was gratified at the diffidence with which Ellis listened to the exposure of his errors.

They would part, Davidson concluding that Ellis's silence implied that he was convinced by his arguments. And then the next time they met, Ellis would continue the elaboration of his version of Hintonism, as though Davidson had never said a word.

The old man found it infuriating. It was understandable that a young man with no training in logic should make the sort of mistakes that young Ellis made. But it was unintelligible that he should be so stupid as to persist in those mistakes when they had been pointed out. Davidson had a profound belief in metaphysics. The perception of the nature of the universe, he was willing to concede, might be a matter for some non-intellectual faculty, vision, insight, intuition, Divine guidance, but the explanation of the nature of the universe must, in Davidson's view, be logically consistent and coherent. He detected in Ellis with horror a metaphysical nihilism which denied the existence of all absolute truth. What he had mistaken for the woolly-headedness of an indisciplined mind, he discovered was a deliberate attempt to catch by analogy truths which Ellis thought died when pinned down in words used logically. He considered also that what Ellis said was at variance with what he believed in his heart; that below communion with the Not-Self by a soul which was co-existent with the body was a deeper belief in a personal God and an eternal soul. He expressed this in a letter written from Rome on 18 February 1884. "I grieve deeply that you should so uncompromisingly assume the position that you do, a position which I cannot distinguish from a rather elevated secularism. To confound the eternal with the phenomenal seems to me the worst of heresies. It is one too in which you, in your best moments, don't really believe."

"It is utterly vain to attempt a system of practical morals without a clear knowledge of the human spirit," he had warned in an earlier letter, "and such knowledge cannot be reached by any brilliant guessing or synthetic ebullience, but only by long and careful analysis."

Earlier in that same letter he attacked Ellis and Hinton for their abuse of the meaning of words. "I cannot agree with your philosophical views, in any sense that I can attribute to your expression of them. That 'this world is the only actual and eternal one' is so plainly not true that I cannot imagine any serious man maintaining that it is. Either he is talking paradox intentionally or else he does not know the meaning of the words he is using. Mr Hinton plainly was in the latter predicament. All this cheap talk about theological dreams is mere popular gibberish, unworthy of the attention of any serious man. The truth is 'this world,' the world of phenomena and change, is not actual at all; much less is it eternal. Mr Hinton was so innocent of philosophical training that he could not distinguish the actual from the real, the eternal from the continuous."

The friendship which had begun with a deep mutual regard gradually withered away, Ellis being unable to accept as relevant to himself Thomas Davidson's metaphysical abstractions, and Davidson being unable to see that Hinton's greatest value for Ellis was that he was associated with that conviction of destiny revealed to him at Sparkes Creek. Davidson put his finger on Ellis's weakness when he warned that clear knowledge of the human spirit could not be reached by brilliant guessing and synthetic ebullience; and Ellis detected Davidson's weakness when he accused Davidson of wanting him as a disciple, instead of letting him develop along his own lines. So far from converting Ellis, Davidson convinced him that his own philosophy was a purely personal matter, that the same was true of every philosopher, and every man had to evolve the philosophy consonant with his true nature. From this followed the corollary that Ellis had discovered that he was of the material from which leaders, not proselytes, are made.

But before this break came Thomas Davidson had inspired Chubb and Ellis and a few others to start a small group with the large title of the Fellowship of the New Life. The first formal meeting was held in the rooms of Edward Pease on 23 October 1883, at which sixteen New Livers unanimously agreed to "realise among themselves the higher life and make it a primary care to provide a worthy education for the young."

In November Davidson left England to sow the seed of the new life in a warmer climate, while Ellis, Chubb and seven others settled down to formulating what higher life was to be realised.

After due debate they agreed on the following:

THE FELLOWSHIP OF THE NEW LIFE

Object. The cultivation of a perfect character in each and all.

Principle. The subordination of material things to spiritual.

Fellowship. The sole and essential condition of fellowship shall be a single-minded, sincere and strenuous devotion to the Object and Principle.

This formulation immediately caused a schism in the membership. As Bernard Shaw described it,[1] "Certain members of that circle, modestly feeling that the revolution would have to wait an unreasonably long time if postponed until they personally attained perfection," argued that the aims should be directed towards practical political and economic action. Ten out of the fourteen members present agreed with Frank Podmore, who put this view. The remaining four, including Chubb and Ellis, were left with their Fellowship while the majority seceded to found the Fabian Society to work for "the reconstruction of society on a non-competitive basis with the object of remedying the evils of poverty."

Thus was revealed the fundamental division between those who agreed the old society was wrong. The Fabians believed outer change would produce inner revolution. The New Livers believed in creating "a kind of atmosphere in which it shall be possible for the outward life to be a true exponent of the inward life." But whereas the Fabians could agree on political and economic programmes, it was far more difficult for the New Livers to agree on anything except their disagreement with the Old Livers and the Fabians. There were as many views of the New Life as there were members of the fellowship; and the only reason for joining together was so that each could explain to the others how wrong they were. It was useful to Ellis as a sounding-board for his ideas. But the Fellowship of the New Life proved in the end as unsuitable to a man of his reclusive temperament as the Progressive Association had been.

The people he liked most were those, such as Edward Carpenter, who addressed the Fellowship, gave it his blessing but did not join. That was an example which Havelock followed throughout the rest of his life. He became an enthusiastic blesser but the most reluctant joiner.

[1] G. B. Shaw: *Fabian Tract, No.* 41.

7

A critic who is not keenly aware of all the defects of a lovely thing that ravishes him is but a crude critic, whose opinion hardly counts. My attitude is the same even in love. The women whom I have loved, and almost worshipped, are women of whose defects I have been precisely and poignantly aware.

My Life

FROM THE conversion at Sparkes Creek in 1879 until February 1884 Havelock Ellis was untroubled by any of those hopeless hidden passions which had made his adolescence splendid and miserable. He had found calm in the abjuration of personal happiness and dedication to selfless service. The sexual problem was solved by the acceptance of his limitations. He was not constituted as other men; but the more he studied, the more he was convinced that the conception of the "normal" man and woman was the product of conventional thinking and conventional living. There was an immense range of deviations from the norm, listed as perversions, but as he preferred to consider them, anomalies, which made the human character more beautiful, interesting and diverse. This study, together with his multifarious activities, kept him busy and contented, certain that if ever a woman was destined to come into his life, she would come of her own accord and without his having to seek her out.

In February 1884 he read a novel by Ralph Iron, *The Story of an African Farm*. Its faults were obvious, but they did not matter beside its freshness, its sincerity, its sense of place and people. The parallels between the author's experience in remote South Africa and his own at Sparkes Creek were so startling that Ellis felt impelled for the first time in his life to communicate his gratitude and admiration direct to the author.

The answer came in due course from St Leonards-on-Sea; and Ralph Iron was a woman called Olive Schreiner, *Miss* Schreiner as she confirmed in her second letter.

A lively correspondence started up, each discovering community of interest in Socialism, the Woman Question and so on. Ellis told her about his medical studies, the essay that he had published on Thomas Hardy in the *Westminster Review*, the Progressive Association, the Fellowship of the New Life, the doctrines of James Hinton, the kindness of Mrs Hinton and the intelligence of Caroline Haddon. Olive told him of her ambition at one time to be a doctor and how she had trained for a midwife-nurse at the Women's Hospital in Endell Street, London, till her health broke down, and who the various characters in *The Story of an African Farm* were based on.

Letters bounced back and forth between London and St Leonards like balls in championship ping-pong; and they were old friends by post before they met face to face for the first time in May of that year.

As soon as she arrived in London—and before ever they met—Olive revealed one of her characteristic oddities. She had booked rooms in Harrington Gardens without inspecting them or getting anyone to do so for her. She arrived to find "everyone drunk." The place was filthy and Olive said she couldn't possibly stay there, but the harridan of a landlady caught hold of her and demanded thirty shillings in lieu of notice. Olive paid the money under protest, went off and found some better rooms nearby and then was struck by the horrifying thought. "Supposing Havelock wrote to me at Harrington Gardens? Supposing he sent some of Hinton's precious manuscripts?" She rushed back to Harrington Gardens and the drunken landlady denied that any letters had come for her. But then she would have done that anyway out of spite. Perhaps she had deliberately torn them up! In her huge spidery handwriting she scrawled off an agonised note to Ellis.

This was the first glimpse he had got of the intimate Olive, the woman who never needed to drink because she was always in the sort of state that other people get into after a bottle of champagne, a woman as violently over-demonstrative in her feelings as he was undemonstrative, who could react so quickly to her environment that half an hour in a place she did not like would lay her low with what she called "asthma."

The photograph which Ellis chose of Olive to illustrate his autobiography showed her at the age of twenty-four, a romantic strong girl with long black ringlets to the shoulder and a provocative curl right down the middle of her low broad forehead: a passionate face, full of character, the face of a Corsican bandit's mistress, a sultry Byron or an English noblewoman cross-dressing in the Levant.

But Olive was five years older when Ellis first met her and already past her first beauty. The face showed the signs of nervous anxiety, an almost continuous hypertension. Her short sturdy body had filled out and no longer had the vigorous curves of youth. When he called at her lodgings to take her on to a meeting of the Progressive Association, the sight of her neither exalted or depressed him. Though extremely sensitive to beauty in most of its forms, he was curiously apathetic to purely physical beauty. What mattered was the spirit within, and just as he seldom mentioned physical beauty, he as seldom mentioned physical ugliness.

Havelock Ellis at the time of meeting Olive was an extremely handsome young man, with fine slightly curly hair, a broad high forehead, deep-set eyes, a full broad mouth and a short spade beard which disguised the prognathous ugliness of his chin. Yet when after a brief conversation Olive retired to her bedroom to put on her hat to go to the meeting, she burst into tears. Judging by the vigour of his opinions expressed on paper, she had imagined a man of strength, determination and will-power. And here was this shy young man, who did not look her in the eyes, who spoke in a high weak voice and whose every movement was awkward. "Don't you think there must *always* be some sense of pain in learning to know more of people whom you've known only through their books?" she wrote to him later, partly sounding him on what he thought of her, but also expressing her disappointment at this first encounter.

When two young people fall in love by post, as Olive and Havelock had done, each visualises what the other may give in terms of subjective needs. Havelock Ellis's needs were very simple. He had his journal to which he had confided his yearnings and his misery,

OLIVE SCHREINER AT THE TIME SHE MET HAVELOCK ELLIS

his aspirations and his ecstasy. He had never shown it to a soul; perhaps Olive was the person to read it and to understand what he was and love him despite or because of it. She was his confessor, if she would be.

Olive's expectations were quite different. There were no fears about sexual potency. She had had a terrifying experience at the age of sixteen. She had fallen in love with Julius Gau, a young man whose sister she was nursing. She thought that he had the fine new views of the equality of the sexes which she had absorbed from her books. She missed a period. She became terrified that she was pregnant. And the young man promised that if that was really so, he would make an honest woman of her in the old-fashioned way. But he did not really want to marry her; nor did she want to marry him, when she saw the sort of person he was. She did not want a marriage made not in Heaven but in the maternity ward.

As a result of this experience, she decided to become a writer. It was safer to give birth to books than to babies. Yet because her sexual nature had been awakened, there would be mountings of desire which she exploded of her own accord. She took potassium bromide in large quantities to lessen their frequency, but, perhaps because of guilt, she became afflicted with exhausting attacks of "asthma."

This very depressing life of work, drugs and moral failure went on for ten years, at the end of which she came to England with the manuscript of *The Story of an African Farm*. She went to stay with one of her brothers, who was the headmaster of a school in the Isle of Wight. And once again she fell in love.

This time it was with a man who was a sadist; and she discovered to her horror that she liked being a masochist. It gave her the most acute sexual pleasure, but it left her with a sense of utter degradation. She hated herself and the man and yet she longed for him and the way he treated her, more than she had ever longed for anything in her life. It ran utterly contrary to all her ideas of the equality of the sexes and it made her feel ashamed of herself. But there it was. She despised the man who had found this flaw in her character and yet she wanted him more than she had ever wanted anybody in her life.

All this had happened three years before. The flight to Endell Street Hospital had been an attempt to get away. The collapse of health had been due to the fact that the flight had been only too successful. He had made no effort to follow her. And yet when Ellis had first written to her, she was still in love with this man. Ellis, she prayed, would be the man who could combine intellectual mastery with sexual dominance. The reason why she went into her bedroom and cried was because he quite obviously was incapable of doing that. He was not the man she had hoped he was.

As she came to know him better, she found that he had thought a great deal about sexual "anomalies," as he called them. He was unshockable. He produced the most plausible reasons why she should not be ashamed of any of the things of which she was ashamed. But her father had been a Protestant missionary with very fixed standards, and despite her emancipation she accepted them.

The Hinton circle, for example, smelt wrong to her, especially Miss Jones with her terrible invitations to Havelock of which he seemed completely unaware. With all her South African common sense she did not like it at all. A friend of hers told her that James Hinton had posed as the Saviour of Woman because that was the easiest way to seduce them. Havelock was terribly distressed. She had got it quite wrong. That was the sort of impure talk which you had to expect from philistines.

Well, why on earth did Hinton talk of a man having a number of wives but never a woman having a number of husbands? Olive asked in her downright way. And Miss Haddon gave a lecture on the beauty of a man loving a lot of women at once. What was behind that?

Ellis claimed that he never supported Hinton's views on polygamy. In fact he defended his benefactress, saying to Olive that such an arrangement might be very beautiful. It was the defence of a man for whom sex was only in the head. But it sprang from his desire to help Olive according to the sexual theories which he had evolved from Hinton.

Olive was more impressed by Havelock Ellis himself than by any of his friends except Edward Carpenter. Ellis's ideas might lack universality, but they had brought him the peace of resignation. She was attracted to his idea of selfless service to humanity. It gave expression to that desire for self-sacrifice and devotion which had been starved since she lost her faith in God at a very early age.[1] When Ellis told her that like himself she was not destined for personal happiness but for the nobler task of helping other men and women to happiness, it sounded plausible and attractive.

Yet she herself believed in the possibility of personal happiness, difficult though it might be to combine with the writer's life. It was possible that Havelock's theories were merely rationalisations of his abnormal shyness. Olive lifted up her face for Havelock to kiss when next they parted. Havelock shook her by the hand, but as he walked away he thought that Olive had lifted up her face almost as if she wanted him to kiss her. The next time they met, she left him in no doubt. She took his head in her hands and kissed him and he was filled with joy. Olive was the woman he had been waiting for. He asked if she would like to read his journal; and she said she would.

This was the great moment of self-revelation that he had first dreamed of that night in Grafton when miserable with unspoken love for May Chapman. Yet though he trusted Olive more than anybody in the world, he waited until she left London at the end of June before giving her the journal.

He was working hard for one of his medical examinations, but he arranged to spend two weeks in the middle of August with Olive, immediately after the examinations were over. It would give her time to read the journal and to recover from any of the shocks which its revelations might give her. For though to anyone reading it to-day, the journal appears a rather sad and poignant chronicle

[1] Olive was devoted to her younger sister Ellie. Ellie died at the age of two, when Olive was ten. She slept for a night in bed with the little corpse and from that time she believed there was no God. By definition God was good, but no God could be good who let Ellie die.

of a difficult adolescence, Havelock regarded it as the revelation of himself in all his spiritual nakedness and a proposal of love to the woman he asked to read it. He awaited Olive's reactions in dreadful suspense.

He had no cause for fear. No woman could have read the journal without feeling compassionate to its author and deeply touched at being the only person to be asked to read it. It confirmed Olive in her view that Havelock was abnormally shy and utterly inexperienced in sex. Given love and reassurance, he would grow out of his difficulties and be able to give some woman, perhaps herself, a rare combination of physical satisfaction and spiritual companionship. It remained for their holiday together to prove whether she was right.

On leaving London, Olive was as restless as ever. She took rooms at Woburn, Beds., but she hated the low ground and the July rain beating on the trees. So she moved up to Wirksworth in Derbyshire, where she was "close to God." She was also close to two friends of Havelock's, Dr Aveling and Eleanor Marx, the daughter of the author of *Das Kapital.* They were living together in unhallowed bliss, moving from place to place to keep one step ahead of the broker's men. It was to Wirksworth that Havelock came after his examination and began what was in part a walking tour and in part a protracted search for lodgings in which two unmarried people might enjoy the freedoms of man and wife without occupying the same bedroom.

In his autobiography Ellis gave a very vague account of his relationship with Olive. "It is necessary to be precise. She possessed a powerfully and physically passionate temperament which craved an answering impulse and might even under other circumstances—for of this I have no personal experience—be capable of carrying her beyond the creed of right and wrong which she herself fiercely held and preached; while, as she once remarked, if I were ever to do a bad action it would be deliberate. For a brief period at this early stage of our relationship there passed before her the possibility of a relationship with me such as her own temperament demanded. But she swiftly realised that I was not fitted to play the part in such a relationship which her elementary primitive nature craved. I on my side recognised that she realised this and knew that the thought of marriage, which for one brief instant floated before my eyes, must be put aside. I have had no reason to regret that inevitable conclusion. We were not what can be technically, or even ordinarily, called lovers." [1]

Though it is not necessary to be very precise about what happened during the holiday in Derbyshire, greater precision is needed than Ellis gives us in the above passage. My belief is that Olive tried to initiate Havelock into the art of love, but without success; that Havelock was content with those amatory skirmishes which he describes as sex-play, but found (or confessed) himself incapable either of consummation or performance in the area of love-pain which to Olive was a shameful but impelling anomaly.

The holiday had very different effects on each of them. Olive had hoped against hope that she would teach him the physical art of love and so combine what had split sides of her nature, the sexual attraction towards dominating unintellectual men and the spiritual attraction towards what she called "men of fine drawn thought." The days in Derbyshire convinced her that this could never happen with Havelock. She was still spiritually drawn to him, calling him her "other self." She valued his friendship as highly as ever. But there was no more element of sex in it than there was in her love and friendship for Edward Carpenter.

Havelock on the other hand found nothing frustrating in their relationship. He had caressed and fondled a woman in the splendour of nakedness. He had achieved a degree of intimacy greater than he had ever imagined himself capable of achieving. It was beautiful and lovely and utterly satisfying. It was something he wanted to do again and again. And he was pained by the fact that Olive was not particularly interested in his form of sex-play, becoming as time went on repelled even by the thought of kissing him.

Olive never again loved Havelock so much as she had when he came to see her at Wirksworth in August 1884. But Havelock's

[1] *My Life*, Eng. ed., p. 185, Am. ed., p. 230.

love for her increased, like those in the past, more and more as he came to realise that it offered him no physical fulfilment. From February 1884, when he first wrote to Ralph Iron, until that Wednesday in October 1889, when he waved her good-bye as she returned to South Africa, she was the one woman in the world for him apart from his mother.

But Havelock was not the one man in the world to Olive. He was still an obscure medical student, she was the authoress of a novel which was read and discussed by all intelligent people. Mr Gladstone had never heard of Henry Havelock Ellis, but he knew the name of Olive Schreiner, admired her book and later invited her to lunch. She met George Moore and Oscar Wilde, who remarked to W. B. Yeats, "Olive Schreiner is staying in the East End because that is the only place where people do not wear masks upon their faces, but I have told her that I live in the West End because nothing in life interests me but the mask."

People quoted her remarks, such as "There are more than one sort of angel" and "A woman is a ship with two holes in her bottom." If she had wished, she could have been a great social success. But more than social success she desired to come to terms with her own nature, so sadly divided between work and life, spiritual aspiration and sexual urges.

Her correspondence with Havelock was more voluminous than ever. There was seldom a day without one letter, many with two and sometimes even three. They enjoyed being with one another, going to art galleries, concerts and meetings, discussing books, Havelock teaching her French. She considered that Havelock had genius and it was possible that though he could not solve her problem physically, he might do so spiritually. She threw herself desperately into the pursuit of selfless service.

But she did not regard Havelock as the only source of truth. Edward Carpenter, for example, had a great deal to teach her and was in many ways a far warmer friend than Havelock. Then there was a doctor whom she had consulted about her bewildering psychosomatic ailments, a gentle creature called Donkin, who fell in love with her and proposed marriage. And there was a young

Professor of Statistics at London University, called Karl Pearson. She was shown some pamphlets of Pearson's during the winter of 1884–85 by a friend called Mrs Cobb, who like her was staying at St Leonards. They were on the controversial subjects of the day, socialism, sex and the Woman Question. The clarity of Pearson's thought and his calm scholarship filled Olive with admiration. She saw in it a counter-balance to Ellis's contradictory paradoxes which turned thought inside out, and the gentle but vague wisdom of Carpenter.

Olive was introduced to Pearson by Mrs Cobb, when she came to London in August 1885, and was vastly attracted to him in what she considered to be a selfless Hintonian sense. Ellis had by that time succeeded in so confusing her ideas that it is now impossible, at least without the aid of certain letters to which I have been denied access, to follow Olive Schreiner's emotional life between the time she first met Karl Pearson in August 1885 and her escape to Europe in December of the next year in order to forget all about him.

Karl Pearson despised the Hinton group, including Ellis. He thought they were flabby-minded, unhealthy and immoral; and he must have stressed as proof of this the fact that in the summer of 1886 Howard Hinton was tried at the Old Bailey for bigamously marrying a woman called Maude Weldon with whom he had spent a week in a King's Cross hotel and by whom he was the father of twins.

On the other hand, Olive, who had been shocked by Caroline Haddon's advocacy of polygamy, rallied to the aid of Maude Weldon and Howard, saying that the only person in the case for whom she could have no sympathy was Mrs Howard Hinton, the mother of Howard's three legitimate children.

Her spiritual love for Karl Pearson was entirely coloured by Ellis's ideas of selfless service. She regarded him as a brilliant young man, dying of tuberculosis,[1] whose few remaining years it was her selfless duty to solace, even if need be (though it wasn't) by giving herself to him physically. She felt for him nothing but

[1] He died in 1936, at the age of 79.

spiritual love in its purest form, and so as to feel close to him spiritually, it was necessary to keep physically apart, etc. Or so she told Havelock Ellis, who was wildly jealous and thought that Pearson's influence on Olive was as pernicious as Pearson thought his was.

Exactly what was happening between Karl Pearson and Olive Schreiner during these months is a matter more for any future biographer of Olive Schreiner than for the biographer of Ellis, for whom it is enough to know that Olive did her very best to remain loyal to both her friends without telling too many lies, and that while Olive remained the most important person in Havelock's life, the most important person in Olive's was Karl Pearson from the time she first met him to a considerable time after she left England in 1886.

Of Ellis she wrote to Carpenter in the spring of the next year. "Yes, Ellis has a strange reserved spirit. The tragedy of his life is that the outer man gives no expression to the wonderful beautiful soul in him, which now and then flashes out on you when you come near him. In some ways he has the noblest nature of any human being I know."

She asked Carpenter to stick up for Ellis if ever he heard anyone talk against him: "he's one of the quite purest, noblest souls, and people don't understand him."

She wondered whether it would be a good idea for Ellis to join her in Italy as he wanted to, because being with someone whom he loved more than she loved him might make him unhappy; and yet she herself would prefer nearness to a beloved, even if it did hurt.

This visit never took place for quite a different reason. It was in the spring of 1888 and Ellis, who was still not fully qualified as a doctor but needed money, was just finishing a term as assistant to a doctor in Blackburn. A few days before he was due to leave, Ellis examined a man in surgery who complained of a sore throat. On the day that he was due to leave, Ellis himself felt unwell and the doctor urged him not to travel. But thinking it was just a cold and anxious to see the annual Winter Exhibition of Old Masters at

Burlington House before it closed, he insisted on leaving for London. By the time he reached home he was obviously ill and the doctor was immediately called in. It was scarlet fever, a fairly severe attack. His sisters were isolated and his mother nursed him. While he was still in bed, his mother caught the infection. A nurse was called in to tend them both. Havelock recovered and was soon convalescing and editing some plays for the Mermaid Series.

His mother on the other hand as soon as she realised that she had caught it remarked calmly, "I shall not get over it."

To help the nurse when she wanted to rest or take a walk, Havelock would sit in his dressing-gown in his mother's room; and on the morning of April 13, he was sitting there alone in the house with her, his sisters and the nurse all being out. His mother felt better. She had asked for some bread and butter and eaten it with enjoyment. She talked about when she would be up and about again, and with Havelock's aid got out of bed for a few minutes.

When she was back in bed, Havelock took up his book, a German translation of Ibsen's *Peer Gynt*. He had never read the play before and with a strange sense of coincidence he came to the scene of Peer Gynt at the deathbed of Mother Aase. He was absorbed in this wonderful scene, when he heard the sound of difficult breathing from the bed. He got up and applied the brush, nearby for the purpose, to his mother's throat. She unconsciously sucked it. He withdrew it and put a few drops of champagne in her mouth. A little later a slight convulsion passed across her face. Then there was nothing.

He stood by her a little while. In hospital and practice he had seen many grievously ill; but the first person he had seen die was the person nearest to him in all the world. He had in a sense killed her. If he had diagnosed that the man in the Blackburn surgery had scarlet fever, or if he had not been so anxious to see the Winter Exhibition at Burlington House, she would still have been alive. Then he went out and lay on his bed, waiting till the nurse returned and he could tell her what had happened.

While she had lived, there had always been "awe" in his "affection" for his mother. He wrote Carpenter that he never realised till after she was dead how deeply he loved her. And more than a year later he confided to his journal that he still could not look at her photograph without tears rolling down his cheeks.

To return to Olive. Though it is true that after the holiday in Derbyshire Havelock was the lover and she his beloved, whose heart was soon engaged elsewhere, Havelock was the person to whom she turned in moments of crisis. In March 1889 she was staying in Mentone when there arrived at her hotel a party of rather vulgar South Africans who had themselves been at Dordrecht at the time of her first disastrous love affair with Julius Gau, or had heard all about it as gossip. She felt that she had to get away, was being "hunted to death." Even the servants wouldn't talk to her. Her only friend was a prostitute to whom she had been kind. She had a number of people on whom she might have called, both women friends and men, but she turned instinctively to Havelock, sent him a cheque for £20 and arranged to meet him in Paris at the Hôtel d'Oxford et Cambridge in a few days' time. He was the one person who knew all about her and the one person who, because of or despite that, she could be certain would give her sympathy.

After Olive Schreiner returned to South Africa in 1889, she continued in correspondence with Havelock Ellis for years, the frequency of their letters diminishing partly through the separation of distance but also because Ellis, compared for example with Carpenter or W. T. Stead, was a dull letter-writer. He lacked the vitality, the ability to express rapid changes of mood and the rapid changes of mood to express.

Gradually they drifted apart. Olive still admired his nobility of character but she lost belief in his genius as a writer. "What a terrible deadly theory that Hinton theory is," she had remarked during Howard Hinton's trial, "like a upas tree blighting all it comes in contact with because it is false to human nature." Maybe it worked with Havelock himself. *Fay ce que vouldras* was all right for him. "Do what thou wilt" might benefit anybody who didn't feel capable of doing very much. But it was a terribly dangerous doctrine for a person like herself, a creature of violent emotions, and a doctrine which she thought wrecked the life of the woman whom Havelock married.

She became frightened of Havelock. There was this desire to make everything public, to prove that private life was far stranger than ever admitted in public places. That was something which everybody except apparently Havelock himself accepted. He had published her case-history with a suitable disguise in the volume of the *Studies* devoted to Auto-erotism. What might he not do with her letters, when she was dead? She asked him to return them to her or to destroy them.

Ellis went through her letters, destroying some in entirety and cutting bits out of others. But he did not destroy them *in toto* or return them for Olive to burn. He believed that Olive Schreiner was a woman of genius and that these letters of hers belonged to posterity, to whom he owed a loyalty which overrode his loyalty to Olive.

Olive died in 1920 and her husband, S. C. Cronwright-Schreiner,[1] asked Havelock Ellis if he would write Olive's life. Ellis rightly refused. He had none of the biographer's gifts, but he promised to help in any way that he could. He felt that Olive had meant a great deal in his life and he also knew that he had meant something important in hers. There was a large number of people, however, who thought, perhaps rightly, that Olive's life should not be written so soon after her death, and certainly rightly that Cronwright had none of the talents necessary for a biographer. The Schreiner family refused to co-operate, and so did most of those

[1] He was a younger man than Olive and she insisted, on their marriage, that he should take her name, not she his. He was a South African farmer-politician, the nearest approach she ever found to a man who combined physical dominance and intellectual power. The marriage was not very successful. She could never live where he had to work, and he could never work where she could live. There was one child, a baby who lived less than twenty-four hours, dying in circumstances somewhat hard to understand. Cronwright-Schreiner seems to have had an ambivalent attitude to his distinguished but not too successful marriage.

who knew Olive intimately in South Africa and England. Her life had an inner coherence which Cronwright was incapable of understanding, and which even if he understood would have appeared as a sort of *chronique scandaleuse* in the 1920s. It was far better, most people thought, to keep quiet for the moment. A time might come later when intimate revelations about a woman who after her death was still an important force in South African politics would cause no harm. Other people, such as Karl Pearson, were silent for the further reason that they had families and academic positions to consider. What would be the position of the Professor of Statistics in London University if a series of letters written by the author of *The Story of an African Farm* about her emotional problems was circulated among his pupils? Pearson thought Olive Schreiner the most intelligent woman he had ever met. But her letters were on two levels; there were the very few which were thought-out letters designed for publication, and the myriad which were the scribbled conversations of a very solitary woman who loved to burble by post.

Finally there was Edward Carpenter, to whom Olive wrote almost as many letters as she did to Havelock, and with more freedom because there was no sexual element in their companionship. Carpenter had no objection to Cronwright's using any of his letters, but at the time he was changing house and it was hard to get at his papers.

So both *The Life* and *The Letters* of Olive Schreiner were compiled almost entirely from the documentary resources of Havelock Ellis and Cronwright, with the latter culling some reminiscences from acquaintances who did not know that the family had put their ban on publication. Both volumes gave the erroneous impression that there had been only two men of importance in her life, Havelock Ellis and Cronwright. There was no mention of any reason why this was an unbalanced presentation of the facts of her life, nor any expression of the hope that later on members of the family and friends of hers would revise their decision to observe her expressed wish that her personal letters should be withheld from publication.

The opinion has been expressed by some[1] that there was a deliberate plot between Cronwright and Ellis to denigrate Olive, the suggestion being that Ellis resented first the rejection of his love and later Olive's repudiation of his genius, and that Cronwright wanted the world to know the sacrifices which he had made in marrying such a difficult woman as Olive. If one judges by the books themselves, such a theory seems plausible. Olive's letters, dashed off on the spur of anxiety or transient emotion, appear hysterical and often fatuous. To print them was as unfair as to take a tape-recording of a casual conversation and then broadcast it as a public debate. There were significant letters among those which Ellis handed over to Cronwright, such as the appeal which she wrote Ellis from Mentone when the South Africans arrived. From this letter Cronwright deleted a phrase, relating to amenorrhoea. I think he did this out of a sense of decency. He did not want to offend the reader. But in fact the phrase he deleted contained the reason for her panic flight from Mentone. Its deletion makes Olive appear a demented woman. As editor Cronwright should either have omitted the letter altogether or printed it as it stood. His action might be interpreted as due to a deliberate or unconscious desire to make his late wife appear crazy; but I think it far more likely that he wanted to give as much as possible of the letter, which is an interesting one. He failed to understand the implications of the deletion.

In the same way, a case could be made that Ellis, prompted by his inadequate sex-life, wanted to claim that he was one of the great loves of Olive Schreiner's life. But I do not think this is consistent with his character. He was very proud of his friendship with Olive and very grateful to her for releasing him in part from the cage of his shyness. What mattered to him was that their love did survive

[1] Most notably Vera Buchanan-Gould, whose biography of Olive Schreiner, *Not Without Honour*, is chiefly valuable in stressing the autobiographical elements in *From Man to Man* and *Undine* as well as *The Story of an African Farm*. Her account of the relations of Havelock, Olive and Edith Ellis is completely without foundation; and the revelation of the existence of a mysterious Julius Zaar of Dordrecht is due to a misreading of Olive's handwriting. For Zaar she should have read Gau.

despite Donkin, Pearson and others. Thus the only reference to these rivals in *My Life* is an aside in a sentence affirming the constancy of their relationship. "After a leap of four years and after *much emotional turmoil in which several men and women were mingled*, she still writes (3 September 1889): 'Fancy, when I think of leaving England the thing I mind most leaving is you. Isn't human affection a funny thing!' "

I think that the intentions of both Cronwright and Ellis were innocent of malice. But they did a grave disservice to the woman to whom they thought they were paying homage. Olive, despite the psychosomatic disorders with which she was tormented, was at her best a very sane and commonsensical woman. She was right to ask Ellis to destroy her letters precisely because she knew the damage which might be caused by the injudicious publication of fragments. She had seen how unaware Ellis was of the effect which the cumulative case-histories of the *Studies* might have on a reader, and she was terrified of the results of leaving this material in his hands.

If I have gone further in this chapter than Ellis himself went in his autobiography, it is because the damage has already been done. The privacy once violated, the alternative is truth; not the uneasy mixture of revelation and suppression Cronwright and Ellis allowed themselves, or the wild speculation indulged in by Vera Buchanan-Gould, but the rounded, balanced truth to be presented by some future biographer. My interest is confined to the significance of Olive Schreiner in the life of Havelock Ellis. How momentous that was one can see by comparing the young man who first wrote to Ralph Iron in February 1884 with the young man who waved good-bye to her in October 1889. The first was resigned to a life of selfless service without any physical intimacy, without any chance of talking to another human being about intimate personal problems or of expressing the loving sentiments locked in his heart. The second, still abnormally shy, dreamed of the possibility that another woman, who would come as Olive had done and kiss him, would find delight in the sort of sex-play which he loved, would exchange with him their innermost secrets and share a similar spiritual companionship.

Perhaps it was not a long way to have come by the age of nearly thirty. But he accepted the slowness of his development as he accepted all the other facts of his nature. He did not know what the future held, but he believed that whatever it was, it would be sent for a good purpose, which it was his duty to perceive.

8

When I want to see Velasquez's pictures I go not to you but to Madrid. But if you could only tell me how he came to paint them!

An Open Letter to Biographers

DURING THE years of his love and friendship for Olive Schreiner, Havelock Ellis was laying the foundations of his literary and scientific career. His medical studies did not engross his whole activity. He took seven years to qualify as a doctor, two years more than was usual; and even then he was only an L.S.A., or Licentiate in Medicine Surgery and Midwifery of the Society of Apothecaries, a qualification, which, though adequate, was without prestige.[1]

Ellis's slowness in qualifying was due only in part to his inability to concentrate on any subject which bored him. The most important reason was that he regarded his medical degree merely as a testimonial to his scientific competence. During his student days at St Thomas's he pursued his broad plans of literary and scientific study, devoting more of his time to these studies than to medicine.

After the publication of *The Law-Breaker*, he undertook editorial work for the Camelot Classics, a series being put out for the Walter Scott Publishing Company under the general editorship of Ernest Rhys. He edited and wrote introductions to three volumes of Walter Savage Landor. He translated *Florentine Nights* for the selection of Heine's *Prose Writings*, which he edited and introduced ; and he also introduced *Pillars of Society and Other Plays*, which was the first translation of Ibsen to appear in English.

[1] Nearly fifty years later, at the instancy of Lord Horder, the Royal College of Physicians made him an honorary fellow. It was proposed that the fellowship be conferred at a formal banquet. But Ellis said he would rather forgo the fellowship than speak in public. A compromise was reached by Horder and two of his colleagues taking him out to an informal dinner.

HAVELOCK ELLIS AS A MEDICAL STUDENT

He reviewed theological books for the *Westminster Review*, for which he also produced occasional articles on such diverse subjects as "The Novels of Thomas Hardy," "The Changing Status of Women" and "Diderot." He reviewed novels and poetry for the *Indian Review* and wrote occasionally for other small periodicals.

In 1886 he proposed to the publisher Henry Vizetelly that the time had come to reissue some of the best of the Elizabethan plays in a popular unexpurgated text, suggesting the Mermaid as the title for the series. Vizetelly had been a journalist before he turned publisher and Havelock had met him through his friend Eleanor Marx, who had translated *Madame Bovary* for him. Vizetelly himself had translated and published some of Zola's novels in a rather bowdlerised form. His reputation was that of a courageous, if rather *risqué*, publisher, prepared to undertake work from which stolider and better established publishers would sheer away.

Vizetelly accepted Ellis's scheme and agreed to his acting as general editor, on the condition that he could succeed in roping in some big names for introducing the early volumes in the series. For a young man of twenty-seven Havelock Ellis was remarkably widely read and the remuneration for which he asked was equally remarkably modest. But his name was unknown except to a very small circle.

Ellis enlisted the aid of Swinburne and John Addington Symonds from among the older critics, and Arthur Symons, one of the most brilliant and sensitive of Ellis's contemporaries. He himself undertook the volumes devoted to Marlowe, Middleton, Ford and Henry Porter.

In planning the Mermaid Series, Havelock Ellis approached the Elizabethan drama in a different spirit from that in which the earlier revivalist Charles Lamb had done. Lamb's interest had been concentrated upon the poetry and drama of the Elizabethan age; Ellis was equally concerned with the effect that these dramatists with their vigour, outspokenness and bawdry might have on the Mrs Grundyism of the late nineteenth century. He was separated from Lamb by the watershed of Victorianism.

A simple illustration will make plain the difference in attitude.

John Aubrey in his *Brief Lives* relates of Edward de Vere, the seventeenth Earl of Oxford, that "This Earle of Oxford, making of his low obeisance to Queen Elizabeth, happened to let a Fart, at which he was so abashed and ashamed that he went to Travell seven yeares. On his returne the Queen welcomed him home, and sayd, 'My Lord, I had forgott the Fart.' "

Lamb, Coleridge and Wordsworth would have laughed at this, because of the profound psychological truth concealed in it. If Edward de Vere had returned to court the day after his misadventure, it would have been forgotten in seven weeks; his nicety of feeling made it remembered after seven years. Havelock Ellis would probably have laughed partly for the same reason, but he would never have been able to forget that this was precisely the sort of anecdote by which Queen Victoria was not amused. In the reaction against Victorianism, bawdry had become infected with puritanism; it was purposive, a blow struck against Mrs Grundy.

Mid-Victorians such as Dickens and Thackeray found the prudery of the age distasteful. They accepted it publicly but privately they felt a nostalgia for the coarseness and belly-laughter of earlier times, for Fielding, Smollett, Congreve, Wycherley and Ben Jonson; and if they had to justify themselves, they would have said it was natural for men among themselves occasionally to talk coarse.

The late-nineteenth-century reaction against Victorianism, led by people such as Ellis, rejected the prudery but accepted the idealism of the mid-Victorians. The Victorian ideal of purity was wrong, attaching itself to acts and objects, and leading to such perversions as putting stockings on the legs of tables and tying mats to the base of cats' tails to hide the rude anal orifice. But instead of sweeping this nonsense away in gusts of gargantuan laughter, Ellis sought what real purity was and enlisted his literary ancestors to fight on his behalf.

Whereas Thackeray hankered after the past, Ellis hankered after the future. The *laissez-faire* belief in the inevitability of human progress was clearly wrong. But science, thought, knowledge and foresight might make at least material progress possible. Man could control his destiny, provided that he recognised the nature of his humanity. And the Elizabethan and Restoration dramatists were closer to human nature than the Victorians tormented by puritan ideals, to fall short of which wracked the conscience and to live up to which distorted the full being.

Havelock Ellis disclosed his purpose too fully in the first volume of the Mermaid Series, his own edition of Christopher Marlowe. He printed as an appendix the full transcript of the scandalous charges of atheism and perversity brought against Marlowe by an informer shortly before his death. The manuscript of this denunciation was in the British Museum, but had never previously been published. Ellis accepted the denunciation as a crude and ignorant rehearsal of views actually held by Marlowe, and added that Marlowe's atheistic views were those "substantially held more or less widely, by students of science and the Bible in our own days."

This was a trick which Ellis was to play more subtly over and over again in his career, to assume that what he wanted to prove had already been accepted by enlightened people, the invitation to join the company of enlightened spirits and no questions asked. But in this instance he did not get away with it. Swinburne, no friend of Christianity, was outraged. John Addington Symonds, whose sexual proclivities were those of which Marlowe was accused, protested. Without a word to his irresponsible young editor, Vizetelly, the publisher of *Nana* and *La Terre*, cut the offending appendix from all except the presentation copies which had been sent out.

Time has proved that Ellis's theory with regard to Marlowe was substantially correct, and Havelock Ellis always regarded the suppression of his appendix as the first attack on his outspokenness by the reactionary forces of Mrs Grundy. In fact what shocked Swinburne and Symonds was less what Ellis had to say of Marlowe than the deliberately provocative statement that Marlowe's views as travestied in this document were more or less widely held by students of science and the Bible. These were the words not of a scholar but of a propagandist using the mask of scholarship to make a debating point.

Despite this error, Ellis made a very good job of launching the Mermaid Series. By 1888 it was well established. But the disaster, which John Addington Symonds had foreseen and warned Ellis against, overwhelmed Henry Vizetelly. For his translations of *Nana*, *The Soil* and *Piping Hot!* he was prosecuted at Bow Street on the charge of publishing obscene literature. He was fined and imprisoned for three months and his business went into liquidation. The Mermaid Series was acquired by T. Fisher Unwin, who dropped Havelock Ellis as General Editor without even informing him of the fact and omitted his name from the volumes produced under his general editorship.[1] Havelock Ellis had increased his reputation, admittedly; but it was not a solid reputation. He was dangerous, a rebel who needed to be watched carefully, not a man who could be depended upon to play safe.

Ellis did not long repine on losing the editorship of the Mermaid Series. It was well launched and he had another, more important scheme in mind.

Diderot was his hero at this time and he saw himself as another great encyclopaedist. To the Walter Scott Publishing Company he proposed a Contemporary Science Series in which "all the questions of modern life—the various social and politico-economical problems of to-day, the most recent researches in the knowledge of man, the past and present experiences of the race, and the nature of its environment—will be frankly investigated and clearly presented."

Ellis was given a free hand and he began by commissioning Patrick Geddes to write a book called *The Evolution of Sex*. Of the other works some were translations of standard European works, like Marie de Manceïne's *Sleep*, Sergi's *Mediterranean Race* and Lombroso's *The Man of Genius*. If no standard work was available, Ellis commissioned direct. Finding that there was no English authority on criminal anthropology, he himself wrote *The Criminal*, a book which to-day has more macabre curiosity than

[1] The Mermaid Series, still the best cheap edition of the Elizabethan and Restoration dramatists, is now published by Messrs Ernest Benn Ltd, who pay due tribute to Ellis as its originator.

scientific value but which in its time was very important because it brought to the attention of the Anglo-Saxon world the fact that there might be a science of criminology. Since that was the purpose for which it was written, Ellis could mark down its obsolescence as proof of success.

The Criminal was published in his thirtieth year, but earlier in the same year had appeared *The New Spirit*, his first literary book.

It is worth while examining *The New Spirit*, because its composition set the model for his later books. It was composed of six essays, on Diderot, Heine, Whitman, Ibsen, Tolstoi and Huysmans respectively, most of which had been previously printed either as prefaces to other books or articles in literary papers; and in the attempt to give form and significance to what was in origin a haphazard collection of literary articles he specially wrote a long introduction and an almost equally long conclusion of a discursive nature.

A book so made can never be a unity. The only thread running through the whole is the sensibility of the author. For Diderot we could as well choose Rousseau, for Heine Goethe, for Whitman Herman Melville, for Ibsen Strindberg, for Tolstoi Dostoievski, for Huysmans the brothers Goncourt, and clamped between the introduction and conclusion, almost unchanged, they could have been presented to the public as *The New Spirit* without the general message being changed. For what was new was the spirit of Havelock Ellis himself and the way he moved through the world of men and ideas.

A percipient critic, reviewing *The New Spirit* at the time, observed that its chief characteristic was a calm and matter-of-fact way of making daring revolutionary statements. "A great wave, with Luther on its crest, swept across Europe, reached at last the coast of England, and left on its shores, as a dreary monumental symbol, St Paul's Cathedral." The key word is "dreary"; but which St Paul's Cathedral is referred to, the Old St Paul's finished a couple of hundred years before Luther was born or Wren's St Paul's, begun over a century after his death, which the

Encyclopaedia Britannica describes as "the finest example of Renaissance building in England," owing very little to foreign influence?

Ellis of course was not concerned with the architectural merits or demerits of St Paul's. He was trying to evolve a theory explaining the periods of renaissance being followed by periods of quiescence or re-death, and in order to fit his theory he had to distort the facts. One sees exactly the same technique in the previous sentence: "In the wonderful thirteenth century, when Francis of Assisi revealed anew in his own person the ideal charm of Jesus, and a group of fine spirits, his fellows, who bore the Everlasting Gospel,—Jean de Parme, Pierre d'Olive, Fra Dolcino and the rest, —sought to rebuild the edifice of Christendom on the foundation of the Gospels, only in the end to deluge the world with a plague of gray friars." By a semantic sleight-of-hand St Francis is separated from his followers, the praise of one being heightened by the damnation of the other.

This was not logical writing. At its best, it had the virtue of the apophthegm. "The tree of life is always in bloom somewhere, if we only know where to look." "Religion knows nothing of the scientific 'nature' or of the ethical 'man'; its impulse is from within and of free grace."

At its worst it begged the very questions that a clear thinker would have been compelled to prove. An interesting example of this can be found in his essay on "St Francis and Others," which was printed in a later collection, *Affirmations*.

Ellis was as deeply attracted to the figure of St Francis as he was to Jesus Christ. It was easy for him to detach Jesus Christ from Christians, but it was more difficult to detach St Francis from Christianity, since there was never a saint more closely linked in communion with the Son of God than he. This was how Ellis did it. "The free play of the individual soul in contact with Nature and men, Francis instinctively felt, is joy and liberation; and if the simple-minded saint went farther than this, and allowed a certain set of dogmatic opinions and conventional abstentions, *we may be sure that herein he had no warrant of personal inspiration*, but was content to follow the well-nigh unquestioned traditions of his day."

The italics are mine; the surety is Ellis's. It is based not upon an examination of St Francis's life and thought but on the fact that if St Francis had had the warrant of personal inspiration for his belief in the Holy Trinity, Havelock Ellis would be wrong.

The question of the way in which the Holy Spirit has moved saints and religious leaders of different creeds has occupied many theologians. Ellis was less concerned with explaining how it was possible. He cavalierly dismissed theogonies and gospels as fairy tales, adventitious aids to illumination. What concerned him was that he himself had had a genuine mystical experience from which he had derived no intellectual beliefs. It was, he felt, the mystical experience which mattered rather than the theological explanation which always follows after the mystical experience.

The weakness of his position lay in the assertion, which he had taken over from Miss Simcox, that such a mystical experience had only a subjective validity. He would have been on unassailable ground if he had said that by introspection he could find no evidence of any objective validity in his own experience, and that it was impossible for anybody to prove that the mystical experience is in fact an illumination of God. In denying the dogmatisms of theologians, he fell into the trap of dogmatising about the purely subjective nature of all mystical experiences, which others had analysed with no less sincerity and seriousness than he had analysed his own.

On the other hand, the majority of Havelock Ellis's readers were men and women like himself whose faith had been slowly and painfully undermined by rationalism and scientific materialism. To them the conclusion of *The New Spirit* held out the wonderful possibility of a mystical communion without having to accept a host of theological dogmas which appeared untrue, meaningless or both. After reading "St Francis and Others," which I have criticised above, Max Plowman for example wrote that Ellis was "like a great, deep well full of wisdom and beauty. The treasures to be found therein are inexhaustible."

And though when he was on his guard Ellis was careful to avoid the use of the word God, preferring the negative Not-Self, he found himself in his simplest and most direct moments using the word. "Men have only to open their souls like flowers wholly to God. . . . We are like flowers, wanting earth for our bodies and water for our minds and sunshine for our souls. . . . Let us open ourselves . . . an open soul is all that is wanted, and nothing will do instead."

Those like Thomas Davidson who expected clear thought from a writer found Ellis unsatisfying. Ellis's unacademic mind shied away from logic like a high-strung horse from a handkerchief. But clarity of thought is not the first or only quality readers look for in an author. There is speculative suggestiveness, the train of thought aroused by analogy or by conjunction of two apparently dissimilar things, the intuitive perception of unsuspected harmonies which has inspired great poets and great scientists. There is the flair for perceiving what is going to be significant in literature, the arts and sciences, the finger on the pulse of the *Zeitgeist*. There is the charm of learning, which makes of Burton's *Anatomy of Melancholy* a work of permanent literary delight though it is valueless as a guide to the depressions, cyclophrenic or involutional. And finally there is "personality" in writing. There are people whom we like to hear talk not because what they say is necessarily true, but because their conversation reveals admirable qualities of character, mind and spirit, courage, nobility, resignation, curiosity, intelligence, originality, vision, the sense of things unseen by ordinary men. The refreshment of conversation with such personalities is something larger than the words that pass. One does not scrutinise such a man's writings, as a customs officer a passport, to see whether his documents are in order. It is not that order of truth which one expects from him. It is both vaguer and spiritually more profound.

In all these qualities Ellis was rich. Ideas sprout and bloom on his pages faster than flowers in the desert after rain. Many die as quickly, others survive; but what is memorable is the miracle of the efflorescence. Ellis was never tired of emphasising that he was not a scholar, that if he had any merit it lay not in facts but in their arrangement; and it would be unfair to criticise him for the failure of scholarship, with which he was credited but which he never claimed. He was perhaps the most widely read man in the world of his time—though by no means the most critical of readers. His erudition often appears as a means of eluding difficulties, a form of what one might call Dogmen-of-Dafurmanship. Faced with difficulty in a straight line of argument, he shifted the area of discourse to the Dogmen of Dafur or took the Trobriand islanders as an example, or considered for a moment the Esquimaux. More persistent thinkers, such as his contemporary Karl Pearson whose brain was academically better disciplined, underrated Ellis because of the way in which he shifted his ground. But there are many types of intellect; and what one might call the lawn-mower brain is not necessarily the only or the best for speculative thought.

Ellis himself thought that his brain moved like a kangaroo, in a series of great but graceful bounds. One should expect from a brain only the performance proper to it. It would be misguided to condemn a kangaroo for not being able to mow a lawn or a lawn-mower for not being able to bound down slopes. And for every thousand mental lawn-mowers turned out by the universities, there is scarcely one mental kangaroo.

But at the same time as appreciating the unique qualities of Ellis's mind, one must also regard the limitations inherent in those qualities.

One of the conspicuous weaknesses, which was to be even further exaggerated in the *culte de nouveauté* of the 1920s, was the confusion between novelty and truth. Havelock Ellis regarded himself as one of the band of intellectual and spiritual pioneers who in every age overthrow the *idées reçues* inherited from previous generations and reformulate the constant truths of humanity in a new and dynamic form, while at the same time driving forward the frontiers of knowledge.

It was a useful image to explain the apparent cycles of rebirth and redeath detectable in the history of human culture. It implied a theory of the relativity of ideas. An idea had, like a human being, a life of its own. It was born, it grew up and it died. But unfortunately it was not automatically interred. It lingered on, decomposing, in the minds of the stuffy, the conservative, the philistine. Part of the task of the pioneer of new ideas was to bury the dead ideas of the past. Only new and growing ideas should be encouraged; the senescent should be given euthanasia. Up to this point the analogy was useful.

But there was a confusion between what was an idea and what was a truth; and a further confusion between a truth newly perceived as a vital part of consciousness and one accepted so long that the truth of the truth was subjectively dead. That roses are red and their leaves green are facts which are constant from the point of view of normal human vision, but at Sparkes Creek Havelock had seen more acutely than ever before or after how red roses were against leaves how green. At that moment the flowers were redder and the leaves greener than ever before. That formed the element of novelty which made the moment important. Yet in fact it was Havelock's vision which was different, not the roses, which had inspired Robert Burns with the image of a great love poem and turned Lucius Apuleius back from an ass to a human being.

In so far as they affected himself, Havelock Ellis saw that age-old truths could become suddenly new in his consciousness; the sun shining, the flowers bursting into flower, the sea breaking upon rocks.

It was equally true that the statement "God is Love," repeated by many people so often that it had become devoid of content, might in a moment of illumination become filled again with a content so vast that the meditation of a lifetime was insufficient to explore it fully. Ellis preferred to turn it round and say "Love is God," which had an effect of novelty in Victorian times though he himself explained that it was the view of certain early Christians.

The early Christians who held this view were regarded as heretics, because instead of extending the vision of God they were distending the nature of Love. Love is one aspect of man's apprehension of God, as beauty, truth and goodness are others. One can say God is Truth, Beauty, Goodness, but one cannot say Love is Truth, Beauty and Goodness.

"Love is God" was capable of many interpretations. It could help a Christian rediscover the meaning of his faith. It could restore belief in the divine principle of love to the unfortunate who had lost faith in the Godhead. Or it could be inscribed over the lintel of a licensed house by a Madame who wished a blessing on her trade. But Ellis himself intended it as the elevation of Man and Woman to the Divinity of which he believed them capable. As a doctor he could not believe in the possibility of spiritual consciousness existing apart from the body. The individual soul must perish with the body. And yet the mystical experience at Sparkes Creek had proved to him that it was possible "to know God."

The importance of *The New Spirit*, *Affirmations* and *The Dance of Life* lay in the fact that Havelock Ellis, the epitome of the New Man interested in all the rapidly emerging sciences of anthropology, eugenics, sociology, psychology and so on, normally associated with materialism, believed in the supremacy of the spirit and the mystical communion with God or the Not-Self. Scientists had attacked religion. Christian apologists had attacked science. Havelock Ellis had effected a reconciliation in his person, and through his writings made the plea, none the less stirring for being imprecise, that science and religion were not antagonistic but complementary.

9

After thirty, if so far you have fulfilled that task, what is there further left to tell? The rest is but the liberation of a mighty spring, the slow running down of energy. The man recedes to give place to his deeds, whether such deeds be the assault of great fortresses or the escalade of mighty sentences. There is the same heroic effort and achievement, whether on the walls of Jerusalem when Godfrey scaled them or on Flaubert's sofa at Rouen.

An Open Letter to Biographers

ELLIS HAD no intention of practising as general practitioner or specialist. But his medical degree helped him to secure various temporary jobs either as *locum tenens* to a G.P. or medical superintendent to a hydropathic establishment whose principal was taking three months' leave. At these jobs he found leisure to pursue his own work and accumulated the capital to take excursions abroad.

He had made great friends with Arthur Symons, with whom he shared rooms in the Temple when he was in London. Though Symons' interests were purely artistic, they had much in common. Both were in revolt against parental puritanism, both favoured an aesthetic approach to life, both were uncompromisingly *avant-gardiste* and both talked in high voices.

In September 1889 Ellis took Symons on the latter's first visit to Paris, and in the spring of the next year they returned for a longer stay. Ellis had published *The New Spirit* and completed the writing of *The Criminal* and decided that a sojourn in Paris would put him abreast of scientific thought in France.

As it happened, he did little work in that field. He went to a few hospitals and lunatic asylums, attended a meeting of the Anthropological Society, explored the School of Anthropology, met Dr Berrillon, a successful hypnotic therapeutist, and saw Charcot give a demonstration of hypnosis at Salpêtrière. Charcot's "powerful, but rather antipathetic personality" impressed him as that of an outsize Napoleon. But the famous neurologist had on him nothing like the effect he had produced on Sigmund Freud four years earlier.

Symons brought with him a sheaf of letters of introduction through which they met Rodin, Verlaine, Mallarmé, Huysmans and others. Most of the talking from the Englishmen's side was done by Symons, who had none of Ellis's shyness. But this personal contact with men whose works he had read and admired was of great importance in giving body to his conception of their thought.

Returning from Paris, Ellis for the first time in his life visited Cornwall, which was to become one of the most treasured places on earth to him. He had secured a job as *locum tenens* for Dr Bonar of Probus, near Truro, while he went on his week's holiday. After that, he was to stay with his old friend Agnes Jones, who had bought a house at Lamorna Cove.

He was due to arrive on August 13; and on that same day Edith Lees arrived at Miss Jones's with her faithful servant Ellen Taylor. The two of them were on a walking tour and they called on Miss Jones with whom Edith Lees had been in correspondence about the Fellowship of the New Life, of which she was organising secretary. Miss Jones asked them to stay the night and they had accepted before Miss Jones let drop that Havelock Ellis would be coming that afternoon to stay the night also.

Edith Lees had already met Havelock Ellis. She had been roped in to the Fellowship of the New Life by Percival Chubb, who had met her at the house of the Reverend Stopford Brooke. She had been working in the London slums with Stopford Brooke's daughters and was looking for a change of activity. The Fellowship, with its blend of idealism and modernity, seemed just the thing.

This was in 1887, when the Fellowship had been going for three or four years. Ellis's ardour had cooled off, but he attended occasional meetings and usually went on the excursions into the country which were organised from time to time. It was on one of these excursions that they first met. "Who's that?" she asked Chubb. "That," answered Chubb impressively, "is Havelock Ellis."

Edith Lees was not impressed. She liked men who were well-dressed and she thought Ellis's clothes ill-made.

They were introduced to each other and walked along together for a few minutes, talking of indifferent things and sizing one another up. She was small, compact and active, under rather than over five feet in height, fine skin, well-shaped head with curly hair, square powerful hands, very small feet and most noticeably large, pale blue eyes, which were beautiful if you liked blue eyes, but Havelock didn't. He preferred green or grey. What appealed to him most was her voice, strong, resonant and full in tone.

Edith did not think very highly of Havelock, his embarrassing shyness, his awkward movements, his high thin voice, his habit of not looking you in the eyes and his utter lack of small talk.

They came to a little chapel in a remote spot and went in to look at it. Havelock found a bell-rope and began to toll it. He thought it was funny, but she didn't. It was irreverent and rather silly.

They saw very little of one another after that, because Ellis was drifting away from the Fellowship. But in March 1890 a friend of hers presented her with a copy of *The New Spirit*. She read it while staying on the Norfolk Broads and enjoyed it immensely. It revealed a spiritual quality which she had never imagined in the shy young man in ill-fitting clothes who tolled solitary church-bells as a joke.

Hearing from Miss Jones that this young man was coming to stay, she retired to her room with Ellen Taylor and told her that a man was coming to stay whom she did not like, and wouldn't it be better for them to push on to Land's End? Ellen begged to stay. Her feet were sore with walking. This house was really comfortable, not like some of the places they'd had to put up at, and a rest would do them both good. Edith agreed, reflecting that it would anyway look rather strange to refuse an invitation which she had already accepted.

Dislike may have been the word she used to Ellen Taylor, but it did not accurately describe her feelings, which combined repulsion from the awkward ungainly man and attraction towards the spirit manifest in his book.

The first of these feelings was confirmed by the appearance of Dr Ellis in the late afternoon, carrying his bag and wearing a silk hat and a torn mackintosh; and the second by the conversation after dinner in which, despite the presence of Miss Jones, they achieved an intimacy with one another.

Next day he and Miss Jones accompanied them on the first stage of their journey to Land's End, and a few days later he met her, whether by accident or design he could not remember, in St Ives, as she and Ellen returned along the northern coast. They walked together, leaving Ellen Taylor to bring up the rear, as far as Hayle Ferry, talking more intimately in the absence of Miss Jones. They discussed modern marriage, discovering a pleasant identity in their views. Marriage must be the union of equal partners. The wife must be economically independent of her husband. (Edith had a small private income.) There must be no secrets; everything open and above-board; no jealousy—a vile, degrading emotion. Marriage must never be allowed to become stale, as it did when man and wife lived together day after day, year after year. There must be no emotional demands on the partner, the bullying dependence of the weaker on the stronger. They united in abusing the Victorian idea of marriage, the barnyard cockiness of the paterfamilias, the tyrant ruling through hold on the purse-strings and then, while demanding chastity from his wife, venting his lusts in the stews.

Havelock waved good-bye at the ferry and went back to Lamorna feeling how mistaken his first impression of Miss Lees had been; and what a lovely vital spirit was hidden beneath her—to him slightly unattractive—manner.

On his mother's death, Louie and he had taken a small house in St Mary's Terrace, Paddington; and on their return to London Edith would pop in to see him, usually by arrangement, but sometimes unexpectedly, always in a desperate hurry but often staying much longer than she said she could. Havelock never went to her rooms in Wigmore Street, but on rare occasions they met in town and went to a concert or a music-hall together. There was no thought of love, no approach to intimacy; it was more the companionship which Havelock had achieved with Olive Schreiner after he had recognised that Olive could never love him in the way he loved her. Edith had a genius for friendship which astonished him. In thirty-five years' correspondence with Edward Carpenter Havelock never addressed him more familiarly than "Dear Ed Carpenter" or "Dear Edward C." Edith Ellis began her correspondence with "Dear Edward Carpenter" and in the next letter it was already "My dear Edward." She knew dozens of people by their Christian names—at a time when the use of the Christian name was rare outside the family circle—and Havelock found himself at a loss to put surnames to this host of friends.

Havelock was very willing to keep their friendship on an impersonal basis—he did not need a confidante. Olive's reading of his journal had cured him of that for life.

But one day Edith burst into his room and started to confide in him the fact that she had been in love with one of the leading spirits in the Fellowship, a man whom Havelock knew. This man had never paid any attention to her or recognised that she was in love with him; and now he had left England and she would never see him again.

He was the only man she had ever been in love with. There were several men in love with her. She had had a number of proposals of marriage—including one from a butcher called Cobbledick at whose mother's farm she had stayed a few weeks on her way back from Cornwall, and another from a solicitor named Algernon—but she had never felt anything except friendship for these suitors. Whatever other passionate attractions she had felt had been for women.

These confidences were followed by others on later occasions, the natural growth of a sympathetic friendship. The details came out piecemeal as Edith chose to relate them, and Havelock felt no curiosity in fitting together the story of her life as he had with Olive.

She was two years younger than Havelock, born 9 March 1861 at Newton in Cheshire. She was christened Edith Mary Oldham, the only child of Samuel Oldham Lees and Mary Laetitia Bancroft. The Lees family were thoroughly Lancashire in type and character; the Bancrofts came from Mottram in Cheshire, and from them she inherited the vivacious qualities which made many people regard her as Celtic.

Edith's mother was reputed to be a woman of singular sweetness and charm. Unfortunately during her pregnancy she met with an accident to her head and, perhaps because of this, Edith was born prematurely at seven months. Ellis considered this "doubtless a fact of much significance, for she remained in some degree undeveloped, in temperament as well as physically something of a child, and with the undue nervous sensitiveness and susceptibility of one whose textures had never had the chance of acquiring completely normal powers of resistance to noxious influences."

In my opinion Ellis tended always to overstress hereditary and congenital determinants of temperament and character and to understress environmental influences. More important than the prematurity of Edith's birth seems to me the prematurity of her mother's death. Mary Laetitia Bancroft Lees died shortly after giving birth to Edith. Edith never knew her mother but she worshipped her throughout her life and to the end kept a large portrait of her mother above her desk. This loss of maternal love must anyway have produced a trauma which it would have taken great love from her father and whoever acted as foster-mother to heal.

The Lees family came of vigorous but unbalanced stock. Edith's great-grandfather, Oldham Lees, made a fortune by stinting himself and his family. He was tyrannical to his son and kind to animals, thinking nothing of staying up all night to sit with a sick horse. He left thirty thousand pounds to charity, twenty thousand to his grandson, Samuel, Edith's father, and nothing to his own son, Silas, who according to Edith was a collier who chased his wife with a carving-knife when he was drunk.

Edith's father was sent to the university, where he acquired intellectual tastes and a love of books. He had no business ability and every scheme he embarked on ended in failure. When his first wife died, he married again, presumably as much to get a foster-mother for the child as a wife for himself. He seems to have repeated much of the pattern of his self-made grandfather. He had no love or understanding of children. He was short-tempered, cruel, despotic, venting upon others the hatred he felt for himself.

His second wife tried to turn his anger from herself by directing it against the child. The child who needed more love than the normal child was given less, the target of a neurotic father's violence and a stepmother's cutting sneers. In sheer self-defence she fought back with the weapons used against her. To love and joy she would have responded joyfully with love. Tormented, she learnt to torture; and her stepmother's sarcasm sharpened Edith's tongue. The worst in their natures brought out the worst in hers. She became a "difficult child" like so many who have difficult parents.

At twelve she was sent to a convent school in Manchester. The nuns were gentle and kind and for the first time in her life she had a glimpse of happiness. She told her father she wanted to become a Catholic and a nun. Mr Lees, an agnostic disciple of Tyndall, was horrified at this lapse into faith. He took her from the convent school and placed her at a school near London, kept by a Madame Thesma, a German lady of sound free-thinking principles. Madame Thesma cured her of her love of God and gave her a love of Shakespeare in its place. Edith, who had a natural sense of drama and a talent for mimicry, was always given the chief male part, playing Romeo opposite Aida Jenoure, who subsequently became a well-known actress. Edith left school with two or three good friends, whom she kept for life, and the vague prophecy of Madame Thesma that she had "a great future."

Edith, who by that time hated her stepmother because she was not her real mother, and loathed her father because he was her father, went to live with her grandmother, whom she did not dislike so much because she was only her grandmother. She went out daily to teach pupils. She was bored and uncomfortable in her grandmother's home, but not so bored and uncomfortable that she accepted the hand of the local doctor who proposed marriage to her.

At twenty-one she inherited a hundred pounds. It appeared to her as a vast fortune. She gave expensive presents to all her friends and almost before she knew it the money had gone.

She decided to leave her grandmother's and start a girls' school of her own in the London suburb of Sydenham. As a teacher she was not such a dismal failure as Havelock. At any rate she ran Girton House, as she called it, for three years before she collapsed with a nervous financial breakdown.

Two friends came to her aid. A wealthy old lady called Mrs Drake, whom she came to regard as her "second mother," paid the debts. And Honor Brooke, the eldest daughter of the Reverend Stopford Brooke, nursed her back to health, introduced her to the Brooke home in Manchester Square which at that time was a distinguished intellectual centre, and then turned her reviving energies towards social work in the slums.

It was, however, some time before she made her recovery. What she was suffering from, though she did not know it, nor did the doctors of that day, was the first bout of cyclothymic or manic depression, or circular madness as it is sometimes called. This is characterised by phases of euphoria, in which energy, confidence and hope are unbounding, and of depression in which doubt, despair and listlessness make life seem unbearable. She had started Girton House and run it on the tide of optimism; now alone at nights in a little attic off Manchester Square she fought desperately against the doubts and terrors which assailed her, fortified only by a saying of Stopford Brooke's, "courage is a habit"; no great consolation for a mental illness which is now alleviated by electric-shock therapy.

Havelock Ellis knew nothing about the nature or the possible treatment of cyclothymic depression either at this time or during Edith's lifetime. He saw her as a person with enormous capacities for love and friendship whose life had been blighted by a poor heredity and a bitter childhood. He did not in any passionate sense love her, but he came gradually to the conviction that she was the person he ought to marry and he was the person she ought to marry. There were many reasons for this; their views on economic independence coincided. He earned only enough money to support himself, so he could not marry a woman he had to support. She had an unearned income roughly the same as he earned. He hated to dominate; she hated to be dominated. He regarded his work as his main task in life, to which the demands of a wife were subordinate. She was fiercely keen on preserving her emotional freedom. He did not want to have children, the support and education of whom might force him to work for money instead of getting money from what he wanted to do. Edith's doctor said that she ought not to have children. He was not at all confident of his sexual performance; she seemed to consider the sexual side of marriage the least important. The differences between their natures struck a sort of balance; in her words he was her opium and she was his champagne. And finally there was his conviction that he was not an ordinary man. He knew that he could never make an ordinary woman happy, nor could an ordinary woman make him happy. He remembered a remark which had been made earlier by Margaret, James Hinton's daughter, who sometimes went to play the piano to the women patients in the Bethlem Hospital for the insane. Asked what the patients were like, she said some were "like that Miss Lees." This was before he proposed marriage, and though he never repeated the remark, he never forgot it.

The announcement that they were going to get married did not cause anxiety purely on account of the disabilities of Edith Lees. A number of Edith's friends and Havelock's warned her against marrying him. Mrs Hinton said he was like James Hinton, and "that was not necessarily a recommendation." There was a vague sense that he was not a very desirable husband. One of the accusations which stuck was that Havelock was still in love with Olive Schreiner and was only marrying her for second best. In June 1891 Edith wrote from Carbis in Cornwall that she couldn't take symbols for realities or a part in place of the whole. Marriage for her meant a complete and permanent union of body and soul.

Ellis replied: "We have never needed any explanations before, and that has always seemed so beautiful to me, that we seemed to understand instinctively. And that is why I've never explained things that perhaps needed explaining. This is specially so about

Olive. I have never known anyone who was so beautiful and wonderful or with whom I could be so much myself, and it is true enough that for years to be married to her seemed to me the one thing in the world that I longed for,[1] but that is years ago. We are sweet friends now and always will be; but to speak in the way you do of a 'vital relationship' to her sounds to me very cruel."

Having followed the story of Havelock's life from the inside, one is liable to lose sight of how he appeared to other people. His association with the Hinton circle, Miss Haddon, the open advocate of polygamy, giving him money for his medical studies and his going about with Olive Schreiner, were matters for gossip and speculation. In the matter of sexual freedom most people practised far more than they preached, and these people did not always understand that Havelock preached so much because he had practised so little.

Ellis had told Edith nothing of his private life and never showed her the journal, the last words of which described his farewell to Olive at the dockside, only eighteen months before. "I keep seeing against the stanchion the little figure that holds so much that is loveliest to me in the world and my heart is heavy." Havelock himself felt there was nothing inconsistent in this and his proposal of marriage to Edith; but Edith might have misunderstood. Instead he gave the following explanation of the failure of his relationship with Olive. He may have believed it to be true, though I am certain that Olive would have denied its objectivity. "Because one has loved somebody who did not love one enough to make the deepest relationship possible—is that a reason why one must always be left alone? I only explain this to show that I am free in every sense—perhaps freer than you—and that I haven't been so unfair to you as you seem to think. The thing I wanted to tell you about that has been bothering me was this. I had to decide whether it was possible for me to return the passionate love of someone whom I felt a good deal of sympathy with, and even a little passionate towards. She would have left me free, and it hurt me to have to torture her.

[1] *My Life*, Eng. ed., p. 238, Am. ed., p. 276. This remark conflicts with the earlier statement in *My Life* that "the thought of marriage fleetingly occurred" to him.

But I had no difficulty in deciding; the real, deep and mutual understanding, which to me is more than passion, wasn't there, and the thought I had constantly in my mind was that my feeling towards you, although I do not feel passionate towards you (as I thought you understood), was one that made any other relationship impossible—I wonder if you understand that."

It is possible for us, with all that we know about the urolagnia, the failure in Derbyshire, etc., to understand what Havelock Ellis was hinting at. But it was impossible for Edith, who had heard far more from friends of Ellis as a free lover than she had heard from Havelock about his sexual limitations, to realise that he had found he was physically and psychologically incapable of being Olive's lover. Nor did she realise the implication of the next paragraph in answer to her statement that her ideal of marriage was "a complete and permanent union of body and soul." What he meant to say was that all he could offer certainly was a union of soul, which he hoped would last.

"Now I've got to explain what I feel about our relationship to each other—and that will be all! Perhaps the only thing that needs explaining is about the absence of passionate feeling. I have always told you that I felt so restful and content with you, that the restless, tormenting passionate feeling wasn't there; and I have seen that you didn't feel passionate towards me but have said over and over again that you didn't believe in passion. So we are quite equal, and why should we quarrel about it? Let us just be natural with each other—leaving the other feeling to grow up or not, as it will. It is possible to me to come near you and to show you my heart, and it is possible to you to come near me; and (to me at least) that is something so deep and rare that it makes personal tenderness natural and inevitable—or at all events right.

"In reference to marriage: I said (or meant) that I did not think either you or I were the kind of people who could safely tie ourselves legally to anyone; true marriage, as I understand it, is a union of soul and body so close and so firmly established that one feels it will last as long as life lasts. For people to whom that has come to exist as an everyday fact of their lives, then the legal tie

EDITH ELLIS ABOUT THE TIME OF HER MARRIAGE

may safely follow; but it cannot come beforehand. . . . Surely, Edith, you, too, understand that you *can't* promise to give away your soul for life, that you can't promise to love forever beforehand. . . .

"Tell me where you don't feel with me, and tell me quite honestly, as I have told you, how you feel towards me. We aren't so young that we need fear to face the naked facts of life simply and frankly."

Havelock believed that they had enough in common spiritually to form the basis for a marriage in which it was possible some physical element would arise, but if it didn't, no matter; they would get on without it. It seemed to him a perfectly normal thing, because he had been living with his handicap for many years, and this appeared a possible solution of it. Its language, however, was so vague that Edith could not be blamed if she failed to understand exactly what Havelock meant. There was only one point on which she could take a stand and there she got her way. If they were going to be married, they had to be married legally in a registry office and not by any of these new-fangled "free unions."

In July 1891 Ellis went down to stay for some weeks at Lamorna. Miss Jones had lent him the house while she was away, and Edith joined him there for a week, the first of many honeymoons. Then Edith went on to Carbis, where she had taken a cottage on a long lease. Though they were not married until December of that year, Havelock was already evolving the pattern of life which he wanted to pursue after marriage. There was to be no invasion of the other's privacy. They would jealously guard their private lives, and meet only occasionally together under the same roof. So marriage would stay fresh, the theory was. What remained to be seen was whether the times each wanted to be alone or together would coincide.

They went along to Hatton Garden to buy a wedding ring, Edith paying her half of it according to the true principle of equality (or so she always said, and Havelock couldn't remember). Then on the morning of Saturday, 19 December 1891, Havelock with his sister Louie as witness went to Paddington Registry Office, where they were joined by Edith with Evelyn and Sybil Brooke. Edith was nervous and alarmed at the decision with which Havelock said "I do." ("Would he turn out one of those bullying husbands after all?") The ceremony was over in a few minutes and the bride and bridegroom separated, Havelock to return to St Mary's Terrace, Edith to her rooms in Wigmore Street. There was no wedding breakfast. Edith always used to say her only wedding breakfast was porridge. But for the afternoon Edith invited all her friends to an At Home at the Fellowship House in Doughty Street. The only person who didn't want to accept was Havelock. Edith told him he would have to turn up, but to spare him discomfort arranged that he should come late. Next morning they left for Paris.

Havelock did not take her to the Hotel Corneille, where he always stayed when he was with Arthur Symons. He took her to a rather more English and more central hotel he knew of, the Hôtel d'Oxford et Cambridge in the Rue d'Alger.

10

> No one could be less like a feather bed than Edith; I was sometimes made to eel that she was more like a little porcupine. That perpetually recurrent external discordance made always a thread of tragedy running through the love of two people who remained at heart, always, lovers and comrades, united in an intimacy of confidence that can be but rarely attained.
>
> *My Life*

I WISH that, to counterbalance Havelock Ellis's account of his marriage to Edith, we had an account by Edith of her marriage to Havelock. He tried, as honestly as a man has ever tried, to be truthful and objective. But the more intimate one is with somebody else, the more difficult it is to see oneself from the point of view of the other; even the image of the beloved seen from too close cannot be viewed in perspective.

It is quite clear that before marriage Havelock Ellis had formed precise ideas of what he wanted from a wife and what he was prepared to give her. His work came before anything else, and his wife must accept that as he did himself. It was not selfish to demand this, because his lifework was a selfless devotion to humanity, in his own view.

His wife must not interfere with that lifework. She must leave him alone to do his study and writing. She must have enough money to support herself, and interests of her own to occupy her while he was working. These must not be the interests of the ordinary housewife, because he was used to looking after himself and it fussed him to have anyone around when he was working; nor that of a mother, because children would impose economic and other burdens, which he did not want to incur. What he looked for from a wife, and what he hoped to give her, was a spiritual comradeship of the sort which he and Olive had shared, and possibly some sort of physical intimacy going at least as far as he and Olive had gone in Derbyshire, and maybe further; of that he was not so sure. He knew precisely what he needed, and fairly precisely what he could give in return.

Edith Ellis, I think, was far less certain of what she expected from marriage. She was terrified of any man, or any action, which reminded her of her father, and she loved Havelock for his gentleness, the complete absence from bullying in his nature; and though she found his unsociability at times infuriating, it amused her at other times and set off her own genius for friendship. She valued more than anything his sensitivity, his tenderness when she was overwhelmed by her moods of depression, his unshockability, his undemandingness and his apparent certainty that things would be all right, when it seemed to her that they were impossibly wrong. He had absolute faith in the ability of the spirit to surmount all physical difficulties. It was this that made her say over and over again, "Havelock is my rock. Without him I should die."

On the other hand, though he constantly told her that she was no ordinary woman, she was more ordinary (or perhaps more womanly) than he would admit. It was all very well for her doctor and Havelock to say that she ought not to have children from the eugenic point of view, but she wanted to have children. At that first premarital honeymoon at Lamorna, there had been some sort of physical intimacy, and Edith wrote to him exactly a year later, "My love, do you know that by the day of the week this is the day a year ago when you and I went to our little house with the foxglove towers and gave ourselves to ourselves. I look back and it seems years and years ago. I was shy and frightened and *cried over my wee babe that was never to be*, and you!—you made me think of how beautiful men could be."

The passage I have italicised shows a very normal desire for children, and it was one which persisted throughout her life. In 1909, for example, she wrote to Edward Carpenter, "A new and beautiful person has come like a bolt from the blue into my life and is *as my son to me*. A starving artist of 21. He tramped all the way from London to Penzance. He is illegitimate but with an inheritance from the skies of a mystical mind and such serene grit he entrances me. His kiss last night effaced all the barrenness. What matter who bore him? He is mine now." (My italics.)

With her cyclothymic disposition Edith could clearly never have been an easy wife to live with, and Havelock Ellis thought she was temperamentally unsuited to maternity. Since he gave her no children, it is a question that can never be decided. What is certain is that like many women she found the hygiene of birth control messy and inhibiting, and Havelock did not prove a satisfactory lover, in a physical sense.

Their honeymoon in Paris was delightful, in that Havelock could initiate her into a city which he knew and she was visiting for the first time. Edith's quick response warmed his heart, as much as her loud expression of pleasure, surprise and curiosity at times embarrassed him. The cafés and restaurants, theatres, concerts and pictures galleries laid the foundation of common memories which were built up in the years to come. "Perhaps our happiest and most exalted moments were in listening to music, side by side. Always music was as it were the sacrament of our spiritual union." But, at least on Havelock's side, there was none of the ecstasy and delight in the exploration of his beloved's body. He could not echo Edith's words and say, "And you!—you made me think of how beautiful women could be!" The sacrament was music, not sex.

They came back to London, Havelock to St Mary's Terrace, Edith to her own rooms, from which she prepared to wind up her secretaryship of the Fellowship of the New Life. She had handed in her notice when she announced her marriage. "Fellowship is Hell," she was fond of saying afterwards. The New Life henceforward was what she made, or explored, with Havelock. She turned from organising to lecturing. She had a good voice and a powerful delivery. But there were not enough calls on her to satisfy her bounding energies. She tried her hand at writing and had a lecture called *Democracy in the Kitchen* printed. After a year of marriage she wrote a pamphlet called *A Novitiate for Marriage*, of which she ordered a first printing of a thousand copies. Only a small proportion of these were sold, and though many were given away, the remainder followed her in a large heavy box at every house removal until her death, when they were destroyed.

Another outlet for her energy was letting cottages. She had rented one at Carbis before marriage. Now she acquired several more, decked them out tastefully and cheaply and let them off to holiday-makers. It was a useful supplement to her income, which she always tended to overspend.

Marriage brought no children, no blossoming of sex; but it brought her the sort of restful love which had never been satisfied in infancy. "You rest every fibre in me and suit me, sir, and I crow like a wee child at the breast, and I'm happy, happy in you, my true Heart." Havelock was a mother to her at some times, and at others her child. "My Boy, my Boy!" A strange mixture of hitherto unsatisfied emotions of love welled up in her and were bestowed on Havelock, who accepted them calmly and gently, unless they threatened his independence.

He went out of his way to stress that independence. "Louie and Symons came to the conclusion the other day that I had not been at all spoilt by marriage; you'd hardly know, Symons said to her, that I was married. Rhys,[1] on the other hand, they decided, had been spoilt. Although better groomed than formerly (or perhaps because!), he looks pale and depressed, and has no spirit for anything; always has to be with his wife."

"I shan't be able to go to the Alhambra with Symons or to meet Signorina Legnani (the most delightful of all ballet dancers) on Tuesday! I'm afraid that I'm not altogether sorry that I shan't be able to go with you on Sunday. Somehow or other the very thought of it made me feel ill and helpless. Now I feel quite happy! And then I don't at all like to feel that you are at all dependent upon me in any way except of love. I don't feel dependent on you in those things and I'm sure I could never have loved you if I hadn't felt that you were strong and independent. You are *really*, my sweetheart, are you not?—I can't bear to think that you are ever such a tiny bit like those wives who hang round their hus-

[1] Ernest Rhys, editor of the Camelot Classics and later of the Everyman's Library.

bands' necks like millstones. . . . Just had a letter from Olive. Is doubtful about coming to England next year, but may. Would like to see you; doesn't much want to see me. But I am the only man-friend she corresponds with regularly." [1]

In re-reading these letters, Havelock Ellis found them "rather strange in places now, both as regards substance and tone." In reading them then, Edith must have found them both strange and forthright. Ellis made plain his terms: he would not meet her friends unless he wanted to; he must have his own social life, his meetings with famous ballerinas, his friendships with famous women novelists, his periods of separation; he would give her love, but he did not intend to be tied to her apron-strings. If she did not accept those terms, which he had made plain from the beginning, then she wasn't the woman he thought he had married.

Edith had found that she wasn't. As she came to love him more deeply, she wanted him far more than she had expected, and especially at night when the reaction from the social excitement of the day plunged her back into the terrors of depression. It wasn't that his love was not enough, but there was not enough of his love. She needed to be held and caressed and cherished; and he would be in London and she at Carbis, or in the cottage they had rented from Rollo Russell in Haslemere.

In the letter about the foxglove towers and the wee babe never to be, and how beautiful men were, Edith went on: "So long ago and yet only a year, it seems as if every phase of life has gone on in me and I'm years and years older. I think when I'm dying I shall see that house and smell the fern-roots and look into that blue sky and see the gulls and feel as near the heart of a great mystery as I did then. I've been reserved, more than is my nature to be, with you and have come to you inch by inch, but I shall never go back, and if you ever leave me, I shall try the other mystery."

But though there was such reliance on him—which he loved when he was free as much as he resented it when he was busy—there was the conflict between their different natures, between her

[1] *My Life*, Eng. ed., p. 261, Am. ed., p. 307. It was reassuring of Olive to say this, but in fact she wrote as frequently to Edward Carpenter.

excessive sociability and his excessive reclusion—which made for frequent quarrels. He could not write when there was any noise and they never occupied a house big enough for him to withdraw in solitude while she entertained. He would make a protest; she would snap back with "stupid naughty words," he would sulk in silence and she would be reduced to a state of despair, "almost on the verge of brain-fever." And it is no use speculating whether Edith would have been more settled if she had been given children, because the patter of tiny feet would have made Havelock tear his hair.

"The beauty and intimacy of our relationship," Havelock Ellis wrote in *My Life*, "was built on our separations, separations without which the relationship might perhaps have dissolved," and dissolved because Havelock thought that he could not live long with anybody, however much he loved them, especially a woman as obtrusive as Edith.

During one of these separations—it is difficult to date because Ellis is imprecise, but apparently early in March, 1892, less than three months after their marriage—Edith wrote from Carbis Bay to Havelock in London to say that an old friend of hers, called by Havelock Ellis "Claire," had come to stay with her and she found that instead of the old feeling of friendship she felt a passionate attraction to her. "She wrote to tell me of it with all her native trustful confidence, simple, direct, and spontaneous. If I remember right, she wrote with a misgiving hesitation at first. (There was, as I now look back, a pathetic wonder and beauty in that appeal to my comprehending love, as though addressed to a divine being superior to the weakness of a human husband.)" [1]

The letter clearly gave Ellis so much pain that it was not one he kept. It is a pity, because his recollection of it was hazy; and one knows, from other letters which he does quote, that his appreciation of their undercurrents was sometimes faulty.

If we had that letter, it might show that it was addressed not to

[1] *My Life*, Eng. ed., p. 263, Am. ed., p. 309. The passage I have included in brackets was, I think, one of the marginal glosses which Ellis added at a later date.

a divine being superior to the weaknesses of a human husband, but to a human being capable of the strength of a husband; that it was a cry from the heart of a woman separated from the love and affection that all her being wanted from her husband, saying, "Look. Help me! See what these awful separations are driving me to." I think it possible that if he had said it would have to stop, she would have answered that it had only started because she was left so much alone, and why couldn't they live closer together. And that was something which Ellis was not capable of doing.

Instead, he wrote and gave his blessing to them both. "The response, as her letters show,[1] was the response she desired and expected. But it by no means came from a godhead, but from a suffering and human heart. It is true that—(though I cannot now be sure)—I do not think my pain was immediate. My emotions work slowly. I think the first effort at self-conquest seemed successful, (but was less successful than it seemed,) and that it was not till the spring of next year that, (as I still vividly recall,) I restlessly paced up and down my study at Paddington with heart aching over letters from Carbis." [2]

If I am right, the argument in Havelock Ellis's mind, when he first gave his blessing to Edith and Claire, was that he had not succeeded in satisfying Edith sexually, though he had succeeded in establishing a spiritual love-relationship with her which had brought both of them great benefit. He could not demand that she should not receive from a woman what he was unable to give her himself. And according to his beliefs at this time, the physical was unimportant compared to the spiritual.

The fact that Edith had chosen a woman rather than a man saved his pride. If she had chosen a man, he would have told her that he would give her a divorce and she should marry him. Part of the reason why Edith chose a woman instead of a man was that she knew this. She wanted Havelock more than she wanted

[1] Though this seems to show that he kept the letters from Edith about Claire, he did not quote from any before February 1893, eleven months later. By that time Edith had become reconciled to the *modus amandi.*

[2] *My Life*, Eng. ed., p. 263, Am. ed., p. 309. Once more I have put brackets round what seem to me later marginal glosses.

anybody in the world, and she was serious in saying that if he left her she would kill herself. So if Havelock was unable to continue to give her the sexual satisfaction, the need for which he had wakened in her, she preferred to take it from a woman who would not provide such a sexual challenge to the man she loved.

This analysis is wrong in the sense that it makes self-conscious what must have been a psychological process of which Edith can have been only dimly aware, and it ignores the fact that Edith's girlhood and youthful attractions had been towards her own sex. On the other hand her two latest loves had been of the opposite sex, Havelock and the man from the Fellowship, who went abroad. According to Kinsey standards which reckon homosexual attachments from 0 for no homosexual attachments to 6 for no heterosexual attachment, Edith's at this time would have been a Kinsey-rating of 4. She was not, that is to say, a totally inverted person. She was making the transition, rather later than most people, because of her prematurity and her unfortunate childhood, from adolescence to the adult sexual pattern. And then, because of Havelock Ellis's own limitations, she lapsed. She assured him that the only reason why she lapsed was because he left her so much alone. But he, who knew so much more about sex from books and so much less about it from personal experience than almost any man of his age, assured her that there was nothing to worry about. Like Edward Carpenter, John Addington Symonds, Michelangelo, Walt Whitman, Marlowe, Shakespeare, Socrates and Sappho, she was that rare, wonderful and nothing-to-be-ashamed-of creature, a congenital sexual invert. He understood, he sympathised and he loved her just the same. There was no reason why she should not be perfectly happy if she accepted her anomaly purely and nobly as he had accepted his urolagnia. It was really a very beautiful thing. And she could tell him everything and it would make no difference at all.

"I told Claire you would be trusted with all," Edith wrote in the first letter of hers which Havelock quoted, eleven months after the "blessing." "She smiled, 'You *are* two odd people!' It is her purity and sweetness which have made me love her; she is so child-like and unprudish, and gives me like a child a love which has rested and comforted and strengthened me in a way which amazes me." And nearly a month later she wrote: "It is so wonderful to have married a man who leaves a woman her soul. I'm utterly satisfied in you, Havelock. It passes all my comprehension, though, why you love me."

In fact, Havelock, despite the promise which he had made that he would keep no secrets from Edith, had hidden from her how deeply hurt he had been by her infidelity with Claire. It was another of these delayed reactions of his, like his physical ardour for Olive rising months after hers had died away. His natural reactions were as distant and as solemn as echoes in the Grand Canyon. By the time that Edith had become reconciled to the startling licence he had given her, he was beginning to react as Edith had expected him to react in the first place. Why should this woman Claire take his wife away from him? he felt. He hadn't the slightest jealousy against Claire. (How could he when he had given her his blessing?) Yet the spiritual hold which he had on Edith—despite all those theories of the supremacy of the spirit over passion—was being sapped by the physical hold of Claire.

Havelock's letters began to show his discontent and unhappiness. And Edith immediately sensed it, though she did not understand yet this delayed mechanism of the man she had married. He was always so confident, so calm, so utterly accepting; and now suddenly for a reason she could not understand, this cloud of resentment burst on her. She was up in Manchester lecturing for Edward Carpenter at Ancoats when the storm burst. She was so hurt that she stumbled through her lectures. She became ill but at the same time she felt that she must see Havelock as soon as possible. She was stung to resentment. For this man who had encouraged her to make a lover of Claire now suddenly turned against her. She reacted with the trigger-anger with which she had hoped he would react to the announcement that Claire was her lover. He knew that she really loved him better than anybody else; and she learnt that he was not indifferent, but a tortoise of a man—and she was a lizard. "Love is funny and I am funny," he wrote in recantation. "It needs its wife's breasties every two hours like a baby, and if they seem far off,—it do shrike! (But you know, my Love, when the mother hears her baby, and knows she has that within her to soothe it, she doesn't feel that she must yell too!)"

At that time nobody knew very much about the causes of what is usually called homosexuality, but which he preferred to call sexual inversion. Even to-day it is debatable whether it is entirely congenital, entirely environmental or combinations of the two. Havelock Ellis decided that there were two types of homosexuality, one congenital sexual inversion and one pseudo-homosexuality. What seems more likely is that there is a large number of intermediates, who are more easily classified in terms of the curable and the incurable. Roughly speaking the curable lie more fully in the Kinsey-ratings 1 to 3 and the incurable from 4 to 6. Edith Ellis with a Kinsey-rating 4 was difficult, and on the other hand she wanted to be cured, and from a non-dominant man like Ellis she felt no noticeable physical repulsion. On the other hand, Ellis's conviction that she was an incurable sexual invert and his lack of desire to cure her thrust her back on a path which she had already traversed. She felt that he was making her a sexual invert because he had not got the sexual potency to make her normal. At the same time he possessed a spiritual quality which she valued more highly than anything. She had something for him and he had something for her, which nobody else on earth could give either of them. He was her opium and she was his champagne.

Two shocks awaited her. The first was that he began to collaborate with John Addington Symonds on a book about sexual inversion. He began to ask her about her homosexual friends. She felt he was using her for his work, was making her into a Lesbian in order to find out the feminine side of the business instead of trying to help her out of her troubles. In a way he was—which made her accusations the more wounding—but at the same time it was the only way in which he was able to help her. Havelock Ellis's acceptance of Claire and her successors may have raised Edith's Kinsey-rating, turned her back to a form of emotional expression which she had been growing out of. But it must be remembered that it was Havelock Ellis who had brought her as far as she had gone through the qualities he had developed in accepting his limitations. Without those limitations he would not have possessed the qualities; and though Havelock overstated his case when he said that he had married "the most difficult woman in the world," it is hard to think of another man who would have loved, cherished and protected her as devotedly as Havelock did.

This, however, did not prevent his administering the second shock to her. To explain how it happened a digression is needed.

The only friend whom Havelock had made among the students at St Thomas's Hospital was a man fifteen years older than himself called Barker Smith. He was an analytical chemist who decided somewhat late in his career to qualify as a doctor. He was already married and had a small daughter, whom we may call Amy as Ellis did in *My Life*. John Barker Smith would often invite Havelock to his house; it became in fact a sort of second home to him. He did not pay much attention to Amy, but as she grew up, Amy paid more and more attention to Havelock, conceiving for him a humble Martha-like devotion. If Edith was a prickly little porcupine, Amy was the feather bed of a woman that Alphonse Daudet thought the ideal wife for a literary man.

About a year after Havelock had given his blessing to Claire, and Edith had come to accept the arrangement as normal, Havelock's delayed resentment began to rise. He felt that he was losing Edith spiritually.

Edith was down at Rollo Russell's cottage at Haslemere and Havelock spent his time between there and London. Edith's nocturnal depressions were bad, and when he was away in London she liked to have one of her friends in the cottage to be on call in case of need. But it chanced that there were none of Edith's friends available, so Havelock suggested Amy as Edith's companion.

With the two women together, both of whom he knew well separately, Havelock began to make comparisons between his wife's tireless (and tiresome) energy and Amy's quiet, unobtrusive feather-bed-like womanliness. They were not entirely in Edith's favour; and when he took Amy for a walk to Hindhead, he gave her, with her approval if not at her suggestion, a kiss.

Remembering their agreement that there should be no secrets between them (though in fact he had kept secret his resentment of Claire), he told Edith of this kiss on his return. He was astonished and wounded by the fact that Edith immediately flew into a rage against this "femininity," as she contemptuously called Amy. Let this femininity get out of the house at once.

Amy said nothing. Quiet and demure, she knew that with every outburst Edith was cutting more ground from under her own feet. Havelock retired into stolid silence. His sense of justice was outraged. He had accepted Claire without demur. And now there was this insane outcry against a harmless little kiss to a chaste young girl of twenty-four. It seemed the most elementary justice that if Edith, a congenital invert, had a sexual relation with Claire, he should be allowed the licence of an extra-marital kiss. What I think he did not realise was that Edith did not consider herself a congenital invert. She thought of herself as a woman who had married a fine and splendid man, who unfortunately was sexually crippled and had nobly acquiesced in her taking women-friends as lovers, because he was unable to satisfy her himself. She had accepted his assurances that he did not feel passionate towards her, because she believed that he was incapable of feeling passionate towards anyone; but his kissing of Amy showed that he did feel passionate towards Amy. Havelock was so inhibited in his demonstrations of affection that a kiss from him was as violent an action as near-rape by anyone else. And that femininity, simpering in silence, was obviously out to hook him if she could.

There was an element of justice on both sides. Each had a strand of truth entangled in rationalisations and self-justification. And each used literature to state his case. The argument running through the *Sexual Inversion* volume of the *Studies* was Havelock's explanation of what was wrong with Edith and how she could be helped by society to turn her anomaly to useful ends: and while he was writing this, in Edith's view worthless and unscientific, book, she was writing a short novel, put out first under the dank title

AMY

Seaweed, and later successfully republished under the title of *Kit's Woman*. *Kit's Woman* is a work of fiction. In Ellis's words it "was a real work of art, well planned and well balanced, original and daring, the genuinely personal outcome of its author, alike in its humour and its firm deep grip of the great sexual problems it is concerned with, centring around the relations of a wife to a husband who by an accident has become impotent. (I say it was 'genuinely personal,' but it is not, I now add, till long after I wrote these words that it has seemed to me that the story was consciously or unconsciously inspired by her own relations with me and of course completely transformed into a new shape. In that shape it splendidly presents exactly what I have attempted to present in the preceding pages: the triumph of a deeper passionate love over physical passion.)" [1]

Kit's Woman presents Edith's view of her marriage. The wife is normal and is driven by physical passion to find a lover (in the novel a man, not a woman) but returns to her paralysed husband because despite his affliction he possesses unique spiritual power and understanding. Though the point of departure in *Sexual Inversion* and *Kit's Woman* is different, each writer concentrating on the abnormality of the other, both arrive at the same conclusion. It is the conclusion which is important, however necessary it may be to establish their different starting positions.

Both of them had the confidence that whatever the other might do, it would not be ugly or ignoble. Havelock himself admitted that if Edith had not made such an outcry over that first kiss, the relationship might have gone no further. It was his sense of fairness rather than passion for Amy which led him forward; and the way when he was in London she would slip round from her father's house, which was close by, and make herself unobtrusively useful. "After months, even years," they drifted into an intimacy which Amy found perhaps the more binding because Havelock insisted that she must be absolutely free and that he wanted to have no hold on her life. And Edith came to accept her, because Amy gave Havelock

[1] *My Life*, Eng. ed. pp. 293–4, Am. ed., p. 348. Brackets suggest the later marginal gloss.

something—not very important—which she could not give, but which seemed to soothe him. She thought Amy was stupid and dull and lacking in fire, not really the sort of person who belonged in their set. But Havelock found in her qualities of sweetness and gentleness and physical satisfaction which soothed him when Edith's violent alternation between euphoria and despair had stretched his nerves almost to breaking-point.

11

When you are dealing with the adult hero in the midst of his work, the one great service you can do, and that which is your most proper function, is to tell us, not about this work, but about the conditions under which it was achieved.

An Open Letter to Biographers

PART OF Ellis's revelation at the age of nineteen had been that his vocation lay in the study of sex. His qualification as a doctor was the first step in that direction. The second was the publication in 1894 of *Man and Woman*, a study of their secondary sexual characteristics. He had started work on it, while a medical student twelve years before, firstly because he knew of "no full and unprejudiced statement of the precise facts" and secondly because it "was intended as an introduction to more elaborate study of the primary phenomena of sex on the psychological side. As such the book was undertaken for my own help and instruction, more than for that of others." It proved, however, useful for others, and the German sexologist Iwan Bloch described it as "a classical work" which formed "the foundation for all later research." F. H. Marshall, the English specialist in the physiology of reproduction, found it "a fund of valuable information." In the sixth edition, which it had reached by 1926, Ellis summed up his conclusions. "The sexes are perfectly poised; men and women are at every point different and at all points equivalent. There is no reason why men should be anxious to do everything that women do, or women be anxious to do everything that men do; but there is likewise no reason why each sex should not be absolutely free to develop the possibilities with its own proper nature, even when the development is along exceptional lines."

Several of the people he knew and loved at the time of writing *Man and Woman* had developed along exceptional lines. The beloved Edward Carpenter, for instance, had never felt any sexual attraction towards women but had been strongly drawn towards men. Carpenter had at first regarded these feelings as an unnatural perversion, but later he had come to regard his inversion as a congenital thing which he must accept and turn to the best use he could. He formed friendships with men of a similar temperament, Urnings as he called them in the words of K. H. Ulrichs.[1] If they did not object to there being a physical bond, neither did he.

Then there was John Addington Symonds, who, though married, had discovered a strong streak of inversion in himself. He had made a study of paederasty in the ancient world and privately printed a monograph on the subject, *A Problem In Greek Ethics.*

Very soon after Edith had confessed her passion for Claire, Ellis received from Addington Symonds a letter suggesting that he should do for the Contemporary Science Series a volume on *Sexual Inversion.* Ellis had by then learnt more caution and, while approving the subject as one which ought to be treated, rejected it for the Contemporary Science Series. After some negotiation, a collaboration was arranged with Symonds to provide historical material and case-histories he had collected and Ellis to provide the weight of his medical degree, further case-histories and the preparation of the purely medical chapters in the book.

The two collaborators never met because Symonds lived abroad, but their letters have been preserved, so we can see how they reached their conclusions. They had little difficulty in agreeing what should be the attitude of the law to sexual inverts. It was in substance what the Wolfenden Committee recommended over sixty years later, but which the British Government has not had the courage to implement, at the time of writing; namely that the same definition of public decency should be applied to intercourse between adult males as to that between adult male and female, though the age of consent might be placed higher to safeguard against corruption of youths who might otherwise develop on normal sexual lines. Sexual practices between man and man in private should be a matter not for the law but for individual conscience, in exactly the

[1] Ulrichs coined the word from *Uranos,* Heaven, his notion being that Urning-love was of a higher order than the love of man and woman.

same way as it was between man and woman, and woman and woman.

Then as now there remained the far more difficult question of how sexual inverts should be regarded. Was sexual inversion a psychic disease, either congenital or contracted? Or were sexual inverts perfectly normal individuals of what Carpenter called an Intermediate Sex, as different at every point as heterosexual men and women but at all points equivalent?

Whichever of these views was held, the argument for the revision of the law was valid. But social and medical attitudes differed according to whether you regarded inversion as a personal characteristic, such as red hair, as an arrested development, such as an undescended testicle, as an irremediable lack, such as colour-blindness, or as a curable psychic disorder.

The truly scientific attitude would have been to admit that it was impossible at that stage to discover what factors were congenital, what environmental or how many, if any, cases of sexual inversion could respond to treatment.

On the other hand Carpenter and Symonds were both convinced that there was a hard core of congenital sexual inverts and that anyone who was "cured" of inversion belonged to a different category, that of "the environmental homosexual," such as the schoolboy, the serviceman, the prisoner who indulges in homosexual practices *faute de mieux*. The Freudian theory that a man might become a confirmed homosexual as a result of some fixation was of course not considered by Ellis, Symonds and Carpenter, because it had not yet been advanced.

Ellis was inclined to accept the Carpenter–Symonds position, because it accorded with his own views. He had both "a germ of perversion" and a shyness that might be considered to verge upon the pathological. He had not sought to cure them, but had accepted them as conditions of his nature and turned them from weaknesses into sources of strength. They were not abnormalities in his opinion, but anomalies.

This predisposition based on Ellis's early personal experience had been strongly reinforced by Edith's passion for Claire. If

Edith was a congenital invert, the reason for the sexual failure of their marriage was clear-cut.

At an early stage in the collaboration, Symonds and Ellis reached agreement on the sort of line to pursue. "That sexual inverts are often neurotic persons there can be little doubt," Ellis wrote to Symonds on 21 December 1892; "that suggestion is sometimes a factor in the causation I am quite prepared to believe, though I agree that suggestion alone can scarcely play a very important part; the fact that both neurotic conditions and suggestion are so common would certainly not prove that they have no connection with sexual inversion. The causation is probably complex. . . . I think it will be best to admit that it is impossible at present to attach great importance to any one theory of causation."

Symonds came back with the suggestion that inversion might be compared to colour-blindness.

"An analogy with 'secondary sensations' (coloured-hearing, etc.) would perhaps be still better," thought Ellis; "such sensations may be either congenital or acquired, and it is not easy to distinguish one class from the other; the subjects of such sensations sometimes, though by no means invariably, show minor neurotic characters or a neurotic heredity, while at the same time it is possible to argue (as some of the subjects of such sensations do argue) that colour-hearing indicates a further step of human development. I think we may regard sexual inversion as a psychic abnormality in just the same way as colour-hearing is. Although neurotic or degenerative signs are found—there can be little doubt—more frequently associated with such psychic abnormality than in average persons, the association by no means necessarily implies that the neurosis is the *cause* of the psychic abnormality."

It is interesting to see how Ellis worked up this material for presentation in *Sexual Inversion*.[1]

"A correspondent compares inversion to colour-blindness; and such comparison is reasonable. Just as the ordinary colour-blind person is congenitally insensitive to those red-green rays which are

[1] *Studies in the Psychology of Sex, Sexual Inversion*, 2nd ed. F. A. Davis Co., Philadelphia, pp. 186–7.

precisely the most impressive to the normal eye, and gives an extended value,—finding that blood is the same colour as grass and a florid complexion blue as the sky,—so the invert fails to see the emotional values patent to normal persons, transferring those values to emotional associations which, for the rest of the world, are utterly distinct. Or we may compare inversion to such a phenomenon as colour-hearing in which there is not so much defect, as an abnormality of nervous tracks producing new and involuntary combinations.[1] Just as the colour hearer instinctively associates colours with sounds, like the young Japanese lady who remarked when listening to singing, 'That boy's voice is red!' so the invert has his sexual sensations brought into relationship with objects that are normally without sexual appeal. And inversion, like colour-hearing, is found more commonly in young subjects, tending to become less marked, or to die out, after puberty. Colour-hearing, while an abnormal phenomenon, it must be added, cannot be called a diseased condition, and it is probably much less frequently associated with other abnormal or degenerative stigmata than is inversion.

[1] Since this chapter was first published (in the *Centralblatt für Nervenheitkunde*, February, 1896), Féré has also compared congenital inversion to colour-blindness and similar anomalies (Féré, *La Descendance d'un Inverti*, Revue Générale de Clinique et Thérapeutique, 1896), while Ribot has referred to the analogy with colour-hearing (Psychology of the Emotions, Part II, Chap. V p. 11)."

On examination this passage is scientifically less impressive than it may appear on first reading. We at first infer that Féré and Ribot arrived at their conclusions independently of Ellis, whereas it is probable that they read his article and took over his analogies as a convenient way of suggesting in non-sexual terms that inversion might be an abnormality rather than a disease.

The comparison between colour-blindness (which in fact is not always congenital but may be caused by disease or injury to the eye) and sexual inversion does not stand up to scrutiny. Since Ellis's day the study of colour-blindness has made great progress. It has been found that there is an indefinite number of gradations between full trichromatic vision and total colour-blindness, which reduces everything to gradations of grey. Schjelderup recognises as many as eighteen different types which need explanation by any theory of colour vision. The three main types of colour-blindness are anomalous trichromatism, dichromatism and monochromatism. The first, anomalous trichromatism, is probably more a colour laziness than a defect of vision. Just as a great painter can analyse the colour-content of what he sees more fully than someone with average trichromatic vision, so there are other people who possess trichromatic vision but are not interested in exercising it. The form of colour-blindness with which Ellis was familiar was dichromatism, the reduction of all colours to mixtures of two of the three elementary stimuli. But there is also the condition in which there is no discrimination of colour wave-length, which is called monochromatism.

Even with the knowledge of colour-blindness which Ellis possessed, Symonds's comparison with inversion was just as unreasonable. It was however useful in diverting the reader's mind from the more sordid elements of the subject raised by the Wilde trial, the stains on the sheets and the catamite picked up by Wilde on Worthing front, the squalor of male prostitution which bedevilled not only the subject but passages of the saintly Carpenter's and the less saintly Symonds's lives abroad. It was not, even the innocent Ellis knew, just as simple as colour-blindness. But if the law and public opinion could be changed, then it might be.

Ellis himself preferred the analogy between the synaesthesia of coloured-hearing and inversion. But that does not stand up to examination. Ellis argued that certain people were attracted to their own sex rather than the opposite sex, in the same way that certain people hearing a sound thought of a colour. But if the analogy was accurate, it would have had to be that the Japanese lady heard nothing but saw red.

Coloured-hearing is quite different from colour-blindness. Colour-blindness can be explained in terms of loss of function in the nervous optic system, so that any two persons with the same degree of loss see in the same way. But coloured-hearing seems to be a matter of association. Some people associate all tones within certain regions of the scale with a colour, but most associate each tone of the scale with a different colour. But within either of these groups few people agree on the colour which they associate with each tone or region of tones.

What is more, the synaesthesia of coloured-vision is only the beginning of this confusion. Huysmans, whom Ellis met in Paris with Arthur Symons, made his hero in either *Là-Bas* or *A Rebours*, I forget which, orchestrate scent and taste. He claimed to be able to play a fugue in scents and liqueurs. But I would bet a pound to a penny that where Huysmans brought in the incense, Baudelaire would have drunk the absinthe, Verlaine the cognac and Mallarmé gone for a good sound scent.

But though this key passage of *Sexual Inversion* turns out to be scientifically unsound, it did the work which Havelock Ellis intended it should. It undermined public prejudice.

Ellis believed that paederasty and acts of gross public indecency between man and man were both aggravated by the public attitude towards all manifestations of sexual inversion. Denied virtuous outlets to their desire, inverts were driven to vice.

The public abhorrence of these practices sprang from the fact that most case-histories of homosexual love came from the records of the police and lunatic asylums. If our views of heterosexual love were derived solely from the same sources, our picture of the love relations between men and women would be equally inaccurate and horrifying.

By using the analogies of colour-blindness and coloured-hearing, he removed—or tried to remove—sexual inversion from a sphere highly charged with moral feeling to the calmer atmosphere of popular science. The sexual invert was in the biological sense "a sport," exhibiting abnormal variation from the parent stock. There was nothing wrong about that. In fact it was how evolution came about. Some inverts considered they were higher evolutionary types than heterosexuals, though it was hard to see how the human race would survive if everyone reached this evolutionary phase.

Ellis was far too wise to advance Ulrichs's and Carpenter's

claims to the superiority of inversion; he left it to be inferred by those who wished, and passed to consideration of great inverts of the past, to Michelangelo, Winckelmann, Walt Whitman and Verlaine.

His selection of the inverted was judicious. "It is clearly impossible to deal at all fully with historical inverts," he wrote to Symonds on 3 March 1853, "and not always desirable. In Shakespeare's case, for example, not only does it seem difficult to throw light on the matter but one would arouse the fury of devout Shakespeareans and divert attention from the main point."

After his introduction, he reviewed previous writers on the subject and then analysed the development of sexual inversion in men and in women, illustrating his points from the case-histories provided by Symonds, Carpenter and his wife from their own experience and that of their friends. What distinguished Ellis's case-histories from those published previously was that they were not drawn from police and alienist records but from members of society at large and people of more than normal intelligence.

As in his juvenile compilation of *Precious Stones of the Bible*, Ellis was working on material at secondhand. He was unable to cross-examine the subjects of his case-histories, apart from Edith, Carpenter and Symonds themselves. But even if he had, he would have been more concerned to explore the hereditary background for other cases of inversion, morbid traits, etc., than, for example, the subject's attitude to father and mother.

The scientific value of the case-histories presented to Havelock Ellis were consequently of small scientific interest; and what interest they did have was lost in the form in which they were presented to the public. In order to disguise the identity of the subject, facts were changed and details omitted which were essential to the psychological understanding of the case. Miss H., Case XLII, for example, disguised the case of Edith Ellis, but omitted the death of her mother and the cruelty of her father and stepmother.[1]

[1] In 1925 Ellis produced an enlarged edition with sixteen further case-histories and revisions of the text.

On the evidence produced in the chapters on inversion in men and in women depended the remaining chapters on the nature and the theory of sexual inversion. "The average invert, moving in ordinary society, so far as my evidence extends is most usually a person of average general health," Ellis found, "though very frequently with hereditary relationships that are markedly neurotic. He is usually the subject of a congenital predisposing abnormality, or complexus of minor abnormalities, making it difficult or impossible for him to feel sexual attraction to the opposite sex, and easy to feel sexual attraction to his own sex. This abnormality either appears spontaneously from the first, by development or arrest of development, or it is called into activity by some accidental circumstance." [1]

The sensational thing about this conclusion was that it was so unsensational. To a world which regarded the subject as unnatural and obscene, only to be encountered in the police court and the insane asylum, Ellis presented sexual inversion as a great iceberg only the cap of which was visible, a mass composed for the most part of men and women indistinguishable from heterosexuals. To those whom Ellis had carried with him in his arguments (for the most part themselves inverts) this conclusion was immensely reassuring. There was no need to fear. They did not—or need not—belong to the company of sexual criminals and lunatics but in the distinguished band of Socrates and Sappho. On the other hand those whom Ellis had failed to convince viewed with horror the thought of society riddled with sexual inversion, like some fair-seeming article of furniture eaten away within by white ants.

Careful as Ellis had been in not citing Shakespeare as an invert of genius, he miscalculated the psychological effect of the accumulation of sexual experiences on the lay reader. Dean Inge was a great admirer of Ellis and in an article on "The Integrity of Havelock Ellis," [2] he wrote, "His books fill nearly a shelf of my library; I have them all, with one exception. The exception is his great

[1] *Sexual Inversion*, 2nd ed. F. A. Davis, p. 192.

[2] Condensed from an article in the *Evening Standard* and reprinted in *Literary Digest*, Autumn 1947.

work on *The Psychology of Sex*. As a classical scholar, I have many books on my shelves which would be confiscated by the police if they were written in English instead of in Greek or Latin. But I must confess that I burnt the first two volumes of *The Psychology of Sex* as being too unwholesome."

Margaret Sanger, Ellis's devoted friend and admirer, defined more clearly what Inge dismissed as "unwholesomeness." "At one gulp I swallowed Havelock Ellis's *Psychology of Sex* and had psychic indigestion for months thereafter. I was not shocked, but this mountainous array of abnormalities made me spiritually ill. So many volumes were devoted to the exceptional, and so few to the maladjustments of normal married people, which were infinitely more numerous and urgent.' [1]

My own view of what is wrong with all the first *five* volumes of the *Studies in the Psychology of Sex* is that they are moral and educational books disguised as science. The climate of public opinion was such that Ellis could not say what he wanted to say to ordinary men and women in his own words. It all had to be wrapped up in the form of quotations from learned authorities, many of whom were engaged in the same sort of sex education, building up their mutual authority by cross-quotation of one another. The "unwholesomeness" one feels when reading the *Studies* or a book like Iwan Bloch's *Sexual Life of our Time* arises from the uneasy sense that the author's real meaning is different from his apparent meaning, like a woman talking about the need to satisfy one's biological urges when she really means she wants you to take her to bed.

After the first World War, when the climate of public opinion had changed as a result of many factors, including the publication of the *Studies in the Psychology of Sex*, Havelock Ellis was able to write openly and directly on matters of sex education. In his *Little Essays of Love and Virtue* and its sequel *More Essays* Ellis expressed himself with a freedom from disguise that began to mani-

[1] *Margaret Sanger, An Autobiography*, W. W. Norton & Co. Inc., 1938, p. 94. This was before she met Ellis. A very brief acquaintance with him was enough to make her revise her opinion of the work. But this merely shows that an important and lovable part of himself was missing from the *Studies*.

fest itself in the last volume of the *Studies*, *Sex in Relation to Society*.

It is probable that in order to arrive at this simplicity he had to accumulate the earlier material. But one gets the impression that in collecting facts—as a numismatist coins for their rarity and completeness without regard for their original purpose—he became so engrossed that he lost sight of the effect that he might produce on his reader. These facts came to him almost entirely at second or third hand, their pain and agony and shame filtered through written words; and since his own emotional responses were always long delayed and held in control, he did not appreciate the effect of what he wrote on others with sharper responses and more vivid imaginations.

Perhaps it was just as well that he lacked this insight and the imagination to foresee that nearly half a century after he had completed his lifework, it would be on sale in rubber shops off the Charing Cross Road at £1 a dog-eared volume and "ten bob back when you've used it." It might have filled him with such disgust that he would have abandoned the *Studies* and left the world the poorer by the loss of what he learnt from writing them.

But though the first five volumes of the *Studies* were overburdened with reference to authority, every so often Ellis himself came forward with his own pronouncements. The conclusion to his study of *Sexual Inversion* bears repetition, if only for the benefit of Members of Parliament.

"The question still remains how far not merely the law, but also the state of public opinion, should be modified in the light of such a psychological study as we have here undertaken. It is clear that this public opinion, molded chiefly or entirely with reference to gross vice, tends to be unduly violent in its reaction. What, then, is the reasonable attitude of society towards the congenital sexual invert? It seems to lie in the avoidance of two extremes. On the one hand, it cannot be expected to tolerate the invert who flouts his perversion in its face and assumes that, because he would rather take his pleasure with a sailor or policeman than with their sisters, he is of finer clay than the vulgar herd. On the other, it might well refrain from crushing with undiscerning ignorance beneath a burden of shame the subject of an abnormality which, as we have seen, has not been incapable of fine uses. Inversion is an aberration from the usual course of nature. But the clash of contending elements which must often mark the history of such a deviation results now and again—by no means infrequently—in nobler activities than those yielded by the vast majority who are born to consume the fruits of the earth. It bears, for the most part, its penalty in the structure of its own organism. We are bound to protect the helpless members of society against the invert. If we go further and seek to destroy the invert himself, before he has sinned against society, we extend the warrant of reason, and in so doing we may, perhaps, destroy also those children of the spirit which possess sometimes a greater worth than children of the flesh." [1]

That was nobly said, and in the England of the 1890s, after the trial of Oscar Wilde for gross vice of the sort which Ellis condemned, it needed courage to speak out. It was a courage which Ellis was given by his love for Edith and his admiration for Carpenter; and Symonds was emboldened to speak because he was a voluntary exile in Europe, beyond the reach of English law.

Symonds, however, did not live to see the book published. And on his death in 1893 his literary estate passed to the custody of his old friend Horatio Brown, who in handling the estate was compelled to regard not only the wishes of the dead man, but the feelings of his living friends and relatives, especially Mrs Addington Symonds and her daughter.

[1] *Sexual Inversion*, p. 216.

12

See what happens to those who, as the men of old days, fight against God. They blindly achieve the exact opposite of that which they vainly imagine they have accomplished.

My Life

It was easier for Ellis to have *Sexual Inversion* published in Germany than in England. Ulrichs, Krafft-Ebing, Moll, Schrenk-Notzing and others had pioneered the way there; and Ellis had already a German translator in Dr Hans Kurella and a German publisher in Wigand of Leipzig. They had done *Mann und Weib* (*Man and Woman*) and *Verbrecher und Verbrechen* (*The Criminal*) in 1894. And in 1896 as volume seven of the Bibliothek für Sozialwissenschaft appeared *Das konträre Geschlechtsgefühl* von Havelock Ellis und J. A. Symonds. Tactically, it was advantageous to secure foreign publication before publishing a book of this kind in Britain, as Carpenter had already found with his less controversial *Love's Coming of Age*, which contained a chapter on "The Intermediate Sex."

Publication in Britain hung fire. Ellis sent the book first to Williams & Norgate, a small firm with a good list which included some serious scientific books. Williams & Norgate gave it to Dr Hack Tuke for his opinion. Though Hack Tuke was an old friend of Ellis's and had employed him on digest and other work for the *Journal of Mental Science* for years, he was a Quaker and disapproved of public ventilation of sex themes. It is possible also that as publisher's adviser he thought that the year following the Wilde trial, when Wilde himself was still serving his sentence in Reading Gaol, was not the best time for a publisher to produce a book which announced "neither 'sodomy' (i.e. immissio membri in anum hominis vel mulieris) nor 'gross indecency' ought to be penal offences, except under certain special circumstances" unless he was prepared to lose a substantial sum of money. Hack Tuke advised against publication and wrote Ellis that he had nothing against it as a book for specialists but he was sure that it could never be confined to specialists, and circulated among others it might exert a demoralising influence.

Havelock Ellis pooh-poohed the idea and in his autobiography quoted half-humorously Hack Tuke's observation, "There are always the compositors."

In reality Ellis did not want to confine his book to doctors and other specialists. The more widely known the facts were, the better. In his General Preface to the *Studies* he wrote "When the rigid secrecy is once swept away a sane and natural reticence becomes for the first time possible.

"This secrecy has not always been maintained. When the Catholic Church was at the summit of its power and influence it fully realised the magnitude of sexual problems and took an active and inquiring interest in all the details of normal and abnormal sexuality. Even to the present time there are certain phenomena of the sexual life which have scarcely been accurately described except in ancient theological treatises. As the type of such treatises I will mention the great tome of Sanchez, *De Matrimonio*. Here you will find the whole sexual life of men and women analysed in its relationships to sin. Everything is set forth, as clearly and concisely as it can be—without morbid prudery on the one hand, or morbid sentimentality on the other—in the coldest scientific language; the right course of action is pointed out for all cases that may occur, and we are told what is lawful, what a venial sin, what a mortal sin. *Now I do not consider that sexual matters concern the theologian alone, and I deny altogether that he is competent to deal with them.* . . . We need to-day the same spirit and temper applied from a different standpoint. *These things concern everyone; the study of these things concerns the physiologist, the psychologist, the moralist.*" (My italics.) [1]

[1] General Preface, *Studies in the Psychology of Sex*, reprinted in *Sex and Marriage* by Havelock Ellis. Ernest Benn Ltd, London, Random House Inc., New York, pp. xi–xii. John Gawsworth in his prefatory note says that this was written in 1897 and that it "preceded the whole work for nearly forty years." It was not in fact printed till the third edition, 1925.

It seems clear that though Ellis was prepared to agree to restricted publication, it was purely for tactical reasons; and he made light of Hack Tuke's fear of its falling into the wrong hands, because he believed that knowledge was more powerful than ignorance.[1]

Instead of trying other firmly established medical and scientific publishers, Ellis sent his book to a new publisher who was recommended by his fellow-scientist, F. H. Perrycoste. Perrycoste had had no personal dealings with the firm, but John Mackinnon Robertson, the socialist and freethinker, had had two books published by them and thought highly of the firm.

Havelock Ellis had a poor nose for publishers. When he had approached Vizetelly about the Mermaid Series, Symonds had warned him that he was taking a risk. The Walter Scott Publishing Company did not last long into the twentieth century, and Messrs Wilson & Macmillan, as Perrycoste's firm was called, should have immediately raised an alarm in a man who had been connected with publishing for over ten years.

The manager of Messrs Wilson & Macmillan was a Dr Roland de Villiers, who, as his name did not imply, was German. He was a "large, gentle, fleshy man with something of the aspect and the stealthy tread of a cat." Ellis enquired whether Mr Wilson or Mr Macmillan took an active interest. "No," said Dr de Villiers. In fact they did not exist. They were just trade names. His principal was his brother-in-law, J. Astor Singer, a very rich man who was interested in the sciences and philosophy, a liberal-minded man who could think of nothing better to do with his spare money than to start a small printing and publishing house to do really important books, like Ellis and Symonds on *Sexual Inversion.*

A suspicion crossed Ellis's mind that the choice of Wilson &

[1] In *Sex and Marriage*, pp. 137–8, Ellis described a boy called Gordon, who read the *Studies* as pornography. His comment was, "Those who fear that new sexual notions will mean greater promiscuity, too easily close their eyes to the fact that promiscuity was everywhere rampant under the old-fashioned education or lack of education in sex matters, and that when we still find it in our days it is mostly among types such as Gordon, still brought up in the old tradition. How frequent it still is parents such as Gordon's remain totally in the dark for the most part, unless some unconcealable disaster make public the consequences, which is far more likely than with enlightened youth."

Macmillan as trade names might have been in order to appear a sort of subsidiary of the better-known Macmillan. But Dr de Villiers was so charming and so eager to look at Edith Ellis's novel *Seaweed* with a view to publication that the only precaution Ellis took was to say that he would like to meet the wealthy Mr Singer. That unfortunately would not be easy, Dr de Villiers said, as Mr Singer was a most elusive man. Always on the move. As might be expected of a man whose interests were so widespread. However he would be honoured to introduce them both to Mrs Singer [1] with whom he shared a house of some grandeur.

Havelock and Edith thought de Villiers was rather a queer character; but as they knew a large number of queer characters, and were not all that ordinary themselves, they did not hold this against him. They decided that Mr J. Astor Singer did not exist and that Mrs Singer was either the mistress or wife of de Villiers. But really what did that matter beside the fact that he had plenty of money, was prepared to take the risk of publishing *Sexual Inversion*, and had accepted *Seaweed* into the bargain? He was at the same time a man of education and of business. *Sexual Inversion* was printed and the advance copies were out, when suddenly Horatio Brown wrote (1 July 1897) to say that he had consulted Professor Poore and Mr Asquith about the advisability of Symonds's portion of the book being published.

Poore said it would do more harm to Symonds's name than good to the cause; better to leave these matters entirely to medical men, who were doing a great deal to modify opinion. Asquith thought the book too literary as it stood. The question would be asked, "Is this a genuinely scientific book?" The answer to that would have an important bearing on the issue of a prosecution. There was "not only a possibility but a distinct risk of a prosecution." Anyone might set the law in motion; and even if the Home Office declined to move, any private individual or vigilance society might take the initiative. The appearance of Symonds's name would do him no good and might call undesirable attention to the book.

As both opinions virtually coincided and pressure had been

[1] Carpenter described Mrs Singer as "a puckered little creole."

brought to bear by Symonds's friends who had seen the German edition, Brown felt he must withdraw consent to the book's being published as it stood. Symonds's name must come off the title-page and his literary and historical material deleted, except in so far as Ellis wanted to draw on it for additions of his own. On the other hand there was no objection to Ellis's using the case-histories which Symonds had sent him.

It was a blow which rankled with Ellis and in his autobiography he tersely stated: "On the eve of publication, the Symonds family seems to have taken alarm and Brown bought up the edition." This was scarcely fair to Brown's carefully reasoned letter; and anyway there was some justice in the family being alarmed, since Symonds's daughter, then a young woman of twenty-two, had no knowledge of her father's proclivities.

Dr de Villiers was not daunted by this setback, if indeed he regarded it as a setback. After all, it is not every publisher who is able to dispose of the first edition of a scientific work to one customer.

For Ellis the withdrawal of Symonds's material was a blessing. Asquith and Poore were quite right. Without Symonds's contribution *Sexual Inversion* was far more of a unity; and published under Ellis's name, it could be incorporated in the *Studies* in a way that would have been far more difficult as a collaboration. Ellis went back and cast the book into its new shape, while de Villiers made new plans for publication. He decided that Wilson & Macmillan was not the right firm to publish a book of this sort. They sounded too commercial. What was needed was the scholarly note. The people to do it were the Watford University Press, a new firm started by J. Astor Singer.

Ellis mildly observed that there was no university at Watford. Dr de Villiers conceded the point. But Mr Singer had laid down an expensive linotype printing plant at Watford and intended to issue books suitable for universities, so that the Watford University Press was an exact description of its location and purpose.

So duly in November 1897 *Studies in the Psychology of Sex, Volume I. Sexual Inversion* was published by the Watford University Press. The format was all that Ellis had wished and it was issued quietly. Announcements were posted to doctors and other suitable readers. Carpenter no doubt provided him with the names of his own correspondents interested in the subject. Review copies were sent only to medical and scientific journals. The few notices it received were respectful, and appreciative. For six months *Sexual Inversion* sold quietly but steadily.

But Dr de Villiers, as Ellis was to discover gradually, was a man of many parts. One of these parts was interested in a small radical society called the Legitimation League, dedicated to the reform of the laws of marriage and legitimacy. The barbarity of marriage in church or before a registrar was to be superseded by a "formal acknowledgment of union," and presumably an equally formal acknowledgment of divorce. By making the position of children born in this new form of wedlock insecure, the insecurity of those born outside it would be comparatively less.

Founder-president of the Legitimation League was Miss Lilian Harman of Chicago, whose organising secretary for Great Britain was a young man called George Bedborough. Bedborough edited the League's pungently progressive magazine the *Adult* which Dr de Villiers published from the Watford University Press.

Meetings of the Legitimation League were held at the Holborn Restaurant or St James's Hall. They were open to the public, and as well as legitimate Legitimatists, a number of anarchists attended. They were welcomed by the Legitimatists, who wanted to make them members of the League of Legitimation; and they welcomed being welcomed because they were too poor to hire halls of their own and they wanted to make the Legitimatists anarchists. Besides, even if they had the money to hire a hall, the police would have been there in force. Far better to use meetings like those of the Legitimation League to propagate their own views at the expense of others.

Scotland Yard became interested in the Legitimation League because of the use to which the anarchists were turning its meetings. The anti-anarchist section of the Yard wanted those meetings stopped, yet it was impossible to sustain the charge that the Legitimation League should be suppressed because its meetings were being abused. An obscenity charge would be easier to maintain; yet in itself the *Adult*, outspoken as it was, was such a piddling sheet that it would be hard to get any court to take it seriously.

Chief Inspector Melville, who was working on the case, told John Sweeney, one of his men, to hang around the Legitimation League and see whether he couldn't rustle up something a little more seriously obscene than the *Adult*. The Watford University Press, after all, were publishing this filthy book *Sexual Inversion*. Roland de Villiers was a shifty character and even if he wasn't using the Legitimation League to peddle the book, he might be provoked to do so.

Sweeney attended the Legitimation League meetings posing as an anarchist. He won the confidence of George Bedborough and when he had all the background information he wanted he called at the offices of the Legitimation League, which were in the living-room of a flat previously occupied by de Villiers and his "sister" Mrs Singer.

Sweeney asked him if he could sell him a copy of *Sexual Inversion*. Bedborough did not have to say that he would try to get one from de Villiers. He had a stock on the premises. He had been pushing them on the sly in precisely the way that Dr Hack Tuke had prophesied would happen.

Four days later Bedborough was arrested by Sweeney and charged with "publishing an obscene libel." Founder-president Lilian Harman was with him at the time. As soon as Bedborough was taken away, she went to the nearest post office and telegraphed the news to Havelock Ellis, who was at his wife's cottage at Carbis Bay.

Later he heard the same news from Dr de Villiers, together with a warning that he, Ellis, was liable to be arrested. De Villiers was very nice. He authorised Ellis to obtain lawyers and to defray the cost of any action and he was only too sorry that his brother-in-law, J. Astor Singer, should have called him to an important business conference in Cologne.

The police did not arrest Havelock Ellis, primarily because they were interested only in suppressing the anarchists and secondarily because they knew that Ellis could bring up artillery which might pulverise their case. They were interested in de Villiers ultimately, but they wanted to take first things first. Sweeney was a good psychologist and he said that Bedborough was a weakling. If they concentrated on him, he would crack.

Ellis had the self-righteous intellectual's view of the police. They were foolish, philistine and crass.

In fact their handling of the Bedborough Case, which in my youth I always accepted as one of the most flagrant injustices of the law, was subtle, flexible and superlatively clever.

The charge was made against Bedborough alone, the weakest link in the chain. Miss Harman procured for him Mr Horace (later Justice) Avory, one of the most brilliant Counsel of his day. Ellis and de Villiers were not cited and could only induce evidence on their own behalf if Bedborough pleaded not guilty.

Bedborough was at first denied bail, but after three days in the cells he was given bail on a surety of one thousand pounds. The police had learnt what they wanted to know. George Bedborough was one of those men who minded imprisonment.

Meanwhile a friend of Bedborough's called Henry Seymour began to organise the Free Press Defence Committee, which was to lift the trial from the plane of the sale to a policeman dressed up as an anarchist of a book which all policemen would think filthy on to the plane where it belonged, freedom to publish scientific work of any sort.

On 13 June 1898 the hearing was resumed at Bow Street. "Criminal" passages were read from *Sexual Inversion*, mostly from the case-histories; and certain passages from the *Adult* cited on the allegation of obscenity. The case was then adjourned, leaving the police to prepare their prosecution, Henry Seymour to rally progressive opinion, and George Bedborough to meditate on prison life.

An impressive committee was formed for the Free Press Defence Committee, including Walter Crane, Bernard Shaw, Edward Carpenter, Grant Allen, Belfort Bax, H. M. Hyndman, George Moore, F. H. Perrycoste, Frank Podmore and William Sharp. Letters of sympathy for Ellis and protest against the authorities came from distinguished American and European alienists and physicians.

Dr Pasquale Penta wrote from the University of Naples, "Dear Colleague, I cannot delay longer to write to you to protest against a prosecution, which is not only an insult to you but to truth itself and to all honest seekers after truth. In other countries, especially in Germany and Italy, such works as yours properly find among magistrates themselves their most numerous readers."

From Germany wrote Ellis's translator, Dr Kurella, "Honoured Colleague. . . . For us on the Continent such a proceeding" as the prosecution "is altogether incomprehensible. What would become of science and of its practical applications if the pathology of the sexual life were put on the Index? It is as if Sir Spencer Wells were to be classed with Jack the Ripper.

"No doubt the judge (unless suffering from senile dementia) will accord you brilliant satisfaction. But in any case the whole of scientific psychology and medicine on the Continent is on your side."

In the public mind the prosecution came to be regarded as a direct attack upon a scientific work and, on August 9 Bedborough's counsel, Horace Avory, attempted to have the case removed from the Central Criminal Court to the High Court of Justice on the ground that the book charged as obscene was a technical scientific work entitled to consideration by superior judges and a special jury.

His plea was rejected; and if we judge the case from the legal point of view it was rightly rejected. Avory was trying to twist the trial in order to secure a legal judgment on the scientific value of *Sexual Inversion*. The police were out to smash the Legitimation League and could quite rightly maintain that in selling Sweeney a copy of *Sexual Inversion* Bedborough was publishing what to Sweeney was an obscene libel.

The form of the indictment was that usual in these cases, but not reassuring to a cell-shy man.

> Central Criminal Court to wit. The Jurors for our Sovereign Lady the Queen upon their oath present that George Bedborough being a

> person of a wickedly depraved mind and disposition, and unlawfully and wickedly devising, contriving and intending to vitiate and corrupt the morals of the liege subjects of our said Lady the Queen, to debauch and poison the minds of divers of the liege subjects of our said Lady the Queen, and to raise and create in them lustful desires, and to bring the said liege subjects into a state of wickedness, lewdness and debauchery on the 27th day of May, in the year of our Lord, one thousand eight hundred and ninety eight, at a certain shop, to wit Number 16 John Street, Bedford Row in the County of London, unlawfully, wickedly, maliciously, scandalously, and wilfully did publish, sell and utter, and cause and procure to be published, sold and uttered a certain lewd, wicked, bawdy, scandalous and obscene libel, in the form of a book entitled *Studies in the Psychology of Sex: Vol. 1. Sexual Inversion* by Havelock Ellis, in which said book are contained among other things, divers wicked, lewd, impure, scandalous and obscene libels, and matters, which said book is, pursuant to the provisions in that behalf, of the Law of Libel Amendment Act, 1888, deposited with this indictment, together with the particulars showing precisely by reference to pages, columns and lines in what part of the said book the alleged libel is to be found. To the manifest corruption of the morals and minds of the liege subjects of our said Lady the Queen, and her laws, in violation of common decency, morality, and good order, and against the peace of our said Lady the Queen, her Crown and Dignity.

There were ten further counts, one for the sale of a lecture by Oswald Dawson, entitled "The Outcome of Legitimation," and the rest for different numbers of the *Adult*, of which Bedborough as well as being editor was the main contributor.

Police knowledge of the psychology of sex may have been primitive, but they understood the psychology of prosecution. A defendant prepared to risk imprisonment for his principles and with a first-class counsel like Avory could have won over if not the Grand Jury at least a large section of the public to the principle of free discussion of sexual problems; and certainly the police would have emerged from such a contest badly mauled even if legally victorious.

But the police calculated that Bedborough was not the stuff from which martyrs are made. I imagine they sent Sweeney or some other detective round to have a chat with him and point out how silly it was for him to stick his neck out, not really for his own principles but for those of Miss Lilian Harman and Dr Havelock Ellis, when the whole question could be settled very simply if he just popped down to Scotland Yard to have a chat.

At any rate shortly before the trial, without consulting his lawyers or informing the Defence Committee, Bedborough did pop down to Scotland Yard and had a chat. They were very nice. They had no desire to put him in prison. All he had to do was to plead Guilty to the first three charges and he would walk out a free man.

The case came up on October 31 before the Central Criminal Court of the Old Bailey. Just before it was due to be heard, Bedborough told his counsel to plead Guilty on the first three charges. The lawyers pointed out that this was impossible. Counsel had been briefed by the Defence Committee to defend him on the plea of Not Guilty. It was impossible to use money contributed for that purpose in order to enter the plea of Guilty.

So Bedborough entered the court undefended by Counsel and pleaded Guilty, while Havelock and Edith Ellis waited in a room ready to give evidence on the scientific nature of the book in question, and the Defence Committee and Counsel debated desperately how on earth they could intervene in defence of a book which Bedborough's confession would rule as obscene.

The verbatim report of the trial is available in Houston Peterson's *Havelock Ellis*.[1] As soon as Bedborough had pleaded Guilty, the Counsel for the Prosecution took over his defence. Bedborough had sworn that he would sever his connection with the Legitimation League and the *Adult* and all similar organisations and magazines, and the Prosecution therefore recommended that he should be bound over on his own recognisances.

Bedborough had placed all blame on de Villiers, as the controller of the Watford University Press and the receiver of the profits from the sale of the books. "That that is the fact there can be no question at all," said the Prosecution. "My lord, Dr de Villiers has absconded. Against Dr de Villiers a warrant has been applied for and granted, and if Dr de Villiers, who I am told is abroad at this

[1] *Havelock Ellis: Philosopher of Love*, Houghton Mifflin, 1928, pp. 249–56.

moment, shall venture to return to this country, he may be quite certain that that warrant will be followed by immediate execution."

Of the author of *Sexual Inversion* not a word was said; of the work itself the Recorder remarked in giving judgment: "I am willing to believe that in acting as you did, you might at the first outset perhaps have been gulled into the belief that somebody might say this was a scientific work. But it is impossible for anybody with a head on his shoulders to open the book without seeing that it is a pretence and a sham, and that it is merely entered into for the purpose of selling this obscene publication."

As soon as Ellis heard the verdict, he went to the *Daily Chronicle* to appeal to Massingham, the editor, for the justice which he had been denied in the Court. Massingham refused to see him and next day published a leader taking the same line as the Recorder. "We cannot take the view that the book has any scientific value whatever . . . it ought never to have been written or published."

In the *Lancet* of November 19 the editor explained why the book, which he recognised as a serious scientific work, had not been reviewed in his columns. "What decided us not to review the book was its method of publication. Why was it not published through a house able to take proper measures for introducing it as a scientific book to a scientific audience?"

"The answer is simple," Ellis answered in the next issue. "None of the medical publishers whom I approached cared to take up a book on the subject of sexual inversion, one or two adding that they would have done so with pleasure had it not been their privilege to live in England."

This statement does not square with what Ellis said in *My Life*, where the only publishers he mentions are Williams & Norgate, who were not exclusively medical publishers. He had probably suggested it for the Contemporary Science Series and perhaps he spoke of the book to some medical publishers, who refused even to look at it.

To make his attitude clear, Havelock Ellis sat down and wrote *A Note on the Bedborough Trial*, which was privately printed by the

Watford University Press. He ended by stating that henceforward he would publish none of his *Studies in the Psychology of Sex* in England. "To wrestle in the public arena for freedom of speech is a noble task which may worthily be undertaken by any man who can devote to it the best energies of his life. It is not, however, a task which I have ever contemplated. I am a student, and my path has long been marked out. I may be forced to pursue it under unfavourable conditions, but I do not intend that any consideration shall induce me to swerve from it, nor do I intend to injure my work or distort my vision of life by entering upon any struggle. The pursuit of the martyr's crown is not favourable to the critical and dispassionate investigation of complicated problems. A student of nature, of men, of books may dispense with wealth or position; he cannot dispense with quietness and serenity. I insist on doing my own work in my own way, and cannot accept conditions which make this work virtually impossible. Certainly I regret that my own country should be almost alone in refusing to me the conditions of reasonable intellectual freedom. I regret it the more since I deal with the facts of English life and prefer to address English people. But I must leave to others the task of obtaining the reasonable freedom that I am unable to attain."

This was a dignified statement of Havelock's position as it appeared to him. One might detect a certain overstatement in maintaining that his own country was almost alone in refusing him the conditions of reasonable intellectual freedom. This implied that his *Sexual Inversion* was available in almost every other country and language, whereas at that time and for many years later the only translation available was the German.[1]

Ellis's faith in de Villiers remained unshaken. De Villiers absented himself from the proceedings admittedly, but he had met all his financial obligations and he acceded readily to Ellis's demand that henceforward his sex books should be published abroad. It was easy to do this by substituting for the Watford University Press, "Leipzig: The University Press." There was no need to tell Ellis that they were still printed in Watford and he was so

[1] Since then it has been translated into many languages, including Japanese.

busy in getting the second volume ready for the press that he did not trouble to enquire.

Ellis regarded himself as a pioneer of sex-enlightenment, and the police regarded de Villiers as an unscrupulous criminal engaged among other things in the peddling of sex-literature for pornographic purposes. Both of them were right. While Ellis let month after month go by, wondering whether perhaps Dr de Villiers was not a little less honest than he might purport to be, Scotland Yard gradually closed in. They discovered that Dr Roland de Villiers's real name was Georg Ferdinand Springmühl von Weissenfeld, the son of an eminent judge. He had been educated at Giessen, where he won high honours in science, medicine and literature. He had married a German lady of good family but had been estranged from his father owing to his dubious conduct. He fled from Germany after forging various cheques and settled in England in 1880 to live by his wits. He served a term of twelve months hard labour for forgery and other offences and then turned to more profitable frauds, such as floating a company for the distillation of brandy, the only visible assets of which were his own person and photographs of other people's vineyards. On the strength of these he raised a sum of about £60,000 from people as greedy for money as he was, to whom he returned their own money gradually in the form of a ten-per-cent dividend. He had so many aliases that he had to keep a card-index system to remind himself who he was when he was doing what and how he signed that particular name. He and his wife had thirty different banking accounts in London alone under different names; and the Watford University Press was a comparatively small part of a vastly shady business.

In January 1901 Havelock Ellis was still undecided about Dr de Villiers, when a strong force of detectives surrounded a large house in the best quarter of Cambridge and then entered with a search warrant. The occupants of the house, Dr Sinclair and Mrs Ella Roland, were at first not to be found. But the detectives knew they were in the house and were not leaving till they got their man. Investigation revealed that the place was riddled with secret closets and passageways.

At last a button was pressed, a panel slid back and there was Dr Sinclair Roland, alias Roland de Villiers, alias George Ferdinand Springmühl von Weissenfeld, with a revolver in his hand. Before he could fire, a detective leapt forward and struck it from his grasp and in less than a minute the handcuffs were round his wrists.

He was taken out into the room and suddenly he seemed in distress. He called for a glass of water, which one of the servants brought him. He took one sip, gasped and fell to the floor. He was dead.

The verdict of the coroner's jury was death by apoplexy, though John Sweeney, the detective in charge of the case, said that De Villiers was wearing a poison-ring which he had boasted a few years before could kill a man and leave no trace. Or perhaps that was a detail added by a crime-reporter ghosting Sweeney's memoirs [1] when he retired. In Sweeney's verdict on the man, "the most amazing criminal of modern times," one detects the writing of a ghostly headline.

In the house at Cambridge several thousand copies of the *Studies* were discovered by the police. They were ordered to be destroyed, a course in which Ellis concurred, since the method of issue was in violation of the agreement into which he had entered.

Ellis regarded de Villiers's publication of the *Studies* as the one disinterested action in the life of a crook, one of those strange uncharacteristic gestures in which human conduct abounds. In my own view, the police and the editor of the *Lancet* were right; de Villiers's interest in the *Studies* was the money which he could make from its sale as a pornographic work. Ellis was the pornographic publisher's dream of an author, a man so pure in heart that he could provide the impure with fare far richer than that of any conscious pornographer.

But the effect of the police action was wholly good. Even Ellis conceded that, though his concept of the Divine wrath belongs rather to the Old than the New Testament.

"Look how the world is made. See what happens to those, who, as the men of old days, fight against God. They blindly achieve the

[1] *At Scotland Yard* by John Sweeney, London, 1906.

exact opposite of that which they vainly imagine they have accomplished. Here was I, a shy, solitary, insignificant student who chanced, a little before his fellows, to feel and to see and patiently to work out a problem which would soon visibly concern all men. But meanwhile what he had done was a crime for which no descriptive terms were too opprobrious, no language of abuse too strong. The mighty engines of Social Order and Respectability were set in motion to crush this infamous thing. What they really accomplished was to enable that infamous thing to crush them. I had modestly chosen to issue my book in the quietest way I could find, almost privately. Order and Respectability killed, not the book, but the method of publication (incidentally also the publisher), and I immediately turned to the United States and placed my *Studies* in the hands of an active medical publishing house with a high reputation and an army of travellers. By the method which Order and Respectability closed to me, my books would perhaps have sold by the dozen; by the method which Order and Respectability compelled me to adopt they have sold, and continue to-day to sell steadily, on a far larger scale, in an ever-increasing circle round the world. The creatures who were the puppets of this show began to fall to pieces when it was scarcely over. The judge died first, suddenly, still in the prime of life, so swiftly after the trial that one might well believe the home truths he could not fail to hear concerning his part in it had struck him to the heart, many of the others soon followed, and Dr Roland de Villiers, that fantastic figure from an alien underworld strangely associated with books whose mission concerned him so little, was destined to end tragically within a few years." [1]

I think that Ellis was right to detect the hand of God in all this, not wreaking vengence on an errant judge, but in keeping the *Studies* out of the hands of those they might harm while directing them to those who could profit by them. Ellis saw himself as God's emissary, but failed to see that the other characters in this drama were necessary to restrain the folly of his blind belief that all the world was ripe for his message.

[1] *My Life*, Eng. ed., p. 311, Am. ed., p. 368.

13

The year of the Bedborough case was in my interior life a turning-point, even the chief turning-point I have ever encountered. It was the end of the upward climb of life, and, as we never seem to be standing still, it was the beginning of what I felt to be the descent. Until then, although I always looked older than my age, I had retained an instinctive feeling of youthfulness. . . . But now, somehow, this instinctive feeling was suddenly and forever killed.

My Life

BEFORE THE Bedborough case Havelock Ellis was known only to a small circle of people. The publicity of the trial brought him to the attention of psychologists all over the world, and, what was spiritually more important, of many people, not merely inverts, suffering from psychological problems which they did not dare confess to doctors or to priests. He received letters or personal visits from unhappy people who looked on him as the Sage of Sex, a healer possessed of rare powers.

He could, if he had wished, have set up a consulting practice, charging for his advice fees that would have freed him from his recurrent financial worries. He did not do so, because he regarded himself as a minister who had chosen Sex rather than the Church for the larger field of prophecy it gave him. It was a labour of love, and it was one of his criticisms of Freud, whom he admired in many ways, that Freud charged money for curing patients. How was it possible to take money for curing someone suffering from a love-sickness? The passing of money would invalidate the cure, Ellis thought. Love-sickness can be cured only by love.

So he wrote letters, gave advice, asked permission to use case-histories with suitable disguises, interested in passing on to other people experiences which might help them to understand themselves. He was the new priest of the twentieth century, the father-confessor of an age too enlightened to believe in Christianity.

He knew that the major act of therapy was to listen to the tale of guilt, as unshocked as a priest in the confessional or a psychoanalyst at the head of the horsehair sofa. He was wise, gentle and moderate, with a beard like a patriarch's and the eyes of a sailor, and if his voice was less impressive than his appearance, that was reassuring. If he had boomed, the effect might have been overpowering.

When male inverts came to him, Ellis would advise them of books to read, and if he thought them safe he would write off to Carpenter or some other male invert, giving details of the case and suggesting they might get in touch with the man if they thought they could help. It was a dangerous thing to do, because there was always the chance that the male invert in distress might be a policeman in disguise.

It was not really ironical that a man whose sexual life was so tortuous and so bereft of the usual outlets should be called on to heal others. In fact it was his personal experience rather than his extensive study which enabled him to help others. His method was precisely the opposite of that employed by Freud and the psychoanalysts. Where they tried to unravel the root causes of, shall we say, a perversion such as urolagnia, and by helping the patient to relive the experience to disentangle the sexual and scatological confusion, Havelock Ellis accepted it and saw the beauty of fountains. It may very well have been that, having disentangled the confusion, Ellis would still have appreciated the beauty of fountains and at the same time have been able to enjoy the physical delight of sex more fully, giving to Edith the marital self-sufficiency she suggested; but we are concerned with the actual and not the hypothetical. Many men and women came to him in distress and went away able to cope with situations which had seemed intolerable. He may have appeared a wise and perfectly balanced man. But the basis of his wisdom was the humility of knowing that he was not naturally perfectly balanced, but only through the precarious maintenance of spiritual equipoise.

Though Edith Ellis had professed that *Sexual Inversion* was a work of small scientific value, she had immediately rallied to Havelock's defence throughout the Bedborough trial. However much

Havelock might maintain that she was a congenital sexual invert, her instinct to defend her husband when he was under attack was the same as that of a heterosexual woman. Immediately she heard the news of Bedborough's arrest, she cabled Havelock some money. She was close to him throughout the trial and when it was all over, they went away together, first to Tangier and Morocco and then to Spain.

Her passion for Claire had cooled to the friendship which it had been at first, perhaps because it had worked itself out, perhaps because in Havelock's dependence on her during the trial she found a hope that somehow they might make a new start. Probably, since human motives are never very simple, it was a mixture of both these things.

I think that it was during this journey abroad that Edith made the proposal that they should try to live together again as man and wife, cutting out extra-marital relations on both sides. I cannot be certain, however, because Ellis himself is the only authority for the proposal and he could not remember the exact time. He did not even know whether it was something she threw out on the spur of the moment, or something which she had carefully considered. He knew that what she suggested was something he was incapable of doing, and that the ease of Amy's feather bed was what made it possible for him to bear his little Edith porcupine. He made no answer and Edith never made the proposal again. "The whole matter seemed entirely to pass from our minds," wrote Ellis; "so much remained that it seemed to leave no blank." [1]

It left no blank with Havelock, because the blank was already filled by Amy. The blank left by the loss of Claire remained until they returned to England. As I have suggested, Claire had at the beginning been a challenge to Havelock's manhood, an appeal from Edith to give her more love than Havelock had seemed prepared to give. After Havelock's acceptance of the relationship, it had become a physical assuagement, a compensation for what she could not, but would have preferred to, receive from her husband. Later still, because the physical act of making love makes love, it grew to

[1] *My Life*, Eng. ed., p. 292, Am. ed., p. 343.

be a threat to the more tenuous spiritual relationship which subsisted between Edith and her husband.

On their return to England, there were two choices for Edith: a physical relation with another man, of which she was not capable, because she loved Havelock, despite his sexual limitations and his devotion to his work, more than anyone on earth including herself; or another relationship with a woman, which from the dammed-up fount of passion was liable to be far more violent than her attraction towards Claire.

Soon after they arrived home, Edith fell in love with Lily, an amateur woman painter. Lily had studied art in Paris as a young English lady of means should, without being contaminated by the Bohemianism of the Latin Quarter. She lived with her elder sister in a small house in St Ives, painting pictures that lacked distinction however hard she tried, reading poetry, taking part in amateur theatricals and playing Chopin and Grieg with a delicate skill. She was generally artistic in the fragile way that makes most professional painters, poets, actors and musicians want to run a mile.

But Edith adored her. Claire had been hearty, county and over-determinedly ordinary. Lily, wilting physically and spiritually, appealed to the protective side of Edith's nature, and Edith gave her the love she might otherwise have lavished on a child.

Lily's elder sister was violently protective. She saw what Edith was up to and opposed it vehemently, defending Lily as though she was a teen-age girl straight out of a convent instead of a woman in her middle thirties.

The affair was cloaked in furtive excitement. Edith was forbidden their house at St Ives; but Lily would slip out and meet her in a quiet copse half-way to Carbis. Or she would come to Edith's studio at Porthminster. Or Havelock would pander to them by giving up *his* studio at Hawkes Point so that they could picnic there alone. Rare were the nights they could spend together, when Lily "would hurry to Carbis with her little nightdress at a late hour when she had almost been given up."

Lily was the great love of Edith's life. There were many "dear

LILY

friends" later, but no other woman so wrung her heart as this weak wilting creature who was so different from herself.

Havelock rather despised Lily—as Edith despised Amy. He did not see that the weakness of the beloved may make a stronger bond than strength, because it taxes the strength of the lover. Edith was able to mother Lily as Havelock mothered *her*. All Havelock noticed was that after Edith fell in love with Lily, she stopped calling him "sweetheart" and saying that he was "man and woman to her." Now he was just her "boy," her "child," her "comrade" and "the one person in the world who understood" her.

A year or two after Edith met Lily, Lily was diagnosed as having Bright's disease. By June 1903 her end was near. Edith wanted to be close to her more than anything else. But the sister said that Lily didn't want to see Edith. She rationed her visits and seldom left them alone. Edith thought for a time that the sister was doing this out of jealousy. Then she heard from friends—who are seldom reluctant to pass on news that will give pain—that Lily was making fun of Edith, finding perhaps her passion and earnestness irksome at the approach of death.

Havelock believed what her friends said, because he had noticed earlier in Lily a slighting, taunting attitude to his own love for Edith, which showed that she had no conception of the strains and stresses to which it was subject. But he pretended to Edith that it was the sister's influence gaining supremacy over Lily as her health failed. He so convinced her that Lily became after death a radiant and unstained symbol of purity. Edith raised her to the point of worship, adoring her more every year that passed, keeping her photograph on desk or bedside closer to her than Havelock's or her mother's.

This private cult started in a strange way. At first she treasured the things which Lily had given her for purely sentimental reasons, her cushion, cup, looking-glass, table-cloth and the brooch which she always wore, even to her cremation.

What raised sentiment to adoration was a queer incident. Edith was standing with a friend in the main road at Carbis when a strange woman who was spending a few days at St Ives came up to them both and asked to see what ornaments Edith was wearing. Edith, puzzled, showed her and the woman fixed on Lily's brooch. "I have a message of consolation from the friend who gave you that," the stranger said and walked away as abruptly as she had come. She was never seen by Edith again.

If the friend with Edith had not confirmed the story, Havelock would have written it off as an hallucination. He could never explain it and Edith needed no explanation. It was a message from Lily.

Shortly after this Edith met a woman medium, who practised not for money but as a vocation. In her trance-state the medium would speak to Edith in what seemed the voice Lily had used in life. She spoke of things only Edith and Lily knew. She foretold the future. She gave advice, which in Havelock's opinion was usually good. She uttered words of comfort, encouragement and love. She foretold that Edith's lecture tour in the United States would be successful and rewarding, which it was, up to a point and at a price. Some years before her death, she said Edith would publish eight books; which was literally true, because the ninth, though written, had only just been sent to the publisher when she died. Shortly before Edith's death "Lily" announced that Edith would either die very soon or live for seven years more.

Havelock considered that it might be possible to explain these psychic messages as the transference of thought from Edith to the medium. But he did not pay much regard to them. They made Edith happy. She was more interested in vague messages such as "What seems an impediment is a star" than in practical guidance, which she took more as confirmation of the rightness of her own decisions.

Edith said that sometimes, without the aid of the medium, she felt Lily close. She saw nothing, heard nothing; but Lily was there. The only evidence—if it can be called that—was that when her favourite cat was with her, it behaved strangely "as though some mysterious presence pervaded the room."

While Lily was still alive, Edith had thought of compiling an anthology called *The Lover's Calendar*. After Lily's death, Edith turned this consciously into a memorial to their love, as a union of spirits not only on earth but after death. She called it an "epitome of a love-history" and tested each inclusion by its applicability to Lily and herself. She made *The Lover's Calendar*, in Ellis's words, "an exquisite shrine at which she could carry on a kind of worship of Lily."

Edith found out that she had not been the first of Lily's women-lovers. There had been an earlier lover, though Lily had always denied this. Edith found out the woman's name and her address, which was in New York, and wrote to enlist her in this posthumous cult of Lily. She broke down the woman's prejudice and made of her a warm friend, if a rather Laodicean devotee of Lily.

Havelock must have been galled to find a woman he did not admire in life deified by his wife after death. He tried to overcome his jealousy, with considerable success. He did not bother with the truth or falsehood of Edith's psychic experience. If Edith was right to believe that Lily survived after death, he was wrong to believe there was no personal survival and *vice versa*. He was incurious. It was enough to know that Edith's psychic experiences were not morbid or hysterical—far less so than her everyday behaviour under strain. As he saw it, the revelation of Lily as a source of spiritual succour was Edith's nearest approach to the consoling power of mysticism. "Her egoism was too strong, her sensibilities too acute, her temper too dominant and energetic for the mystical spirit to be natural or easy to her. It could only come through the crushing shock of love swiftly passing to loss, and even then she was not entirely subdued to it. But such as it was, it was her religion, the only real religion she ever had, the true Heaven of her soul, and there was nothing to feel but reverence." [1]

Reverence was not an emotion which Edith felt towards Havelock as a sexologist. "His sex books are nothing," she would say. "He is a poet and a philosopher and all the rest is nonsense." This judgment must have been coloured by her personal experience,

[1] *My Life*, Eng. ed., p. 332, Am. ed., pp. 395–6.

including the fact that whereas Havelock devoted a whole volume of *The Psychology of Sex* to the study of Sexual Inversion, he devoted only one paragraph to the subject of sexual impotence. She set some store by his sociological works, like *The Nationalisation of Health*, *The Task of Social Hygiene* or *The Nineteenth Century: a Dialogue in Utopia* and more by his speculative essays in *Affirmations* and *The Soul of Spain* than by more narrowly scientific works like the *Studies*, *The World of Dreams*, the *Study of British Genius* and *The Problem of Race Degeneration.*

In the long term Havelock agreed with her that his literary work stood the best chance of survival and especially those writings which were most himself, *The New Spirit*, *Affirmations*, *Impressions and Comments* and *The Dance of Life*. But this did not mean that he regarded the more ephemeral books as unimportant. Any contribution to knowledge, in so far as it is accepted, becomes out of date, and Havelock Ellis did not write so much in the hope of ultimate recognition by posterity as with the aim of changing the social, moral and aesthetic values of his own time. "If the deeds are real they will speak for themselves in history or verse or other shape that men will not let die," he advised biographers in his *Open Letter*. All his writings were merely the fruit of his life. Living was the art in which he strove to make himself a master.

Yet the cumulative effect of his writing, especially about sex, was that his relationship to the outside world changed increasingly after the Bedborough case. He who had found it impossible to establish intimate contacts with even close friends was now approached by strangers bursting to confide their most intimate secrets to him. He who had thought himself younger and less wise than his contemporaries was now treated with a reverence which he could accept without conceit because he humbly recognised that the source of his strength was his weakness.

This reverence irritated Edith. She thought it ridiculous the way disciples would hang upon his lips and she went out of her way to snub him. If anyone protested, she said that it was good for him. He was being spoilt by success. When he was dreamy and absent-minded, she would treat him as a small child, incapable of looking after himself.

Havelock was hurt by these attacks, but he made no protest. He felt as embarrassed for Edith's sake as he did for his own. He put it down—in so far as he tried to explain it at all—to Edith's uncertainty about herself; but he seems to have been too generous to recognise that his wife felt jealous of the public figure he was cutting.

This jealousy had been present from the beginning of the marriage, as it is in most marriages where one partner is more famous than the other. From the beginning of the century the ambition to equal and even outdo her husband became as strong as, and sometimes stronger than, her love and admiration of him. At first it took the form of being more practical than he was. As well as letting cottages to holiday-makers (which she would advertise as "One outside privy, with four-roomed cottage adjoining"), she ran a smallholding at Carbis. She even overcame her natural loathing of butchery, had her pigs slaughtered on the premises and cut them up herself.

Then she began to write short stories, beginning with sketches from real life and working up to more imaginative fictions. She was successful in having these published in newspapers and book form; and she was not such a feminist that she used her maiden name or even Edith Ellis. She wrote as Mrs Havelock Ellis, and secured the more attention because she did so.

She was naturally a mimic rather than a story-writer. Her characters were entirely Cornish and her dialogue was difficult to read, because she tried to transliterate every nuance of dialect. "I'm certain sure o' that, for what's nothin' but a bit of a prank wi' one is devil's own ark wi' the other," is hard on the eye because the author was trying to be too true to the ear. Her talents were really those of a playwright, and one morning convalescing in bed from a severe illness she dramatised a short story called *The Subjection of Kezia* and sent it to the manager of the Court Theatre, London. It was accepted almost by return and scheduled for immediate production as a curtain-raiser.

Edith was too ill to see the production, but it was well received and on the tide of Edith's euphoria the Ellises reorganised their lives. All the cottages in Cornwall were to be given up, except one small *pied-à-terre*. Cornwall was bad for Edith's health, which had been steadily deteriorating. Havelock (in the autumn of 1909) took a largish flat in Dover Mansions, Brixton, and Edith rented a room from him. "I should not disturb you a bit," she promised, "as I can always cook my own breakfast, etc."

They had never shared the same roof in London before. In the country they kept the same hours, early to bed and early to rise. Havelock did not change his habits when he was in London, but Edith, arduously social, stayed out late at night and then had great trouble getting back to Brixton in the small hours. She never did cook her breakfast and Havelock brought it to her in bed each morning.

Edith immediately set about meeting the people who had made her curtain-raiser a success. She became friends with Cosmo Hamilton's wife, Beryl Faber, who had played the part of Kezia. The Hamiltons lived at West Drayton, a village thirteen miles from London. Going down there for the day, Edith fell in love with the Hamiltons' place. It was perfect, just what she and Havelock were looking for in which to pass the evening of their days. Beryl Hamilton told her that next door there were ten acres to let with a clump of cottages in the middle called Woodpecker Farm.

There was nothing for it but that Edith must view it at once. It was a compact half-timbered building, divided into three cottages, with a large solid old barn and stables alongside. There was, as estate agents say, a wealth of old oak, and when it had been built, three hundred years before, it had been a substantial place.

Over the centuries it had fallen into disrepair. Tiles fell off, floor-boards and wainscotting rotted and were not replaced. It was overrun with vermin and so broken down that only the "dregs of West Drayton" would live in it, and they refused to pay rent for the privilege.

To Edith's creative eye the place was heaven. Just next door to the Hamiltons! And what could be done with it! She went straight to the landlady and begged for as long a lease as possible. Before she left she was morally if not legally committed to take Woodpecker Farm.

Back in Brixton she broke the wonderful news to Havelock. He listened with sinking heart. What would it cost to put the place in order?

Edith had anticipated the question. The local builder estimated it would cost fifty pounds, and out of *The Subjection of Kezia*, with three hours' work, she had made a hundred pounds. The hundred pounds had gone to pay doctors' bills and other debts. But with her flair for the drama and Beryl Faber next door to help her, what money-spinners she would write!

Havelock looked over the farm. He could see the place had possibilities, enormous possibilities. His main objection was that the possibilities were so enormous. The landlady's agent was smiling as he listened to the improvements which Edith was proposing to make. The builder's estimate of fifty pounds would not begin to realise them, but Edith was carried away, like a child, thinking only of how wonderful the place would be in the end.

They would have to think it over, Havelock said. But Edith had thought it over. She was morally committed, and if Havelock would not go into it with her, she would get one of her friends with the vision to know a good thing when she saw one.

Havelock knew that if he stood out, he would anyway be responsible in law for his wife's debts, unless he had given notice disclaiming them. He felt he could not do that. He knew also the stream of accusations she would level against him; that he was jealous of her success as a playwright, that he was standing between her and Beryl, that it was she who made the money while he burrowed in the British Museum copying bits out of other people's books to make books of his own which didn't sell.

Havelock Ellis reluctantly agreed. The lease was signed. The tenants were evicted. The bugs were gassed and work started on the house.

Long before he was finished, the Cosmo Hamiltons had moved. They said they had a row with their landlord. But they may have thought that Edith Ellis, who was fun to invite down from London for the day, would be hell to have next door, dropping in any moment to read over her last scene or ask advice on the manipulation of her characters.

But Woodpecker Farm and Beryl Faber and the theatre were not her only fresh interests. Lily's old love, W., came over to Paris in the spring of 1910 and suggested that Edith should meet her there. Edith took her dearest friend of the moment and found that W. also had a dearest friend with her, a singer "as tall as herself, so I look like a hyphen between two big American words."

In the letters she wrote Havelock during her two trips to Paris that year, and in most of the letters in the later years, Edith betrayed a pathetic desire to be loved, admired and spoiled, which is not shown in earlier letters. Perhaps the adulation she complained was spoiling Havelock made her feel less cherished. "I travelled with a charming American girl and gave her the roses Montefiore gave me," Edith wrote for example. "She declared I was not English. 'The Englishwomen are dead—dead. You—oh! you are alive—My! so alive.' When I told her my age, she did laugh! They all spoil me here. W. kissed me once on the lips and pushed her hands through my curls; 'I expect L. rather liked your curls,' she said. Yesterday a funny little look came on her face and she said: 'Do you know, sometimes you have L's identical intonation and, a little, her smile?' "[1]

Americans in Europe, as Europeans in America, are lavish with invitations, the broad Atlantic being an insurance against offers of hospitality being taken up. W. pressed Edith to come and stay with her in New York and suggested that with her voice she could make a profitable lecture tour. Edith returned to London with a second string to her bow. If the theatre failed her, she could fall back on the American lecture-hall. She faced the future at Woodpecker Farm with confidence.

Part of the plan had been that Edith's two old retainers, Priscilla the maid and her brother Bert the handyman, should move from

[1] *My Life*, Eng. ed., pp. 360–1, Am. ed., p. 429.

Carbis up to West Drayton. But Priscilla, after ten years of service, had reached that stage of intimacy which Edith was prone to encourage and then resent. Edith and Priscilla had a flaming row and parted company. There was only Bert and the pony and the donkey and some of the Carbis furniture to provide a continuity between the old life and this new delightful life which was opening up.

Edith followed the work on the farmhouse, brimming with new ideas and oblivious of the money they would cost to execute. She even, to Havelock's horror, had a telephone installed by her bedside. It was hard to say which side of his nature was more shocked; the cautious East Anglian careful to live within his income by the outrageous expense of installing Mr Edison's invention, or the shy scholar by the wilful assault this diabolical triumph of applied science might make upon his privacy. The thought of either was enough to keep him awake at nights.

Yet even he had to admit that Edith had converted the rural slum into a charming retreat. And sometimes her optimism was contagious. Something would surely turn up. And to help turn it up, Edith could, and often would, go daily to London.

Nearly fifty, abnormally slow to mature, Edith had suddenly come into her own. With the assurance of her published books, her theatrical success, her husband's famous name, she had developed new authority in the oldest of her arts, public speaking. Her personality had always been dynamic. Shortly after her marriage an earnest admirer had called her "the light and hope of our Future civilisation," a remark Havelock didn't let her forget. It was a tribute as much to passion and over-seriousness as to her sincerity. Now she had mellowed and shot seriousness with humour, moral indignation with tolerance, and high idealism with broad experience. She was confident and impressive in private conversation, and in public discourse fluent but not facile. She had grown up.

Her sociability, repressed over nearly twenty years of living most of her time with Cornish fishermen and yokels and the reclusive Havelock, burst on the Lyceum Club in Piccadilly.

The Lyceum was a club for women, in those days a startling idea which appealed only to the most progressive and emancipated, Edith loved it all the more for knowing how Havelock would have hated it. She left him pottering at West Drayton with the *Psychopathia Sexualis*, or the last article in German on the Mescal Button, and got away to the Lyceum, where she would meet people who laughed and talked business and drank perhaps a little too much wine at lunch and blow Golden Mediocrity.

And if there was a letter waiting for her, it wasn't from a stranger saying she was the wife of a lecturer at Uppsala University who made her walk round the bedroom wearing nothing but black stockings and high-heeled shoes and was this normal? It was just how to organise the next Poetry Circle and should John Masefield read his own poems or should an actor do it for him?

At these Poetry Circle dinners she used to speak—and speak well—taking more pleasure because she knew Havelock would have rather died than attend one. The wise old polymath had left her the whole range of social activity and she could pride herself that whatever he couldn't do, she could do better. It gave her a full life.

But it did not bring in enough money. During the summer Havelock loved working and eating under the great walnut tree in the grounds of Woodpecker. It was different in winter, when days grew short and fuel-bills rose.

The only way to pay the bills was to take lodgers. Edith found them as she had done at Carbis. But at Carbis they were parked out in cottages and fended for themselves. At Woodpecker Farm they appeared, meal after meal, at the same table with the man who had less small talk than anyone in England and could not even look them in the eyes. It was not, said Ellis, "a proceeding that was really agreeable to either of us." By herself Edith might have made a success of Woodpecker Farm as a sort of guest house, but with Havelock even she had to admit it was intolerable. She had tried to do too much with too little. She had made a demi-paradise that had to be shared with paying guests who somehow never paid quite enough to meet the outgoings.

After two years a wealthy American friend of Edith's, Miss

Emily Grigsby, who shared her passion for the theatre, paid a visit to Woodpecker Farm and fell in love with it. She offered to take it over with everything it contained. Her offer was generous and covered most of their outlay.

She saw its possibilities as clearly as Edith had, and she had the money to realise them. Having bought the freehold and changed the name to The Old Meadows, she brought it to the state of loveliness of which Edith had dreamed. From a vermin-infested slum it was transformed into an historic building which the National Trust was grateful to accept on Miss Grigsby's death.

14

My darling one, I am very ill. Cannot get right at all—somehow. Heart worse than it has ever been in a way, and had fever, and have been in hell. . . . I feel the smash-up I have dreaded for years has come at last . . . and if I die I shall leave all in confusion, and what can I do?

Edith to Havelock Ellis, 28 June 1913

MISS GRIGSBY's offer was generous, but not a penny of it went to Havelock. There were bills to be paid, loans to be returned. Havelock could wait. Not that Havelock was not going to be repaid; but these other charges were urgent.

She set to work on dramatising *Kit's Woman.* It was not so very difficult, because it read more like a play than a book; long slabs of dialogue, interspersed with stage directions, and very little action. If the curtain-raiser had brought her a hundred pounds, what might she not expect from a full-length drama on a far more powerful theme?

Kit's Woman was performed by a Sunday repertory company in London. It was well acted and Edith was called to take a curtain at the end. But no commercial producer would touch it. Impotence, even with a Cornish burr, was no subject for the suburban theatre-goer in 1913. Even Ellis himself felt that it was a subject more suitable to the novel than the stage.

Edith had given up the attempt to live at Dover Mansions. Apart from the difficulty of getting back there late at night, she had discovered there was a slaughterhouse just round the corner. She could hear, or thought she could hear, the death-squeals of the butchered animals. She took a flat in the top of the house in Harley Street where her doctor lived.

Money began to run short again and she asked a friend for a loan. She had done this before, taking out a life policy to guarantee repayment. On that occasion there had been some question of a heart condition, but her doctor at St Ives, who was a good friend, passed her as sound and the insurance company granted the policy. When she had an examination for this new policy, the doctor turned her down. The examination showed traces of sugar in the urine. She might have permanent diabetes, which was a very dangerous disease in 1913.[1]

Their marriage had been coasting along for years, each taking the other for granted. The discovery of glycosuria quickened the relationship. There was a limited time left to them; every day became important. The little irritations seemed less important and they discovered new reserves of tenderness.

It did not change their ways of life or alter purposes, but it intensified them, precipitating the disaster they wanted to avert. Edith resolved that if it killed her, she would get the money to pay her debts before she died. She had failed in the theatre, but she would succeed in the States. She had a message, the acceptance of one's own true nature; she could preach it in terms of Hinton, Carpenter, Ellis. She could arrange publication of her books in the United States, could get her plays performed, prove to Havelock that she was no financial burden, do good and pay her debts.

"Lily" approved, and with a sudden upsurge of manic energy Edith set to work on preparing her lectures. When Olive Schreiner arrived in January 1914, a rotund figure in loose drapery, agonised with asthma, heart-trouble and a stone in her kidney,[2] Edith welcomed the chance of getting Havelock out of the way, so that she could concentrate. She insisted on his going to spend ten days with Olive in Florence.

The visit was a failure. The days when Havelock was a doting medical student and Olive a young literary lioness were beyond recall. They had grown up and old and apart and didn't approve of one another any more. Olive still called him Havelock Boy, but he was fifty-four and felt it. He was glad to be back to spend some days with Edith before she sailed. Both of them knew that it was

[1] Insulin was not discovered till a few months after Edith's death.

[2] Carpenter, whom she informed of this, was so alarmed that he went round to the doctor she had consulted, Dr Alice Corthorn, who admitted that she had examined Olive but had found nothing organically wrong.

possible she would never come back. Edith said good-bye to him in London and then went down to Southampton, where she spent two nights with her dear friend of the moment before boarding the *Minneapolis*, with ten pounds in her pocket to cover her expenses in the States.

During the two days she was in Southampton she wrote six letters to Havelock, and while she was on the high seas letters arrived daily, which she had written and given to the Lyceum Club porter to post in the order which she had named, a demonstration of love rare in a wife married for over twenty years. "And the wonder of it was that all this love and tenderness and passion on a sea of adventures, apart or together, then and throughout, was on both sides without, in the narrow physical sense, any elements of sexual emotion!" [1]

When Edith landed in New York, she found that W., with whom she had planned to stay, had been called to the bedside of a relative dying in Europe. She had made no advance plans for lectures, and the chances of fixing any at this late date was small. She could only regard this trip as a reconnaissance for a longer visit in the autumn.

Having accepted these blows and found herself an alternative home with a Dr Maclean and his wife, Edith began to respond to the American scene with surging ebullience. Interviewed by half a dozen reporters as the wife of the famous author of the *Studies in the Psychology of Sex*, she was at first filled with dismay but then flung herself into the interview with a gusto and frankness that turned the dismay back onto the reporters. The Macleans invited distinguished friends to meet her. "I am the woman of the moment. . . . This afternoon fourteen of the most prominent women of New York are coming here to meet me and yesterday I was at the house of a wonderfully beautiful woman as a *lioness*." "Mrs Maclean says more has opened for me in a week than for most in years . . . your wife is just spoilt to death. Oh! Lily, Lily, how well you knew and how wonderful it all is." "I am the rage . . . I am an utterly different creature already in this dry stimulat-

[1] *My Life*, Eng. ed., p. 396, Am. ed., p. 475.

ing climate . . . Mrs D., the great actress . . . said I had magnetism and a voice that would hold any audience spellbound. . . . I wonder why people love me so."

In Chicago she scored another success, in her own right and as the wife of Havelock Ellis, whom she found was regarded with a reverence which among his friends she had considered foolish adulation. "It is just as if I had died and woke to real understanding. . . . They said things about you I thought would choke me. . . . I said I would drag you over the ocean and the land by your beard if you would come no other way. I've never realised such enthusiasm."

She engaged a lecture agent who said that there was no doubt from the lectures she had given that she had things to say and a way of saying them that Americans, especially American women, wanted to hear. If she came over on November 1, he would arrange a tour of lectures and readings.

The sunny brilliance of her triumph was shadowed by a single cloud. It was common gossip among newspaper men that the conjugal set-up of the Ellises was, to put it mildly, unconventional. Never cautious, Edith had let drop remarks in her interviews which were able to be garbled and misunderstood; and of course it was these that received the widest currency. They came to Havelock's notice and he wrote to Edith saying he thought she had been indiscreet. Edith answered that she had said what she had to clear up misunderstandings she had found in people she had met. He answered that the public correction of private error merely made private error public. The publicity about their "mutual independence and unity" had shocked some English friends and amused some American.

Intoxicated by her success, Edith thought that Havelock was jealous of it. And though she would have liked to think it entirely her personal triumph, she knew that a large part of it was due to her being Mrs Havelock Ellis and not just Miss Edith Lees. "I've conquered," she wrote, "and however much you may hate some of the interviews they were inevitable. I'm booked well for the autumn; I mean to be here on November 1st and want you to venture. I can protect you easily and the sun and warm places would do you good. . . . I happen to have 'caught on' for some reason. Even your name would never have done it alone and most of the women have never heard of you. Now—the men declare—they realise why you have done what you have! They just love me. It is very funny. I ought to lose my head, but it is scarcely touching me, though the feeling that all our worries will be over is a great sedative. I expect I'll just live to pay my debts and fling out to a greater America."

Towards the end of her two months' stay she began to feel the strain. She complained of headaches, fatigue and insomnia. By the time she returned to New York, diabetic symptoms were recurring.

But the voyage home was restful and when she reached London at the beginning of July, she appeared in excellent health. The diabetic symptoms had gone, and the misunderstanding about the press interviews vanished as soon as they met again, leaving only the warning of the dangers of publicity to the private lives of two people separated from each other by an ocean.

The Ellises had rented a tiny cottage in the village of Stanwell not far from London. There they retired to work during the high summer of 1914. Havelock refused at any price to go to the United States with Edith in the autumn; but he consented to write a paper for her to deliver on his behalf. He called it "Masculinism and Feminism" and he composed it with a special regard for her idiom of speech and delivery.

That July was one of the happiest in their married life, to be compared with the premarital honeymoon at Lamorna, yet deeper and tenderer because their love had strengthened and matured in the meantime.

The war broke on them from the blue, something as monstrous as it was meaningless. Ten days after Britain joined in, Ellis wrote: "The sky is a cloudless blue and the breeze murmurs pleasantly through the leaves overhead and the butterflies chase one another idly and the doves coo at intervals and the stream pressed by the water-lilies is almost too languid to move beneath the heat. Perfect peace seems to rule the world and the reign of Heaven begun on earth.

"I note these things and I note them with only sadness. For to-day, it is said, five nations are beginning to fight the greatest battle in the history of the world, and over the whole cradle of human civilisation the Powers of Hell are let loose.

"*Vae victis! Vae victoribus!*" [1]

Woe unto the vanquished! Woe unto the victors! It was what Havelock and Edith felt after ten days of war, but which it took the nations of the northern hemisphere fifty-one months of war and almost as many of subsequent peace to arrive at. War to them was a monstrous, minatory irrelevance. And it made no difference to Edith's plans. In November she was due to lecture, and in October she sailed from Tilbury on the *Minnetonka.*

This time the roles were reversed. She spent the night with her "dear friend" and she wanted Havelock to see her off. She wanted to show him her cabin so that he could visualise how she would be crossing. And also she was more afraid. Havelock was thinking of the physical things, the possibility that the *Minnetonka*, though American, might be sunk by a torpedo-happy U-boat commander; the strain that the lecture tour might put on her physique, her heart, her lungs, her metabolism. Edith was thinking of something far more alarming, "the smash-up which" she had "dreaded for years." There was something about this vertiginous ascent to success in a new place which was ominously like her Girton House venture. The memory of those awful nights after her collapse in the attic off Manchester Square, alone, sobbing in despair the more dark because totally irrational, was perhaps the major reason why she had begged Havelock to come with her. And from those terrible days, she remembered the Reverend Stopford Brooke. "Courage is a habit."

At Tilbury Docks the war was on. How were they to know that the bearded sage of sex hadn't a bomb hidden under his Norfolk jacket? Only passengers might go aboard.

Frustrated, Edith lingered with Havelock at the foot of the

[1] *Impressions and Comments*, 2nd series. 14 August 1914.

gangway. There was so much they both wanted to say which they could not say in public. The war was in the air like a lethal gas. Havelock gave her the dressing-case which she always took when travelling, the case she had had in North Africa after the Bedborough Trial, and in Spain when they made friends with Dolores the dancer, and in Aix-les-Bains when she started writing her stories and, come to think of it, right at the beginning when they went to Paris for the first time and stayed at the Hôtel d'Oxford et Cambridge and her loud shout of joy to see that Parisian cabmen wore white top hats.

She took the case and went up the gangplank, becoming as she went less Edith and more one of a crowd, just a passenger crossing the Atlantic in the greatest war in history. She went along the deck and found a place at the rail and tried to shout down to him something which was drowned among the voices of all the people trying to do the same thing. As Havelock looked up at her and she down at him, there was the same thought in their hearts, that they might never see one another again, or if they did, so different that they might be unrecognisable to one another. She was waving and smiling and trying to joke, and then Havelock could bear it no longer and he waved his hand and turned and walked through the crowd towards the railway station, and all he remembered later was pacing up and down the deserted station waiting for the train to arrive to take him back to London, while workmen streamed across the rails to find their midday dinner.

"I thought I had blood in my throat when that awful moment came," Edith wrote him. "I caught myself moaning while I was trying to laugh and joke. Never mind—it is already so many hours to the time we meet again."

The voyage was "awful." But the moment she landed in New York City, the intoxication of its great, vital exhilaration caught her up. Mitchell Kennerley and his wife, whom she had met in the spring, took a flat beneath theirs, put their secretary to sleep there and told her to use it as her headquarters just as long as she wished. "You've saved me, Mrs Ellis," Mitchell Kennerley said, "and nothing material I can do is worth more than a ripple." Everything was going to be wonderful. The debts would be paid. New York was being taken by storm. She met the famous X, the beautiful Y, and Z the multi-millionaire.

But before she had been in New York a couple of weeks, she was seized with nausea at a lunch. She had to leave the room and was violently sick. She had an important lecture next day at the Cort Theatre. She felt terribly ill and her friends made her feel worse. A woman who believed in mental healing insisted on giving her treatment until 10 p.m., then a friend who believed in massage worked on her till 1 a.m. Finally, with the aid of a wonderful gargle supplied by wonderful Mitchell Kennerley, she tottered round to the Cort Theatre and lectured with great success. But it was a poor start to a gruelling lecture course.

A few days later a nurse was giving her special treatment with ice-packs and only charging her three dollars a session because Havelock Ellis had turned her "from a savage to a human being." The treatment revived her but left her still hoarse and with a desperate night-cough, which she dreaded because of her liability to broncho-pneumonia. She was frightened, because with such a start it looked as if she might die before she earned the money to get Havelock out of her debt.

Havelock's father, dear old boy, died at the end of November, which left Havelock with a lot of odds and ends to clear up. Which made Edith sad, but there she was on December 1, in "Chicago, the wealthiest city, and Lily is doing her work." With Lily's help she was going to earn "a new home;" which would have been as lovely as Woodpecker Farm without bills or paying guests.

But in Chicago in early December it was horribly damp and a bitter wind blew across the lake, and she could not stop coughing. A woman doctor who attended all Edith's lectures examined her and said that with her electrical treatment she could cure her completely and there was no reason why she shouldn't live to be a hundred. She felt a little better, but not all that much.

Then something happened which was so wonderful that it made her forget all about being ill and afraid she might die before the tour was over. The women doctors of Chicago booked the Orchestral Hall for 4 February 1915, so that Edith could deliver her paper on "The Abnormal in Eugenics" to an audience of women only. They guaranteed no worry, no expense and all the profits to Edith after the costs were paid. "They just love us—you and me," wrote Edith, "and this is one of their ways of showing it." Havelock must finish his paper on "Masculinism and Feminism" and get it to her by that date, so that it could be read as his special contribution.

Edith's letters were filled with accounts and press-cuttings of successful meetings. She said that for her lecture on "The Loves of To-morrow" seats were put in every available spot and thirty people were turned away. She was judging by the standards of the Fellowship of the New Life and the various small organisations in England to whom she lectured. The success of such meetings is an equation between how many people try to sit on how few seats. Fifty people trying to sit on thirty-five seats is a packed meeting. A hundred people with two hundred seats to sit on is a failure. After six weeks of intensive lecturing and reading, Edith had earned £110, which she thought "not bad in these war-times." For those United States her draw was clearly very small, because her message was addressed to the comparatively few who would publicly acknowledge they were abnormal. But she was making money, and Havelock's main concern was whether her physique would stand up to the strain.

Later, with the wisdom of hindsight, he saw that throughout the correspondence her mental tension was mounting; but her letters were never so wild as Olive's at her most distraught and he had come throughout the years to discount much of her splendours and her miseries. She on the other hand knew that his smallest exhibition of feeling concealed a surcharge of emotion; that though he might appear calm, he was seething within. And consequently she had every reason for alarm when a new note was sounded in his letters.

In the early part of December 1914 Havelock found among his letters one from an American woman called Margaret Sanger, saying that she would like to have a talk with him. She was a friend of Dr C. V. Drysdale and his wife Bessie, the moving spirits of the Neo-Malthusian Society, and she herself was concerned with the fight for birth-control in the United States. She had read all the *Studies in the Psychology of Sex* and would appreciate the wise counsel of their author.

He invited her to tea at 14 Dover Mansions one day in the middle of the month. She was a red-headed Irishwoman, young enough to be Havelock's daughter; and at first she was as shy of the great man as he was of everybody. But as he carefully made the tea, she was soon at her ease and telling her story, which was one that appealed to Havelock's chivalry and love of rebellion.

She was the wife of an American architect, William Sanger, and the mother of three children. But she was also an evangelist dedicated to the deliverance of woman from the drudgery and dangers of excessive child-bearing. In New York City she had been indicted under the Comstock Act for infringing the laws relating to the use of the U.S. mails for carrying obscene literature on nine counts, all concerned with the dissemination of information about birth-control. If indicted on all counts, she was liable to imprisonment of up to forty-five years. Her counsel had advised her to plead guilty—in which case she would get off with nine months or perhaps a fine. But she would not plead guilty. Her own mother had died from bearing too many children too quickly without enough money to support them. On Margaret had fallen the duty of mothering her brothers and sisters, and she refused to admit that in telling other women how they might avoid a fate like her mother's she was doing anything wrong. She fled across the border into Canada without a passport, took passage for Liverpool, where they threatened to send her back, and blarneyed her way to London, where she obtained a false passport under the name of Bertha Watson. She intended to study the literature and practice of contraception in Britain and on the Continent, and with the information obtained return to New York City and defend her innocence in court, indicting the United States in general and

Anthony Comstock in particular for being in this matter vastly behind the progressive countries of Europe.

Ellis listened, fascinated by the young woman's story, by her courage, her devotion to an ideal, her fire, her vitality and beauty. He had never been so quickly or completely drawn to a woman in the whole of his life. And as for Margaret: "After those first few moments, I was at peace, and content as I had never been before." [1] It struck seven o'clock before she realised how late it was. As she left he invited her to come again.

"On me this first meeting," wrote Ellis many years after, "simply left a pleasant impression which, aided by sympathy with her lonely situation in a strange city far from husband and children, induced me to invite her again. The second visit sufficed to bring us into a relationship of friendship, I may say of affectionate friendship, later combined with admiration and gratitude. . . . An American of Irish origin, she attractively united the good points of both nationalities. They are not my English traits; she was quicker, more daring and impulsive, than it is my nature to be. But we soon found that, both in emotional attitude and mental outlook, we had much in common and never jarred on each other. I had rarely known a more charming and congenial companion and I had never found one so swiftly." [2]

It took months before Havelock kissed Olive and years before he kissed Amy, but on 1 January 1915 he wrote: "I cannot tell in what lurid gloom mixed with what radiant halo this year will stand out from all the years in the eyes of men alive on the earth after us. Yet we, too, are still living, and for all living things hope springs afresh from every despair. So it is that I have begun this new year at the stroke of midnight with a new kiss." [3]

Ellis did not mention Margaret Sanger in his letters to Edith for some time. His reasons for not doing so are unconvincing. He says that he merely felt sympathy for her. Yet with Edith in America meeting the sort of people who were interested in family

[1] *Margaret Sanger, An Autobiography*. W. W. Norton & Company, p. 134.
[2] *My Life*, Eng. ed., pp. 429–30, Am. ed., p. 520.
[3] *Impressions and Comments*, 2nd series. Constable, 1926, p. 64.

MARGARET SANGER

limitation, he would naturally have mentioned her if he hadn't suspected that his feelings ran deeper. Later on, he said, he did not mention her because it had all happened so quickly he did not know if it would last. "The relationship—I speak more specially concerning my own attitude in it and she showed herself beautifully willing to accept my attitude—was one of calm friendship, even though there was a sweet touch of intimacy about it. There was thus no trace of guilty consciousness to spoil its delight. It was not my habit to practise deceit, but here I never even felt the need for secrecy. Yet it was some weeks before I mentioned my new friend in my letters to Edith. To form a friendship so quickly was such a novel experience in my life . . . that I needed to know first exactly where I stood."

Havelock's first letter mentioning Margaret arrived in Chicago on February 3, the eve of the great meeting in the Orchestra Hall, which was to be the combined triumph of Havelock and Edith Ellis. Edith was shattered. Amy she had reconciled herself to with reluctance, because the intimacy he had with Amy was physical and did not encroach on her spiritual relationship with Havelock. But Margaret was a double challenge, giving Havelock more than Amy spiritually and more than Edith physically. She had little sleep, worrying, and at 5 a.m. she got up and wrote Havelock what he described with astonishing unawareness of its undertones "a long and sweet letter of six large pages . . . a little sadly but with no bitterness."

"My darling Boy,

Here on the great day of my public life I awake at five and write my English letters, for never am I alone now. I got all three of your letters and read them when resting after my Turkish bath. Of course I got a fearful jump when I realised there is another ——.[1] If it makes you happy I am glad, but somehow it is a kind of strange realisation which makes it still easier for me to die. I *want* to die, and yet I am at my zenith, and if I can only live two

[1] What term of abuse Edith used, the reader must guess for himself. It was clearly stronger than the "feminity" she used against Amy; or Havelock, the great opponent of Bowdlerisation, would not have Bowdlerised it.

more months I shall not die in debt. Everything is opening, as Lily said. . . . Thank God someone has put life and joy into your sad face. . . . Be careful, for I realise so much here how hero-worshipping is like drug-taking. I've had to cope with it, and even sometimes had to be brutal, in a way, as it is mawkish. A curious aloofness from the world makes me feel sure that at last I am nearer leaving it than I thought. . . . I am terrified of tonight. It is a huge hall, but my voice carries, even in a whisper, almost all over it. They are all crazy over my voice. Isn't it dear of these medical women? . . . I wonder how you spent your birthday, Dear One. Which of the —— came, or did they come in relays? . . . With my dearest love and all tender hope for your happiness,

Your Wifie

P.S. I drank to you and your new —— in a cocktail last night."[1]

Having once mentioned Margaret to Edith, he wrote about her in letter after letter, the concerts they went to, the books he was recommending her to read in the British Museum, the times they had spent together, the beautiful qualities she had. He wrote to Edith daily, and as it took some ten days for the mail to cross the Atlantic, he had written twenty or more letters about his wonderful new friend before he received Edith's reply to his first announcement; and each of these letters confirmed Edith in her wildest fears. It was the tragedy of distant separation.

If they had both been living in London, they could have met and perhaps resolved the misunderstanding. I use the word "perhaps" deliberately, because it was more than a misunderstanding. Edith was justified in feeling outraged and threatened. For more than twenty years Havelock had dinned into her that the passionate in the physical sense was unimportant, and what really mattered was the spiritual bond they had between them. Now he protested that there was no need to be annoyed at his friendship with Margaret Sanger because though there was affectionate intimacy there was nothing passionate in the physical sense. The bond between him

[1] *My Life*, Eng. ed., p. 443, Am. ed., pp. 524–5.

and Margaret was a spiritual one. And unlike Edith and Havelock, Margaret and Havelock "never jarred on each other."

Even if her nerves had not been stretched to near breaking-point, this would have been a monstrous blow. There was Edith delivering lectures on the philosophy she had accepted from Havelock for over twenty years; that the spiritual is all-important and the physical does not matter; and she was met with the argument that his relationship with Margaret did not matter, because it was purely spiritual. It made a mockery of her whole life, her message and this courageous bid to get out of debt before she died.

"I wrote," Havelock defended himself, "strong in the security of a sense of loyalty, though—such is the ingenuity of self-torture—it was for Edith the very fact that my new comradeship was of the soul rather than of the body that made her feel she had been dispossessed in my heart."

For once Amy and Edith were at one. There was enough intimacy in the affection, for Amy to feel "in much the same way, and with equal unreason. So many applications are there of that oft-invoked saying of Pascal's that 'the heart has its reasons which reason knows nothing of'." [1]

Merely by quoting Pascal, Ellis, himself not the most logical of men, did not excuse his failure to understand the effect that his simple, delightful friendship with Margaret Sanger would have on his wife, who had been living for so long in the looking-glass land he had created for her.

Edith felt too tired, sad and bitter to write an account of the lecture. She sent newspapers which pronounced it a great success, though when all expenses were paid, it brought her only £51. She sent him also a card on which various admirers had written Havelock affectionate messages at a champagne party after the lecture. She wrote one of the messages herself and she used "by a strange mistake which she never observed, her usual maiden signature 'E. M. O. Lees,' which she had not used for more than twenty years. It was a revealing little indication of the nervous disturbance

[1] *My Life*, Eng. ed., p. 432, Am. ed., p. 524.

which this life of high strain was producing." He may have been right. I think the signature was deliberate. It was her way of saying "You want to get rid of me. Well, let's say we were never married."

In later letters Edith spoke of their relationship as completely changed. "I always speak nicely of you, but I shall cease saying some things as I've no wish to pose in America as a deluded *wife*. . . . I feel sort of stunned as if the 'belonging' between you and me had got its deathblow. I only want to die because I feel in human nature there is nothing for me any more—only in Nature and music." She decided that she would continue her lecture tour longer than she had planned, so that she could wipe off her debts. Then she could die in peace and join Lily, the only person who returned her love.

She did not receive Havelock's answer to her letter of February 4 until the 24th of that month. It partly reassured her. But though he might discount Margaret, she was still an element in his life that had not been there before. "I do hope M. is out of trouble. People say she is deep and sweet and good, and that is beautiful." Then she added naughtily: "Tell her from me to take care of you always, and Amy too." She enclosed in the letter a medical report on her condition, which she was afraid might alarm him "a little." She was sure she would be better when she got out of all this "terrible noise and rush;" but all the same she was keeping her money in Express notes rather than a banking account, so that Havelock could get it at once if anything happened. "I'm only writing this just to ease you in case I am very ill."

While she was confident of Havelock's love, she wholeheartedly desired to maintain her health and complete the tour. But from February 4, when she first expressed the desire for death, one is aware of the unconscious wish to become ill so as to draw from Havelock some proof that it was she whom he loved best of all women. The refrain of later letters was failure of health, the possibility that she would never live to return to England, longing for death, the sense of being a waif and an alien who should never have been allowed to grow up, and finally, with a mounting urgency, that he should leave Margaret in England and come to her in the States, not as she had begged earlier to share her triumph, but to comfort her loneliness and heal her wounded spirit. "Perhaps when M. is back," she taunted him, "you will feel differently about it."

Letter after letter revealed the mounting of her mental agony and the decline of her body. In Buffalo there was a bad attack of angina. In New York City ulcers burst in her throat and she had to be operated on without an anaesthetic.

Her pleading had no effect on Havelock. "Although my love was doubtless more firmly resistant to the attacks of accident and mood than hers, it was not in my nature, as it was in hers, to feel the acute sudden poignancy of love in emergency, or perhaps even to respond to it adequately when presented to me." He was so used to Edith's ups and downs that he did not take her entreaties seriously. "My own darling Wifie," he wrote when the ulcers burst, "your three letters of 5th, 8th and 9th have all arrived during two days, and tell me how bad you have been with that awful throat and that you now seem to be recovering. Of course I still feel very anxious and long to get later news. I do trust you will be able to convalesce nicely, and wish you were leaving earlier, as the rest and peace of the voyage at this lovely time of the year may do much good. And I trust, too, you will have no worries, financial and other. You speak of fearing complications over here, but do not say what they are, not serious, I hope." [1]

Edith knew that she was married to one of the most imperturbable men in England. She took this letter, which even Ellis admitted seemed "scarcely to show an adequate sense of the serious character of her illness," as just another proof that he no longer loved her. "I've never felt so ill—never—but I'm struggling on." Her handwriting developed an irregularity Havelock had never seen before. She was too ill to sail without a period of convalescence. Doctors and specialists had made a hole in the profits of the lecture tour. But Dr Laura Keisker, of Brookline, Massachusetts, with whom Havelock Ellis had been in correspondence

[1] *My Life*, Eng. ed., p. 452, Am. ed., p. 545.

for more than twenty years, asked Edith to spend her convalescence with her.

Once more Edith wrote begging Havelock to come and fetch her home. Dr Keisker and her sisters "want you to come, but know you can't." She would not go further than that, because if Havelock came, it must be from a spontaneous sense of love. Dr Keisker wrote herself to ask him. But Ellis regarded it as "a kind formality on the part of Edith's hostesses" and in his replies did not even trouble to refuse the invitation. The crisis, after all, was nearly over. A good rest on the boat would make the world of difference to Edith. He would meet her in Liverpool, explain to her about Margaret and get everything in perspective. Then he would take her to London for a few days, and then off for the summer to Speen in the Chiltern Hills, where she would build up her strength. There had been so many of these ups and downs that it was foolish to worry unduly.

15

Even a disordered mind is moved by motives, however unreasonable they may be.

My Life

EDITH BOOKED her passage on the SS *Philadelphia*, sailing from New York on 8 May 1915.

On May 7 a German U-boat sank the *Lusitania* without warning, and the lives of 1,198 men, women and children were lost.

When news of this act of barbarism, more horrifying in those days than in our own, reached New York, hundreds of passengers cancelled passages on Allied liners and transferred to the old tub, *Philadelphia*. Overrun with cockroaches and sickening to a sensitive passenger at the best of times, the *Philadelphia*, when overcrowded with passengers in a blue funk, was hell afloat. A woman journalist, abreast of the gossip, suggested to Edith that Havelock was coming to Liverpool to "break the news," perhaps with Margaret Sanger at his side. In Edith's fevered state of mind, it did not appear impossible. It was consistent with a ghastly sense of openness. So when she saw her sad bearded Havelock Boy waiting on the quayside, her first question was "Are you alone?"

Looking back, Havelock saw in this question a symptom of mental derangement. The idea was so utterly fantastic to him. Yet was it? Edith had been through so many extraordinary phases, being told that she was a congenital sexual invert but it didn't matter because it was beautiful; and it didn't matter because his intimacy with Amy was physical but not spiritual; and his intimacy with Margaret was spiritual and not physical, so it didn't matter. She didn't know what next he might not say was beautiful and didn't matter. All she knew was that she was utterly exhausted in mind, body and spirit. She had come to the end of her tether.

But thank God, Havelock was alone and had booked rooms at the St George's Hotel and the nightmare was over, the lectures and the gossip and the newspaper interviews and the sympathy of friends who were really just trying to find out what was going on between these two extraordinary famous people. She rallied and he thought, as he had expected to think, that she was better at the mere sight of him, and they slept in the same bed together, and next morning she told him she had had the most restful night for weeks.

She had breakfast in bed and said that she did not want to get up. She would like to spend a few days in bed in the hotel before moving down to London. Besides being exhausted, she felt perhaps that in Liverpool they were alone together. She did not want to see people who were in London, and especially Margaret Sanger.

The St George's Hotel was expensive and Havelock had planned they should go to London the next day. Edith could not be really comfortable in bed in an hotel, and he could not be constructively occupied in a city like Liverpool. Why shouldn't they go back to Brixton, where he could work and look after her, and she could rest, and then they would go down to Speen later?

He knew from of old that if she really wanted anything, she would insist on it. But Edith did not insist. He thought later that she gave in because she was tired and weak and had lost her old energy of resolute self-assertion. But perhaps there was another reason. She had asked him to come to her at Brookline, Massachusetts, and he hadn't even deigned to refuse. Now she asked him to stay a few days with her alone in Liverpool, away from Margaret; and again he refused. It was another test of love he had failed to pass.

Before they reached Brixton, she began to show "distressing signs of exhaustion and irritability." Dover Mansions was where Havelock had been while she was going through agony in the United States. She wrote to Mitchell Kennerley, who had squired her through her tour and had tried to ingratiate himself by taking her side against Havelock. She spoke of Havelock's "steadfast

EDITH ELLIS IN 1914

devotion" and—uncharacteristically—made a copy of her letter, which she left lying about so that Havelock was able to see with what loyalty she spoke of him to her friends of the other sex. It showed him that other men liked her but she was faithful to him.

A few days after Edith reached Brixton, Amy dropped in, as her custom was. Havelock brought her in to see Edith, who was lying in bed. They were such old friends that he left them alone for a little while. "Amy with kindly intentions but not happily inspired," spoke of Havelock's care and kindness and hoped he would soon make her strong.

Havelock took Amy out and spent a few minutes talking to her in the hall. Then he went back to Edith. She was looking rather strange. "Is anything wrong?" he asked.

She said, "I've swallowed the morphia tablets."

He looked at the bottle. It was empty.

Havelock rushed out, mixed an emetic. Edith swallowed it without protest. The tablets were returned. "I think she was rather pleased at the concern I showed," he remarked.

She was. He wouldn't come to America for her. He wouldn't stay in Liverpool for her. He wouldn't keep his old —— out of her bedroom. But at least he did not want her dead. Havelock realised that "her nature had been undermined and the fibres of her soul as well as her body weakened."

A few days later they went down to the Old House at Speen, where they had spent a few weeks together between her two visits to America. There they were alone and much together and would have been very happy if it had not been for the book on James Hinton. Edith had been working on this book for years and in the States she had signed a contract and received an advance on account of royalties. The publisher was starting to agitate for delivery. James Hinton was not an easy man to write about at any time. But he was even more difficult to write about when her husband who had taught her most about Hinton seemed to believe in the darker side of that shifty prophet. She found it hard work and insisted that when she was working in the revolving shelter on the lawn, he should be always in view. It was just the opposite of his natural method, which was to be always out of view when working. It might have meant that Edith could not see enough of him; or that she could no longer trust him out of her sight.

It is hard to think of a subject worse for her mental health than the study of the sex-obsessed ideas of a man who died of a cerebral tumour. But when all objective psychic pressures are taken into account, one must still recur to the cyclothymic depression, the circular madness, which had already overwhelmed her once, before her marriage, and which had been the *leitmotiv* of all her activity since, the passionate enthusiasms and the bottomless depressions, the bustling days and sobbing nights, the surging confidence and the low-tides of doubt. In America she was right to claim she was in zenith. Now she was approaching the nadir.

In the old days after a visit to London she might come back tired, but after dinner with a glass or two of claret or burgundy, she regained her spirits and laughed and joked. Now she did not respond to food or drink. As the day wore on, she sank into deep melancholy; and if her energies rallied, it was only to rehearse his spiritual infidelities and betrayals with an anguish which no argument could allay. At night she might have been quieted, if he could have lain holding her in his arms, but as usual they had chosen their cottage badly. The bedrooms were too small for double beds. Their closest intimacy was the opening of the connecting door. As he lay in his single bed and she in hers, they must have had strange thoughts of that so carefully planned independence, which was to bind neither of them involuntarily together, but now bound them involuntarily apart.

One morning Havelock woke up and saw that Edith was missing. He went downstairs and found her. She had woken in the dawn, she said, and gone to the well which lay underneath Havelock's window and tried to pluck up the courage to throw herself in. "Courage is a habit" Stopford Brooke had said. But it was not that sort of courage.

From this time Edith's behaviour conforms to what is now recognised as the classic pattern of manic or cyclothymic depression. She was sailing away from life on a course which has since been charted. But in Edith's time the trade-routes of the departing spirit were unknown; and Ellis with his love of dignifying any aberration as a beautiful anomaly was not a good person to diagnose mental disease. It is possible that there is a physical connection between cyclothymic depression and some disharmony of the thyroid gland. But at that time endocrinology was in its infancy, and Ellis was still thinking largely in terms of the therapy of love, according to which manic depression became a mental disease only if a person desperately in need of love failed to receive it.

This second contemplation of suicide was like the first, a plea for more love. It was nothing more than Edith telling him that she had wanted to do away with herself. It might be near-madness, but it was still on the sanity side of the watershed. Havelock gave her all the tenderness of which he was capable; but there was such a sad look in his eyes that Edith knew the joy had gone from his love of her to the deep calm friendship with Margaret Sanger.

Havelock tried to revive the old pattern of separations. Edith had her good friend Yvonne, who could come down to Speen on her motor-bicycle and stay with Edith and give her massage while Havelock went to Somerset with Amy or met Margaret in London. "I shall think of you with Margaret tomorrow," Edith wrote him. "Say I hope she will come here before she sails. *I mean this*. I've waged it out at last."

She and Margaret met not once but several times. They might have liked each other, if it had not been for the man who linked them. Margaret, unaware of the circular madness, thought Edith extremely difficult and selfish. Edith envied Margaret because she had succeeded to the love which was hers by right of marriage. When Havelock was with them both, there was constraint. "He seldom talked to her when others were around him or her," Mrs Sanger wrote me. "He wanted her all to *himself*. She also wanted him in the same way, she said. He was shy, and *very* shy toward her or anyone else when she was near by."

Edith dreamed of returning to the United States for another

lecture tour; but this time Havelock *must* come with her. Edith appealed to Margaret, who said she thought he ought to stay in England. She was thinking of the awkward figure that fine-looking man might cut in public. Edith was thinking of the comfort Havelock's presence would bring her, and turned to Olive Schreiner for help.

"What does Havelock want to do?" asked Olive.

"He wants to stay in England," Edith said.

"Then of course he should stay," Olive said.

It shows Havelock's passivity that Olive was the first to think of what he might want to do. But Edith was not satisfied and she gave him no peace until he made a sort of half-promise that if she went again he might join her in California or Bermuda. He knew it was unlikely to happen anyway.

Summer passed between Speen and London, Havelock and Yvonne, the Hinton book and visits to the doctor. The accepted explanation of her life was that she had been very ill but was getting better. Both knew really that something very serious was wrong, which was difficult to diagnose. Was it Edith's heart? or diabetes? or general debility? or neurasthenia? or Havelock's friendship with Margaret?

By the time he wrote his autobiography Havelock Ellis knew something of cyclothymic depression; but in 1915 it was lumped under the heading of neurasthenia, a vague terrifying illness, the cause and cure of which were both unknown.

The tenancy of Rose Cottage at Carbis fell vacant in the autumn. The best thing, Havelock decided, would be to spend the winter in Cornwall. Edith resisted the idea violently; the thought of it was horrible.

"Then what *do* you want to do?" he asked. "Where do you want to go?"

"I don't know," she said. She wanted to go back to America, taking Havelock with her. But even she knew it was impossible.

"Then we go to Rose Cottage," he said, taking the decision for both of them once again, as he had done when they left Liverpool for London.

Though Havelock was the healthy one and Edith the invalid, it was Edith who had to go to Carbis in advance to make the cottage ready. She took with her as a maid an American girl whom she had met and liked as a servant at the Lyceum Club. Millie's family had come from Cornwall and it seemed a nice idea to take her back there.

It wasn't.

Rose Cottage had been left in a filthy condition and it exhausted Edith to put it to rights. Millie began as a treasure and ended as a terror. She had been attracted by Edith's friendliness and high spirits. She had not seen the dark side of her nature, the black moods and outbursts of rage and abuse. Millie was used to the democracy of domestic service in the States. Edith, for all her socialism, treated servants *à la grande dame* when she was roused.

Rose Cottage was very small, and for the sake of privacy they rented a bedroom for Millie in the cottage next door. But Millie lunched with them every day. Ellis found the pure stream of his meditation polluted by Millie's babble; or alternatively Millie sat silent and oppressed by this formidable couple, the old man who looked like somebody out of the Bible and the unpredictable woman with the bulging eyes. Millie could not stand it, and one day early in the New Year she sassed Edith with "such unrestrained rudeness . . . that she had to be told to leave the house at once."

That, said Millie, was something she'd do with the greatest of pleasure. She bounced down the stairs, flounced out of the cottage, slamming the door behind her. Then she opened it again and shouted up that she was very sorry for Havelock being married to that woman, a mark of sympathy which he "curtly repelled."

In happier days that incident would have been woven into the fabric of reminiscence, becoming funnier with each repetition. But now it gave Edith the last push beyond the frontier of sanity.

While she looked for another job, Millie went on sleeping next door. Edith said she was the enemy. She was traducing her to the neighbours. Havelock pointed out that Millie was a stranger while Edith had been known in Carbis for a quarter of a century.

Edith said he did not understand. Millie was spreading foul lies.

Millie was putting it about that she was a drunkard. To prove how wrong Millie was, Edith stopped drinking any alcohol.

But then she thought the neighbours were in a new plot. They were going to break into the cottage and take all her precious things. One by one she smuggled her treasures into St Ives and gave them into the safekeeping of her friends.

Living not far from Rose Cottage was an Irish doctor. When he heard what Edith was doing, he took Havelock on one side and said that he took a very grave view of Edith's health. "What do you mean?" Havelock asked. The doctor said, "I mean that Mrs Ellis is becoming insane."

Havelock refused to believe him. But the chance remark made by Miss Hinton years before came into his mind, that some of the inmates of Bethlem were "like that Miss Lees." "You'll see," said the Irish doctor.

As the days passed, Havelock saw the fire die in her. She never teased him as she had in the best days; never even ranted about his infidelities, as she had at Speen that summer. She never spoke a harsh word to him, was tenderness itself, could not bear him away from her. But at the same time she lost all will-power. Till he got a daily woman in Millie's place, Havelock found himself doing all the housework and looking after her.

Every morning he made breakfast and brought it to the little bedroom where she lay in bed with the cat on the table beside her. Later the daily woman arrived and heated water which was taken to the little room that served as bathroom. She insisted on a daily bath but had lost the ability to take it. Havelock would take her to the room and leave her by the tub and then go down and walk in the garden for half an hour, hoping that being left alone she would muster the will to undress and bathe. But when he went back, she was standing where he had left her, still in her dressing gown, the water cold.

Dressing was even more difficult. She could not decide what to wear. Havelock made suggestions, but nothing was right. What wasn't too old to wear was too good for everyday. She found it almost impossible to go downstairs at one go. She descended a few steps and then sat down, sunk in depression from which it seemed she would never rise again.

She had been fond of food and Havelock took pains to prepare her favourite dishes. But when something was put before her, she would sit looking at it as if she had no idea what it was, while Havelock gently urged her to eat. She took no notice of him, but suddenly she would take a morsel, gobble it up and then push her plate away.

Walking had been one of her delights. She had loved to stride in to St Ives to see her friends. Now she found the strain of the hills too great; and though she went out in the afternoons, it was always the same dull promenade to Longstone and back, which had only flatness to commend it.

The days were a torture, but the nights were worse. When it grew dark, he put her to bed and tucked her up like a child, gave her a good-night kiss and climbed to his own little bedroom above, through the thin floor of which he could hear every sound, every sigh.

She could not sleep except in brief snatches. The melancholy crowded deeper on her in the darkness. The night terrors which had haunted her in the little attic off Manchester Square before her marriage returned with reinforcements.

Havelock lay on his bed listening, trying to rest yet afraid to sleep, seeking an equation between her physical needs and his. He could hear her in the bed below and from time to time he went down and spoke to her gently, hoping to calm her restlessness. But sometimes his exhaustion was too great. He could hear her beautiful voice calling to him through the curtain of sleep and he didn't answer, hoping against hope that she would stop. Or else he would totter wearily down the stairs and get into the small bed and put his arms round her, whispering love-words until she fell into a doze, while he lay stiffly awake, resting only in her rest.

He thought of the translation of the fifth chapter of the third book of St Thomas à Kempis's masterpiece, which he had made and sent to Edith before their marriage. "A great thing is love, a great and altogether good thing; for love alone makes every burden light, and every unequal burden equal. Because it bears the burden without being burdened, and makes every bitter thing sweet and delicious. Like the living and ardent flame of a torch, it ever rises and safely passes through all." This was how he felt it was with him at this time; when he should have been physically exhausted, new strength was given by love. At Speen he was strained and wearied by her recriminations, but at Carbis her tender need supplied the strength to meet it.

Yet her condition did not improve. In a moment of clairvoyance she said to him, "I am sane enough to know that I am mad." Friends coming out from St Ives were shocked at the state of Edith and concerned with the tax on Havelock's strength. They urged in fairness to them both that Edith should go where she could be properly nursed. The Irish doctor had been saying this for weeks, but Havelock did not trust him. He called in Dr Hamilton of Hayle, a Scotsman in whom they both had confidence. Edith did not want to be parted from Havelock, but her condition had so deteriorated that Dr Hamilton suggested that the Convent Nursing Home at Hayle, where the great naturalist W. H. Hudson had been till a few days before, would be a good place. Hudson's room was vacant. Edith was "full of nervous terror" at the thought, but she was calmed by the prospect of being nursed by nuns. She still remembered her happiness at the convent school; and when the move took place, she made no fuss.

Dr Hamilton expressed the opinion that for some days she should have no contact with the outside world. She must receive no letters, flowers or gifts. No one must visit her, not even Havelock to start with.

Havelock took a room close by in Hayle and divided his time between there and Rose Cottage. He had done no work for weeks, because of looking after Edith, and now worry prevented him from concentrating. He was grateful when a letter arrived from Edward Carpenter to Edith about a lecture she was supposed to deliver in Manchester. He wrote back that there seemed to be no chance that she would be in a fit condition to deliver it personally, but he would try to find a copy so that someone else might read it for her. The nearest he came to revealing the agony of the weeks he had lived through was in one sentence. "As I have been most of the time single-handed in the little cottage it has been (and still is) a most trying and anxious time." But his handwriting showed such a marked deterioration that Carpenter did not need to be told more. He wrote a most sympathetic letter back and enclosed a cheque for five pounds, "because his books happened to be making money."

By the time Havelock received it he had been given permission to see Edith. His presence comforted her enormously and she liked him, to the consternation of the nuns, to lie upon the bed beside her, with his body outside the covers and his arms round her. But it was hard to say whether the relief his presence gave her outweighed the grief which his departure produced. He would lie with her until she appeared to be asleep. Then he would gently disengage his arm, ease himself slowly off the bed, tiptoe to the door and open it very quietly, listen for a moment to her breathing and then tiptoe out and close the door behind him.

As often as not, when he thought he had made an undetected get-away, he would hear, as he went out through the main gate, from the room above it where his wife lay, her lovely voice, which could reach so far even in a whisper, cry out with sudden terror, "Havelock! Havelock! Havelock!" and the nurses come running to urge silence on her, but still that voice pealing through the quiet night. And he stood, wrung with the sense of impotence to help her, and then he walked back to his lonely room, the cries not ceasing but growing softer in the distance.

The Convent Nursing Home was for general cases. They had taken Edith out of deference to Dr Hamilton. But they had no experience of mental nursing and it disrupted the Home to have all the other patients woken up in the middle of their first sleep by the screams of Mrs Ellis. Havelock suggested that his wife would be quiet if only they would allow him to sleep on her bed all night; but the nuns were emphatic that this was a breach of the regulations which could not be permitted. The only thing to do was to have Mrs Ellis certified and removed to Bethlem or some other asylum.

Havelock fought against this, pleading with Dr Hamilton to

appreciate that such confinement would tilt the balance of her mind irreparably. He suggested that as his visits had stimulated Edith's interest in the outside world, so if Yvonne sent her some flowers or fruit, without a letter, it might help her recovery by reminding her that there were others who loved her.

Hamilton agreed to the experiment. Havelock wrote and made the suggestion to Yvonne, who duly acted on it.

The parcel was brought to Edith and the nurse told her it was from Yvonne. "So she has found me, has she?" Edith said. She paid no attention to the parcel and lay very quietly in her bed for about an hour. She then said that she wanted to go to the lavatory. She had been bound into the bed with sideboards,[1] probably as a result of the struggles which she had made when Havelock left her at night. Two nurses released her and accompanied her to the lavatory. As they were returning Edith made a sudden excuse, ran back into the lavatory, slammed the bolt home and threw herself out of the window onto the concrete pavement, where they found her with blood streaming from her head, moaning "My foot, my foot." She was taken back to her room and examined. The injury to head and leg was not serious; but the damage to her reputation for sanity was grave.

Before considering the consequences, it is worth while examining the motive for this attempted suicide, which cannot be explained away, like the taking of the morphia tablets and the thought of throwing herself down the well, in terms of a need to be reassured that Havelock loved her. Ellis himself was bewildered. "Why should a token of affection from a dear friend, who was associated with no seriously painful memories, have had this potent influence for evil? Moreover, how far was the act consciously planned, how

[1] There is no mention of Edith being bound in Havelock's account in *My Life*. The detail emerges from Havelock's letter thanking Carpenter for the cheque. "Yesterday morning they thought her unusually quiet, but, taking advantage of a moment when she was *unbound* . . ." The exact form of binding is not clear from this. I suspected a strait-waistcoat might have been used; but Dr Stanley-Jones of Hayle, whom I consulted, said "As a doctor, I would say that anything in the way of a tight-jacket would be quite out of the question. Sideboards on the bed to keep a restless patient from getting out are not unusual, and would certainly fit in well with H. E.'s rather ambiguous word 'unbound'."

far subconsciously accomplished by a sort of secondary personality? She herself, after she regained full consciousness as well as later, would tell me how puzzled she was over this question. She certainly retained no consciousness—and I knew her too well to doubt her honesty—of any suicidal intention on that morning; it is well known that any sudden shock which abolishes consciousness abolishes also the memory of the immediately preceding events. She could only conclude, although unable to understand, that it was an accident. . . . But it certainly was not an accident; she herself, by some force which for the moment possessed her, had suddenly and definitely planned the act."[1]

I suspect that Ellis was led astray by his *cliché* "dear friend." How dear and how reliable a friend was Yvonne? Havelock's discretion Ediih trusted utterly. But if Yvonne had found out her address, she might come to see her. If she came to see her, she would find out that she had gone out of her mind—or that was what the nuns would tell her, and what Yvonne would tell other people, and she would never be able to go to the Lyceum Club or meet any of her friends again without the knowledge that they were whispering this awful secret behind her back. Better death than such a life.

I think it was some such argument as this which provoked her attempt at suicide. The physical damage which she did herself was slight and seems to have eased her mental tension. But the pressure from the Mother Superior for her removal increased. Dr Hamilton saw no way of avoiding her being certified, and in his letter to Carpenter, written the day after, Havelock admitted: "Even at the best it now becomes necessary to 'certify' her. . . . So nothing seems to remain but the asylum which she has so dreaded."

As a delaying action, Havelock suggested bringing from London a trained mental nurse, to which Hamilton agreed, though he warned that the Mother Superior was terrified there would be another, and successful, attempt at suicide. One can appreciate her anxiety, because if that had happened, there would have been an inquest at which the coroner would certainly censure a general nursing home for keeping a mental case.

[1] *My Life*, Eng. ed., p. 484, Am. ed., p. 588.

The mental nurse was a pleasant young married woman who won Edith's confidence. But it was all Dr Hamilton could do to stave off Edith's departure, while Havelock tried to secure Edith's admission to Bethlem as a voluntary patient. A week after the attempted suicide, Dr Hamilton called in the morning to dress Edith's wounds. He went on to finish his morning round and then, getting into his car, he told the chauffeur to drive him home. He leaned back, lit a cigarette and died.

The doctor who took Hamilton's place was not sympathetic. The Bethlem authorities would not accept Edith as a voluntary patient. In that case, said the new doctor, there was nothing for it but to certify her.

The mental nurse had a better idea. She knew a nursing home near the Crystal Palace which specialised in convalescent mental and nervous cases. They would be prepared to accept Mrs Ellis as a voluntary patient and it would be easy for Havelock to visit her from Brixton.

Edith herself wanted to go back with Havelock to the Brixton flat. But Havelock would not agree. It was unsuitable for an invalid. He would have to leave her alone there, and if something happened while he was away the blame would fall on him. He would get no work done. He could not repeat the agony of those months at Rose Cottage. It was a correct decision, but later he tormented himself with the thought that it was a failure of love which Edith would not have been guilty of, if their roles had been reversed.

Havelock took Edith to London on the night train and as soon as they reached Paddington, something happened which showed that her illness had changed course. For weeks she had been submissive, totally devoid of will-power. Now she made for a telephone booth, saying that she wanted to see her friend Dr Ettie Sayer. Havelock took hold of her arm and tried to guide her towards the underground railway. She turned on him with all her old vehemence and Havelock gave way. If not better, she was different.

They breakfasted with Dr Sayer, and then without demur Edith went on to the Crystal Palace. She thought she was entering a general convalescent home and Havelock did not disillusion her.

Edith's depression left her and as she felt her energy return on the euphoric upswing, she thought she was cured. Dr Barker Smith, Amy's father, came to see her and she flung open her arms and embraced him, a thing she had never done before. Unaware of the nature of her illness, Havelock was heartened by the turn which things had taken. Though not quite herself yet, Edith seemed very much better.

Then one afternoon an American woman called at the nursing home. Edith had never met her before, but she had a letter from Lily's dear friend W. in New York City. They liked one another immensely and the woman stayed on and on, till Edith thought what a good idea it would be if she spent the night there. She rang the bell and told the nurse to get a room ready for her friend.

The nurse said it was a nursing home, not an hotel.

Edith lost her temper and called for the superintendent. But the superintendent was off duty. There was violent and acrimonious argument, during which I imagine (though Ellis does not say so) Edith discovered that she was in a home for insane people. At any rate, immediately the new American friend left—which must have been around midnight—she despatched a telegram to Havelock informing him that his wife was leaving the convalescent home forthwith.

At 4 a.m. Havelock was awakened by a hammering on the door of 14 Dover Mansions. He went sleepily to answer it and was handed the telegram by special messenger. He woke up fully the moment he read it. He went back and lay on his bed. There was no chance of sleep, nothing to do but wait and wonder until the first trams started to clatter on the tracks.

Havelock arrived at the nursing home before breakfast. Edith had already packed and was waiting for him. He asked her where she intended to go. She said she would go to a friend of hers in the West End. She had quite recovered. They had breakfast together, Havelock paid the bill and they went their separate ways. They did not quarrel because he did not say she was still ill.

She spent the next few weeks moving from friend to friend, demonstrating to them as she thought that she was her old self again. But she was not her old self, or rather she was such a parody of her old self that people realised that even in the old days when they thought she was bubbling over with high spirits, she was ill. People began to avoid her.

When anyone asked her if she had seen Havelock lately, she said, no, she had given him enough trouble already and did not want to give him any more. Havelock did not know whether she meant this or something quite different. He made no effort to see her, but one morning she arrived with a cab at Dover Mansions and removed all her heavy luggage. She was going to Carbis, she said, to show them she was all right.

Havelock begged her not to do this. He had seen the effect she had had on friends in London and knew that in the gossip of Carbis and St Ives things would be far worse. But she would not listen to him. She thought he was saying she was mad.

He saw Edith's lawyer, faithful Algernon West, and her friend Dr Sayer, and begged them to use their influence with her, as his carried no weight. They refused, saying that they were as helpless as he. While she was at large, nobody could do anything with her. Then he went to ask Olive what he should do. She told him to go to Spain and forget about Edith for six months, as nothing he did could help her in her present condition.

But he knew that she might veer as suddenly back to dependence as she had veered away from him. He had to be near at hand in case he was needed. He compromised by going down to Norfolk for a few days. It rained all the time and he went for long miserable walks through it, thinking this was the first time since he had married that he had ever gone away without telling Edith where he was going.

On the day he left for Norfolk Edith had left for Cornwall without notifying him. She had taken with her "an ambiguous youth," whom she had picked up on a bus. He had told her he had lost his mother and father, so she took him under her wing and called him her adopted son. He wanted to go on the stage, but he had no money, so he accepted all Edith gave him and went with her to Carbis.

To turn up with this adopted son was not the way to restore shaken confidence. The Irish doctor had spread lurid rumours while she was away, and now he went from house to house warning her friends to be careful because Mrs Ellis might be dangerous. Her approach was watched with care from behind lace curtains, and before the door was opened children were hidden away from the homicidal maniac. She called, keyed up for a jubilant reunion, and found only reserve, suspicion and alarm. Even if she had been in her right mind, such a reception would have been disturbing.

As it was, she heard the wild rumours circulating through the district; that she had escaped from the nursing home, that Havelock had taken out papers to certify her and even now "they" were on the way to put her in a lunatic asylum. She flew into a panic and rushed back to London with the boy on the night express. When anyone approached she was certain that it was some attendant from a lunatic asylum looking for her.

When they reached Paddington, the adopted son asked her where they went from there. "We will go to dear Havelock!" Edith said.

The boy said that from all he heard about Havelock he wasn't so very dear. But to Edith for the moment Havelock was dear. So over to Brixton they traipsed and up the stairs of Dover Mansions and rang the bell of No. 14. There was no answer, because at that moment Havelock was still in Norfolk, waiting for the train that would bring him to London. Long before he got back, Edith had been to see Algernon West and told him to draw up a deed of legal separation so that it would be impossible for Havelock ever to certify her and have her put away.

There were many other clauses, most of which were legal recognitions of what was their regular practice, such as that Edith would indemnify Havelock against all debts and at all times keep and maintain herself. But the sole purpose of the deed was to ensure her physical liberty, even if at any time they lived together as man and wife. From Edith's point of view the document was not as fantastic as Havelock found it. There had been a time when

Havelock had thought he would have to certify her. In fact he had fought for her liberty and preserved it. He was glad to have the odious decision taken from him in the future. He signed the deed without demur and took Edith out to lunch after signing it.

But though things on the surface were much easier after the signature, Havelock was in fact deeply hurt, partly because news of the separation got around and made their marriage appear even more farcical than it had before, and partly because he resented Edith's wish that they should continue to regard one another as man and wife, after they had been legally separated. He had no logical justification for his resentment, because at the end of her marriage Edith was proposing to him precisely the same extra-legal relationship which he had proposed to her before they were married.

Having ensured her liberty, Edith embarked on another euphoric excursion, the English equivalent of her American conquest. She took a lease of a flat in Sandringham Court, Maida Vale. The rent was more than either of them had ever paid and Havelock knew she could not afford it. But he had signed away the right to protest. Then she set about decorating and furnishing it. She insisted on Havelock helping her. Havelock was to have his own bedroom (which he privately resolved he would never occupy) and his advice would be invaluable in the choosing of curtains and furniture. (It was not until later that he had the uneasy feeling that Edith thought she would get more credit if she had him with her.)

Then she started on a series of lectures. She saw herself as a sage and teacher who was Havelock's equal. She took the Bechstein Hall [1] at her own expense and was saved from an expensive flop only by the owners withdrawing consent before the meeting. She talked to any little society which would ask her, and converted Havelock's bedroom into a miniature lecture-room in which to talk when no one asked her.

Then she became interested in a brand of Sufi mysticism purveyed by Inayat Khan. She planned to write a book on Emanuel Swedenborg and wanted a private room in the British Museum where she could dictate it to one of the two secretaries she now

[1] Now the Wigmore Hall.

employed. She started the Shamrock Press, employing a firm of Maida Vale printers to run off a sizable edition of *My Cornish Neighbours*, a volume of her short stories, the plates of which she had acquired. Large bales of the unbound sheets still cluttered the flat at the time of her death. To pay for good authors like herself, she decided to publish best-sellers. She hired a private car—for which she never paid—to take her to Stratford-on-Avon where she extracted a promise from Marie Corelli to publish her next book with the Shamrock Press. By the time the female Swan of Avon's agents had repudiated the promise, Edith was thinking of a new scheme for making money. Instead of employing a private-car hire-man whom she didn't pay, how much more profitable to buy a car on hire purchase and let it out to people who would pay the instalments.

Then there was the theatre. For the winter of 1916–17 she thought she would rent the Little Theatre in Chicago to put on worthwhile plays like *The Subjection of Kezia* and *Kit's Woman*, while she was lecturing. Meanwhile there was the British cinema, a golden opportunity for anyone with imagination and artistic genius and drive. She enlisted the support of an actress of some promise and a manager of some experience and set about floating a film company. She offered Havelock the opportunity of investing in this "splendid chance to make money."

Before the project had got under way, a young Frenchwoman was sent round by a Miss Sand in the hope of getting a job acting. She had never done any acting before, but she had paid money to a man in Dean Street to teach her film-acting and he had run off with it. Edith offered her thirty pounds to translate her book *Three Modern Seers* into French. The book was about Nietzsche who was already very well known in France, Edward Carpenter who was almost and Hinton who was totally unknown in France. The young woman, Françoise Cyon, wondered if any French publisher would be interested. "Leave that to me," Edith said. "You set to work. And I'll go to Somerset House and send you a stamped agreement."

Her personality was so contagious and her conviction so great that money would soon flood in from one, other or all of her schemes, that she found little difficulty in getting credit and loans. She lost some of her old friends, but she had a genius for making new ones.

The reconciliation after the deed of separation was only temporary. She hoped Havelock would use the bedroom in Sandringham Court and keep her company during the terrors of the night, but he refused with that cold silence which was worse than anger. She would go to see him, feeling kind and gentle; and then suddenly all the anger and bitterness would well up. "Edith had not been long in the room," Ellis wrote, "when in Yvonne's presence, the old charges were launched again with the old indignation. I bore the invectives gently, with scarcely a word. On their way back, as she later told me, Yvonne reproached Edith for her harshness, and Edith replied: 'But think of the things he said to me!' "

He told it as a story to illustrate how unreasonable Edith was in that last manic phase; or how utterly distraught, if one looks at it with the eyes of someone knowing this sad mental disease. And yet, as he rightly said, "Even a disordered mind is moved by motives, however unreasonable they may be." And I ask myself why, if Havelock was right in his initial diagnosis that Edith was a congenital sexual invert attracted only to women, she should at the age of fifty-five have been taxing her husband, the man of whom she said "If I lost Havelock, the earth would rock," about sexual infidelities, to which she should have been utterly indifferent. I cannot help thinking that when she made provision for Havelock to come back and live with her as man and wife, it was what she wanted more than dear friends or indeed anything except the security that he would not put her in a lunatic asylum.

On 3 September 1916 there was a Zeppelin raid on London. Edith was woken by the gunfire and slipping on a few clothes with a cloak on top she went down to the front entrance of Sandringham Court to see what was happening. She was pleased to find that she was not frightened as most of the people were who were watching.

The woman who was standing by her shivered in the night-cold and impulsively Edith took off her cloak and laid it over the woman's shoulders.

Next day Edith did not feel well. But that happened so often she took no notice. The air-raid had been on Sunday night. On Wednesday she stayed in bed because she had a lecture the next day. On Thursday she was running a high temperature and the lecture had to be cancelled. A friend wrote to Havelock on her behalf to say that she would write as soon as she was able.

Some time before, Havelock had planned to go down to Clare in Suffolk with Dr Barker Smith. Not having heard from Edith, he went to see her on Sunday, the 10th. She was recovering from pleurisy. Her physical condition seemed satisfactory, her mind was clearer than it had been for some time and she told him he ought to go to Clare, because it would do him good. Before he left London next day, he received a note to say everything was going well, and next morning in Clare there was another note to the same effect. He decided to stay on till Wednesday morning.

When he reached home, he found lying on the mat a telegram which he tore open. It read MRS ELLIS DYING COME AT ONCE. The date was the day before.

He immediately took a taxi to Maida Vale. Everything that could be done had been done. The oxygen which had saved her life in America had no effect. She was in a diabetic coma. She could not speak and when he spoke to her there was no sign of recognition. She did not know him any more.

He sat by her for some hours and then went and lay down on the bed which she had provided for him in the next room. He thought how mean he had been never to use it before, when she needed company at night, and especially his; and now she was beyond that comfort.

One of the nurses called him and he went back to her room and examined her. Her breathing was shallow, but calm and regular. "She who had lived so vividly, so eagerly, often so tempestuously, died in perfect peace. Not the slightest shudder passed over her as her spirit sank to silence, merely the breathing grew slower; then there was a pause, then another breath; then no more forever."

After a time he got up and started to explore the place in which this woman lived, who had ceased to be his wife in law even before she had ceased to be his wife in life. He went to her desk and saw that she had been writing something, when she had been taken ill. It was the introduction to some readings which she had intended to give in that little room, intended for his bedroom but converted to a lecture room. He picked up the paper and read. "When many years ago—about 28—I first read *The New Spirit*, I knew I loved the man who wrote it. To-day, in reading *Impressions and Comments*, I realise that the man who has written both books is worthy of love, forgiveness and eternal comradeship, as a fine spirit forges into beauty, however long it takes, and that not one of us but many write not with ink but blood."

16

Grief is one of the great mysteries of life. In losing a beloved person one is plunged into sorrow. Yet at the same time one is raised above all doubts and fears and anxieties into a sphere of joy which nothing can henceforth touch. While the loved one lives there is always doubt whether the love will last; there is always fear of giving or receiving hurt; there is always apprehension of harm to the being who is so dear. Now one is raised above all doubt and fear and anxiety. One enters the heaven of complete and eternal possession which nothing can henceforth touch. To think of the loved one is now of all pleasures the greatest.

My Life

I will have nothing but what you offer; it is the very flower of love.

Françoise Cyon to Havelock Ellis

IT WAS all over; not merely Edith's life, but, as it seemed to him at first, his own. He was in his late fifties and old for his age. He had felt a flagging of his powers since he had finished his lifework, the *Studies*. Edith had been his link with the outside world. Now he could retire into his world of dreams, taking with him his memories of this extraordinary woman.

He could not help being aware that even his nearest friends and Edith's regarded their marriage as a tragic failure, disputing with one another where the responsibility for the failure lay. There had been times when Edith was alive when Havelock himself could only see the suffering which their incompatibility brought on each other. The marriage seemed a battle, in which new wounds were always being inflicted and the old wounds never completely healed.

But after he had seen the coffin swallowed in the vast and seemingly liquid mass of the crematorium furnace, pain was alembified into joy at the glory of the vision. It was right that she whose spirit was a flame should pass in fire and rise to become one with air, with the sea and sky. He shed no tear at her cremation—only later, sometimes years later, a street, a memory, an echo recalling her brought tears brimming to his eyes.

He felt at Edith's death that his life had been lived; but it had not been fully explored. It was as if he had been a character in some quasi-religious mystery, the true significance of which he had not understood at the time. By going back over it, describing what had happened, meditating on it, he would be able to penetrate its esoteric meaning. The autobiography on which he had been working at his leisure since 1900, each year writing up about a year of his early life, became now a more urgent task for him. It also changed its aim. It had begun as a sort of enormously protracted case history in which Dr Havelock Ellis examined Henry Havelock Ellis, his ancestry, paternity and life with a dispassionate scientific objectivity for the benefit of posterity, the natural history of a genius. Now it became an attempt to explain to himself how it was that a marriage which appeared to the world a tragic failure was to him, at least in retrospect, when neither of them could be hurt any more, the most important spiritual experience of his life. In page after page he tried to capture what Edith had meant to him; and he was most successful in the following gloss.

"What I experienced with this woman—I feel now many years after her death—was *life*. She was the instrument that brought out all those tones which the older I grow I feel to be of the essence of life, tones of joy sometimes, but oftener of anguish, not happiness. I smile when I find people cheerfully talking of 'happiness' as something to be desired in life. I do not know what happiness may be, but it is not life, I have lived. And this woman, by her peculiar temperament, by her acute sensibility, by her energy of impulse, by her deep hold of my most sensitive fibres, struck out the notes of joy and anguish which are love and which also are life. For love as I have known it is a passion more of what we call the soul than of the body; unlike the passion that is alone of the flesh, it is a flame that continues to burn even long years after the body that may seem to have inspired it is turned to dust. But it is because I have known love that I have lived and that my life and my work in the world have been one. My work, I am often told, is cool and serene, entirely reasonable and free of passion, but without that devouring passion of the soul my work would have been nothing." [1]

[1] *My Life*, Eng. ed., p. 411, Am. ed., p. 496.

This seems to me most excellently to convey what Edith meant to Havelock Ellis in essentially spiritual terms. Where the book and its author were less successful was in the perception of what Havelock meant to Edith. Havelock was rich in sympathy and poor in empathy; he would feel with people, but he did not attempt to feel his way into other people and look out at the world (including himself) through their eyes. He was too occupied with his own dreams to be preoccupied with those of others. He said that Edith was the most difficult woman in the world to marry, but he never speculated whether Edith may not have found him the most difficult man.

If he experienced with Edith *life*, what she experienced with him was *love*. From his point of view, the brief story of their marriage was that their spiritual love was so deep that it survived her infidelities with many women and his far smaller number of intimate friendships with women. He saw himself as calm, tolerant and reasonable, and Edith as violent, and unreasonably demanding from him a different code of fidelity from that which he allowed her. From her point of view, I think that the brief story of their marriage was that Edith loved his calm, heroically accepting spirit so much that she accepted the limitations he dictated before marriage; no children, separate establishments, long absences. She hated birth-control and Havelock proved an ineffective lover. She tried to provoke him to virility, but when he gave his blessing to her affair with Claire, she accepted what she took to be a confession of impotence. She resented Amy so fiercely because it did not fit in with her theory of impotence. He was capable of some sort of physical relation with Amy which he could not have with her; and she became reconciled, because she saw that she would lose Havelock altogether if she did not accept Amy. When they went to Spain after the Bedborough case, she proposed that she should give up Claire and he should give up Amy and they could start afresh. He refused even to discuss the subject. She fell in love with Lily and after Lily's death had a number of physical relationships with women, which satisfied the side of her nature which Havelock did not satisfy. He on his side had a number of mildly erotic friendships with women, none of which harmed the spiritual love, which Havelock emphasised was the most important. But when Margaret Sanger appeared and Havelock fell in love with her—as he was careful to emphasise *only* in a spiritual sense—the balance of Edith's mind went, though she still preserved above everything her love for Havelock. From her point of view she was quite right to load him with recriminations.

To an outsider like myself the clue to the understanding of the Ellis marriage lies as much in this disparity of viewpoint as in temperamental and psychological differences. Ellis in the years that he devoted to the retrospection on his marriage endeavoured to explain everything satisfactorily from his point of view, but it could only be explained properly if seen also from the points of view of Edith and also of the minor characters involved in the drama.

Even to explain his own point of view satisfactorily, Ellis laboured under a liability which he did not recognise. Though he had "always desired to spiritualise the things that have been counted low and material, if not disgusting," there were certain instinctive emotional reactions which Ellis considered low, material and even disgusting, but which are in fact in moderation as protective as the instinctive blinking of an eye on the approach of a foreign body. Ellis hated jealousy as much as a teetotaller hates wine. Yet jealousy in moderation is the natural and healthy reaction to threatened love; and the beloved is quite justified in suspecting indifference in her lover, if he does not show jealousy in a situation where he ought to feel jealous. His attitude to other negative emotions was equally ill-balanced. He dreaded anger as much as Edith dreaded the night; yet he was never tired of pointing out the interdependence of night and day, light and darkness and even good and evil. There are few marriages which are not improved by a periodic row, but when Edith tried to provoke one, he went into a calm sulk which must have exacerbated Edith's feelings.

But though Ellis started serious work on his autobiography soon after Edith's death, much time and thought had to be given to settling Edith's estate. She owed money to friends, doctors, tradesmen and her landlord. There was no possibility of meeting all her liabilities in full out of her estate, even if he succeeded in placing the Hinton book in England and made another volume out of Edith's unpublished lectures.

He was not legally responsible for her debts, but he resolved to repay all those non-payment of which would cause hardship. A group of Edith's friends banded together to start a collection to honour her memory and help settle her creditors.

Ellis himself was poorer than he had ever been. His earnings while nursing Edith had been very small. In the weeklies he wrote articles around, rather than about, the war. But the payment was small and his predominant theme, that peace should be negotiated soon, was not popular.

Considering that he had been writing for over a quarter of a century, he earned very little from royalties. He had been as unbusinesslike in the placing of his general books as he had been with the placing of the *Studies*. Until 1908 he had been jumping from one unsuitable publisher to another. In that year he had had the good fortune to be taken up by Otto Kyllmann of Constable in London and Ferris Greenslet of Houghton Mifflin in Boston. These two publishers took him over as a "house-author" and set themselves to build up and consolidate his reputation not only by publishing each of his new books as it was finished, but also by acquiring the copyrights of earlier books and issuing them in a standard edition.

Examination of the correspondence between Ellis and Messrs Constable proves an interesting contrast with that of most authors and publishers. Otto Kyllmann throughout was pressing Havelock Ellis to write more and more new books and put as many as possible of his earlier titles back into print. Ellis's was the restraining hand. He would not allow a book to be reprinted if he felt that it had served its day, and he would not be pushed into publishing during the war anything which he felt might be more effective if held over till the armistice.

His chief royalties during the war came from *Impressions and Comments*, which he had published in 1914. These random extracts from his journals were the most happily adapted to his form of thought, which was episodic rather than sustained. His thoughts flowered rather than flew, and these short pieces have the merit of not being worked up in the attempt to sustain too heavy an argument.

"It is inevitable," he wrote in the preface to the First Series of *Impressions and Comments*,[1] "that such leaves cannot be judged in the same way as though they constituted a Book. They are much more like loose pages from a Journal. Thus they tend to be more personal, more idiosyncratic, than in a book it would be lawful for a writer to be. Often, also, they show blanks which the intelligence of the reader must fill in. At the best they merely present the aspect of the moment, the flash of a single facet of life, only to be held in the brain provided one also holds therein many other facets, for the fair presentation of the great crystal of life. So it comes about that much is here demanded of the Reader, so much that I feel it rather my duty to warn him away than to hold out any fallacious lures.

"The fact has especially to be reckoned with that such Impressions and Comments, stated absolutely and without consideration for divergent Impressions and Comments, may seem, as a friend who has read some of them points out, to lack explicit reasonableness. I trust that they are not lacking in implicit reasonableness. They spring, even when they seem to contradict one another, from a central vision, and from a central faith too deeply rooted to care to hasten unduly towards the most obvious goal."[2]

In this last paragraph Ellis brilliantly characterised what does not appear as a flaw in *Impressions and Comments* because of the loose form of presentation he chose, but which is a flaw in worked-up books, such as *The New Spirit*, *Affirmations* and *The Dance of Life*. On those books he tried to impose an explicit reasonableness, but he frequently failed because the act of composition was not a single creative fusion of thought but the arrangement of a large number of short created passages in an attempt to make a significant pattern. The act of book-making resembled that of the mosaicist more than

[1] The Second Series, 1914–20, was published in 1921 and the Third, 1920–23, in 1924. It was Ellis's one unrealised ambition to have the three volumes, which he rightly thought contained "most of himself," published in a single volume.

[2] *Impressions and Comments*, First Series, pp. v, vi.

any other artist. But there was this difference. The mosaicist builds his design out of small pieces which are not interesting in themselves but which become significant by their relation to other pieces. Ellis's original notes, on the other hand, were very carefully designed, resembling finely made pictorial tiles rather than the dull little squares of a mosaic. The very fact that each fragment from which he made his books was more or less complete in itself made it difficult to fit them into a larger pattern. In consequence, one finds that in the worked-up books, the sum of their parts is greater than the whole, whereas with the less ambitious *Impressions and Comments* the whole is greater than the sum of the parts.

In both cases there is an implicit reasonableness, because of the central faith and vision of the author. The thoughts stem from a common centre like the petals of a flower. Artificiality only arises when the attempt is made to join one thought to another, converting the petals into spokes fixed at one end to the hub of the author's vision and at the other to the circumference of a wheel of logical argument.

"From that central core," Ellis continued, "these *Impressions and Comments* are concerned with many things, with the miracles of Nature, with the Charms and Absurdities of the Human Worm, that Golden wire wherefrom hang all the joys and the mysteries of Art. I am only troubled because I know how very feebly these things are imaged here. For I have only the medium of words to work in, only words, words that are flung about in the street and often in the mud, only words with which to mould all my images of the Beauty and Gaiety of the World."

For an artist in writing, words are an enormous treasure on which he can draw without ever falling into debt. To complain of such riches is like a painter sighing because he has only all the colours in the rainbow and all the shapes and patterns that were ever thought of. Words are the bricks from which the writer builds the cities of his fancy, and if some are dirty, so much the better; they will do well for the shambles, the cow-byre and the stews.

But Havelock Ellis, though he could write with brilliance, was not primarily an artist in words. He was a visionary, a mystic who brought to the human beings he loved the sort of reverence that most mystics give to God. Life was the medium of his art and what he wrote was an attempt to translate into words what properly was the language of the Holy Spirit, something ineffable, intangible, invisible, inaudible, and yet once experienced, as he had experienced it at Sparkes Creek, unforgettable. It was never to be caught, but at moments it could be seen as Blake saw a world in a grain of sand and a heaven in a wild flower.

Ellis in *Impressions and Comments* stumbled upon the form most natural to his genius and it found a response in the public. Sales, however, were not enough to help him financially in this crisis of his life, when he was having to meet the most urgent of his wife's debts and at the same time deliberately holding back work of his own which he felt would be more useful after the war.

He sold his furniture, whatever might fetch a price, and bought in its place bamboo and wickerwork junk from the secondhand dealers. He did not mind, because he had grown hardened in the schoolroom at Sparkes Creek, and the camp bed he owned at the age of fifty-nine was far more comfortable than the sacks nailed to the wooden frame on which he had slept forty years before.

Among the letters of distress, he received one from the young Frenchwoman Madame Françoise Cyon, who, Edith had told him, was engaged on a translation of *Three Modern Seers*. Edith had given Havelock the impression that a French publisher had commissioned the translation or that the translator was so impressed by the work that she was doing it as a speculation. From Mme Cyon's letter, however, it was clear that Edith herself had promised her thirty pounds. As the work was not finished, the translator proposed a payment of five pounds and permission to do what she liked with the translation.

Ellis wrote back that the proposal was fair enough, but at the moment he had no money at all. In a week or two he would pay her a little. Then, sensing there was a certain urgency in the appeal, he added: "If before then you *badly* need money, please tell me, and I will send you what I can at once."

Madame Cyon had enclosed a lecture called *The Mental Havoc Wrought by the War*. She had delivered it to a number of audiences and wondered if he had any ideas for its publication. He read it through. It was based on Mme Cyon's personal experiences on both sides of the lines in France and Belgium. She had apparently deliberately left her husband and her child and gone to have a look at the war as it appeared to both sides, and had come back with a violent hatred of war and compassion for war-sufferers on whatever side they were. It ought to be published, he told her, but the only outlet he could see was in the United States, where his friend Margaret Sanger might help.

In a correspondence which extended over seven months Ellis was able to be of little material assistance apart from paying off the debt of five pounds. But the young woman's difficulties as they emerged from her letters were not purely material; her life seemed in a state of protracted crisis from which a few pounds could not deliver her. Ellis, sensing her desperation, suggested several times that she should come to see him, and at last in May 1917 she accepted the invitation.

Françoise was young enough to be Ellis's daughter. She had been born in Northern France, Françoise Lafitte, and grew up in the tradition of emancipation which had been initiated by Ellis's generation, a feminist, pacifist, socialist, naturally intensely religious but without belief in a personal God and with a strong anti-clerical bias. To escape from the cramping influence of home, she had emigrated to England, where she had supported herself by teaching, journalism, etc. She disapproved of the conventional man-dominated marriage and believed that there should be endowment of maternity. Five foot two inches in height, lofty in thought and feelng, she had been badly mauled by life. She had taken a visiting American "trade-unionist" as a lover for a brief period and then when already bearing his child had broken with him, because he did not live up to her ideals. Then she had fallen in love with a Russian revolutionary exile called Cyon.[1] He had been in the Czarist Army and had fled

[1] In *Friendship's Odyssey* she called her husband Aleksei de Ritter instead of Serge Cyon; and herself Delisle, an anagram of "de Ellis". Other characters were also given pseudonyms.

to Britain at the time of the October Revolution of 1905. He moved in socialist–anarchist circles and professed belief in the complete emancipation of women. He had a son by a woman from whom he had parted, and he proposed to Françoise that with their respective children they should get married and start a home.

Françoise agreed, but very soon after marriage quarrels started because Françoise wanted to earn her own living and Cyon revealed the most bourgeois ideas of woman's place being in the home. By Cyon Françoise had a second son.

When war broke out, there was a further conflict between husband and wife. Françoise felt as strongly about pacifism as she did about the status of women. Her husband took a well-paid job as a military commentator on a Fleet Street newspaper. After her visit to the battlefront, Françoise was faced with the choice of living comfortably with a husband whose male dominance she detested and whose job she despised; or going off with her two boys and her devoted maid Bessie and trying to support them all by her own efforts. Cyon refused to give her a penny, because he hoped to starve her into submission.

When Françoise was in this state of revolt, a Mrs Jacoby gave her twenty pounds, some of which she spent on the Dean Street course in film-acting. When that failed, the translation offer from Edith was like a gift from Heaven, a gift suddenly withdrawn by Edith's death.

When Françoise told Havelock that she needed money badly, she was not exaggerating. She was at her wits' end and only prevented from committing suicide by her sense of responsibility to her children and her determination not to give in to her husband. She was a fighter and Cyon's economic blockade was his surest method of defeating himself.

Rather alarmed at what he was doing, Cyon changed his tactics and suggested to Françoise that they should have a council of friends to decide what they should do. It was this which made her accept Havelock's invitation to call on him. She felt that the time was coming when she would need advice desperately.

She arrived, bitterly conscious of the shabby coat she had to wear because of the cold, the shoes with Louis heels she had borrowed which didn't fit, and the blouse which someone else had given her which didn't go with the pinafore-style dress that was the only thing she wasn't ashamed of. She was very shy, but was reassured when she found him equally shy, shabbily dressed and obviously but unashamedly poor.

She had never mentioned Edith in her letters, because Edith had never mentioned her husband to her, and she knew they were separated. Their relations might have been as strained as hers with Cyon.

Now she spoke of her admiration for *Three Modern Seers* and how Edith's warmth and generosity had heartened her. Seeing from his expression that despite their separation he still loved his wife, she spoke of other meetings, reading her translation to Edith at Sandringham Court, and how Edith said the French translation brought out meanings which were hidden in the English; and listening to Edith's readings from Oscar Wilde; and spending nights at the flat to keep Edith company. She did not tell how five nights before Edith caught her fatal chill, Edith told her to come round and spend the night and she would give her £7 10*s*. as her advance and the rest on delivery, and she had only her fare to Sandringham Court, and when she arrived there was no one in, so that she had to walk all the way home, and she never saw Edith again.

Havelock told her about Edith's death and what she had been like when she was well, taking delight in telling someone who had loved her in her decline of how fine she was in her heyday. He lent her *Kit's Woman* and another book of Edith's, asked her to lunch next week, and sent her away without ever mentioning Françoise's personal problems. Yet in a way they had been talking of these all the time, because what she wanted most was sympathy and the courage to be herself.

The reconciliation scene was in the best Russian tradition. Cyon grovelled on his knees, swore that Françoise was the perfect mother and he the imperfect father; but if only she would come back to him, everything would be wonderful, and now that the glorious

Kerenski revolution was victorious they would go back to Russia where important work awaited him and this nightmare would be over.

Françoise said she would think it over. She knew nothing about Havelock except that he was Edith's husband and seemed wise. But she was lunching with him next day and wanted to take his advice.

Earlier I have talked of the sort of therapy which Ellis evolved in contrast to that of Freud. His treatment of Françoise was an example of the flexible technique which he had been refining during the previous seventeen years. At this stage in their relationship, he regarded her purely as another unfortunate young woman whom he might be able to help. He had guessed during their first session that she was on the verge of suicide, but he knew by the time she left she would not do so, because they had established a sympathy.

At her second session he took her into the kitchen-dining-room-study and gave her an excellent luncheon, which he had prepared himself and of which she was greatly in need. While they were eating, he let her discover that he was a doctor, had written some books about sex and was—since she had admired Edith's essay on Hinton—a sort of healer like Hinton. After luncheon he told her to lie down on the sofa and have a rest, and when she was relaxed they began to talk about herself and her troubles. There was really not a great deal of difference between the method and that of a psycho-analyst, except that it was unselfconscious. He did not tell her to say whatever came into her head. She said it naturally. He did not find the resistance of the paying patient to the psychoanalyst, because she wasn't paying and he wasn't a psychoanalyst. He was a friend. She poured the whole story out.

It seemed to her that he was pleased there was a chance of being reconciled to her husband. She pointed out how impossible he was. He reminded her that Cyon might have causes for complaint. She had refused to sleep with him, for example, which a husband might resent. And had she thought that a woman alone with two children might fare worse than a woman with three children and an imperfect husband? It takes two to make a marriage, but only one to break it.

She tried to get him to tell her what to do, but he refused. He just wanted her to face all the facts. And the session ended with Françoise saying that she would follow her husband to Russia with the children if he would go there first and establish a home. And then if she went, she demanded the right to come back after six months if it did not work out right, but meanwhile he must contribute to their support.

Cyon agreed to the terms. He left for Sweden taking his elder son Boris with him, gave Françoise some money and arranged that she should have an allowance from the London newspaper for which he would continue to write.

This semi-reconciliation made things easier for Françoise financially without placing on her the strain of remaking a home with Cyon. Ellis continued to correspond with her, as he did with a number of other people, male and female, about their problems. Sometimes she went to see him, usually when there was something which could not be thrashed out by post. He pursued two parallel lines of argument. He warned her that all marriages went through various trials and would succeed only if both parties learnt from them. At the same time he encouraged her to be independent, because it was good in itself and was also a safeguard against the failure of her marriage.

I have emphasised the identity of Havelock's treatment of Françoise with that of other patients. But there was from the start a difference. His other patients came to him because he was the author of the *Studies in the Psychology of Sex*. Françoise had come because she had liked his wife and was owed money by her. Then she had liked him. Then she had found out that he was famous. This made her a special person. He could talk to her about Edith in a way that he couldn't talk to any of the old friends, who were either on Edith's side or on his. She loved them both, in a way that only that very old friend Edward Carpenter loved them both. And then the fact that Françoise had liked and trusted him because he was himself and not because he was famous was marvellous. And then she was so ripe for his teaching. The spiritual and intellectual problems which she was coming up against for the first time were those which he had had to face twenty or thirty years earlier. He began to lend her his own books instead of Edith's.

Though Françoise had approached Havelock because she needed help, she soon saw that Havelock was himself in need of it. At fifty-eight he looked on himself as an old man with death near and not unwelcome, because he had nothing to live for now Edith was dead. That seemed to her a terrible delusion. Grey-haired, grey-bearded though he was, he was magnificently handsome. He was in such physical trim that he could live for years, given the zest for life again. And he must recover it, because intellectually he was the richest man she had ever known. She prayed that she could help him.

But there were her own troubles to cope with. She took a petty clerk's job licking envelopes in a Pacifist Society office. The pay was small but the cause was good. Money was coming from Cyon and if he did make a home in Russia she would join him.

Then she heard that he had gone to Russia and rejoined the army with the rank of lieutenant-colonel, he the husband of a militant pacifist.

In September 1917 there was an even greater shock. A friend of her husband's inadvertently let out that Cyon had a son of nineteen by his first wife in Russia. Cyon had never told her of this marriage. What had happened to the first wife? Françoise asked. Were they divorced?

The friend said he expected so. But there was no means of telling whether or not she was legally married, except by following him to Russia.

At her next session with Havelock she launched a tirade against her husband, who was guilty if not of bigamy at least of gross deceit. Havelock told her not to judge her husband in absence—the whole thing might be gossip—but at the same time he urged her to strengthen her independent position, by looking for a job in a school, which would bring her more money than licking stamps and sealing envelopes.

The relationship which was being built up can be viewed objectively as a friendship-cure. It appeared to Françoise and to Havelock in quite different lights. To Havelock she was first a patient and secondarily a friend. He had helped many unhappy men and women in this way before and was familiar with the different phases through which the cure was likely to go. To Françoise he was healer and friend in one, a person who had brought sanity and peace into her disordered life. But soon after the first apparent peace had been established on an intellectual level, she became aware of conflict on a deeper level. It was all very well for Hinton to say that Nature was the bride of the Soul. But Nature had not been the bride of the Soul in her own experience. She had failed to reconcile body and soul in the sexual act; and much as she desired it, she could not see how it was done. She told Ellis of her difficulties and he reassured her of their normality and lent her his Essay on *Psychoanalysis in relation to Sex* and later the *Evolution of Sexual Modesty* volume of the *Studies*.

Instead of employing the Freudian couch technique, Havelock would take her on excursions to Kew Gardens and into the country round London, talking as they walked about dreams or anything else which came into her head, enjoying Nature, as Françoise expressed it, as "two liberated spirits." Havelock Ellis was interested in dreams and she promised to write down hers to help him. Havelock Ellis was quite aware that sooner or later it would produce what the Freudians called, in his view wrongly, the transference situation. A psychoanalyst had to regard the love between patient and healer as a purely subjective projection on the part of the patient, because otherwise the analyst would have been involved in an impossible tangle of love-relationships with his various patients. (Incidentally he would be very soon struck off the medical register.) Ellis had greater freedom because he was not practising as a doctor and he was not surprised to receive a letter from Françoise written on 3 April 1918, which began,

"Dear Friend,

I am going to write a very difficult letter. Yet it must be written if I want to find peace of mind. The truth is, Havelock Ellis, that I love you."[1]

[1] The full text of this moving declaration of love is given in *Friendship's Odyssey*, pp. 270–2.

In the course of this letter, she analysed her dilemma. She loved her husband as she would love a child. In loving Havelock, she loved a man. The thing she wanted was to retain Havelock's friendship at whatever cost, even if it meant never seeing him again. "Yesterday I came away from Brixton in a state of high emotion. I went to bed and shouted 'Havelock, I want to be your wife!' If the wind could have carried my words, you would have heard them, though they were only said in my heart."

Havelock wrote on her envelope: "The first real letter." It was the first and only declaration of love Françoise had made to a man, but not the first which Havelock had received. He answered it the same day "in full honesty, and full caution," finding the less difficulty in his reply because he had written similar letters many times before.

"Dear,

I had your letter this morning. It is very, very beautiful, and I am glad you wrote it, because it will help us to understand things and to have everything clear and right. I wanted to put my arms round you when you lay on the sofa half asleep, but I did not want to do anything you might misunderstand, and I should be sorry for you if I do anything you might feel afterwards was not right and that might make you unhappy. I would like to soothe you and comfort and help you, and it is very good for me, too, to be near you, and I felt much better for your visit. I am sure we could be loving friends, real affectionate and intimate friends. But I wouldn't be any good as a passionate lover or husband. You must remember that I am much older than you, and in some ways older than my years, as I have had a great deal to suffer and go through. I am not a bit like the virile robust men of the people in your dreams! I have several dear loving women friends, married and unmarried (most of them just now scattered in various parts of the world, so that I cannot see them), and with some of them I am very close and intimate friends, so that we can be perfectly free and natural and like children together. But there is not one to whom I am a real lover. I don't ever want to be, and if they had a proper lover I should not feel any right to be jealous. That is how I would like to be with you. I feel sure that I am good for you, and I am sure that you suit me. But as a lover or husband you would find me very disappointing. When you know me more you will feel that as an affectionate friend, as close as you like, someone you can be perfectly natural and yourself with, you will have all the best that I can give. It may be all the better for beginning just as it has begun, for that has happened with one or two friends who are very dear.

"But there is nothing in all this to prevent you from being a good and faithful wife. I should be very sorry to do anything that was not fair to your husband, and I should be very sorry for you to have any sort of guilty thoughts. I would like you to feel that the love you have for me is not a love that you feel the least bit ashamed of, or that you have any need to be ashamed of. If you feel that this kind of affectionate friendship is *not* possible, then it would be best for us not to meet. But I think it *is* possible, and that you will find it quite easy and beautiful and natural and helpful. It will be all that to me too. I am, in some ways, understanding as you say, but I am also like a child, and it is lovely to me to be able to be like a child." [1]

The reader of this book will find this letter easier to understand than Françoise did when she received it. She was puzzled by its confidence and its vagueness. She waited a few days before answering. Havelock wrote her a second note, for fear that he had offended her. But before she received it, she had already despatched a long reply, one sentence of which summed up her attitude then and thenceforth. "I will have nothing but what you offer; it is the very flower of love."

[1] *Friendship's Odyssey*, pp. 272–3.

17

A woman may have been married once, she may have been married twice, she may have had children by both husbands, and yet it may not be until she is past the age of thirty and is united to a third man that she attains the development of erotic personality and all that it involves in the full flowering of her whole nature.

Little Essays of Love and Virtue

HAVELOCK ELLIS had met women before who though married were still spiritually virgin. He proposed to give Françoise not that part of sex which she had received from her inept self-satisfying lover and husband but the explorative, caressing, other-satisfying tenderness in which he had become expert because of his primary limitation. He did not intend to usurp her husband's function but to open up to Françoise the continent of psycho-erotic personality, which was *terra incognita* to Serge Cyon. His desire at this time was to awaken Françoise in the hope that she in her turn could awaken her husband.

He proceeded very slowly with her, so that instead of recoiling in alarm, she pressed eagerly forward towards the paradise of erotic delight. Her progress is recorded later in the essay quoted above.

"Up to then she had to all appearances had all the essential experiences of life. Yet she had remained spiritually virginal, with conventionally prim ideas of life, narrow in her sympathies, with the finest and noblest functions of her soul helpless and bound, at heart unhappy even if not clearly realising that she was unhappy. Now she has become another person. The new liberated forces from within have not only enabled her to become sensitive to the rich complexities of intimate personal relationship, they have enlarged and harmonised her realisation of all relationships. Her new erotic experience has not only stimulated all her energies, but her new knowledge has quickened all her sympathies. She feels, at the same time, more mentally alert, and she finds that she is more alive than before to the influences of nature and of art. Moreover, as others observe, however they may explain it, a new beauty has come into her face, a new radiancy into her expression, a new force into all her activities. Such is the exquisite flowering of love which some of us who may penetrate beneath the surface of life are now and then privileged to see. The sad part of it is that we see it so seldom and then often so late." [1]

With Françoise Havelock succeeded more brilliantly than he had done with any friend who had come to him in distress. But his plan for returning her to her husband failed. With the triumph of the Bolsheviks in the October revolution, Cyon was imprisoned in Finland. He escaped to Sweden, where he announced his intention of returning to England as soon as he could secure a visa.

Havelock behaved with great caution. He was not a home-breaker, but a home-mender. He was uneasily conscious that Françoise viewed him with a devotion near idolatry, which none of his warnings could abate. He had only to say the word and she would abandon Cyon. But it was the last thing in the world he wanted, because though he could help her as friend, he could not give her what she needed as husband or lover.

The best thing was to work towards a reconciliation, while taking precautions against its failure. Françoise gratefully accepted what he offered as the flower of love. She lived from day to day, dreading the thoughts of her husband's return. She wrote to suggest that he should try to get a job in Stockholm and when he was settled she would bring the family to him there.

Cyon replied that he could find no work in Sweden and she must redouble her efforts to get him a visa.

Havelock had considered that his life was at an end when Edith died and all that remained was to live with Edith in his world of dream. But Françoise with her problems, her marvellous efflorescence and her absurd but flattering respect for his understanding, pulled him back to life with both hands. He might try to stay

[1] *On Life and Sex*, Heinemann, p. 91.

detached, but inevitably he became engaged in the future of this young woman and her family.

In September 1918 she took her elder son for a holiday to Westcliff-on-Sea. Havelock joined them there. He had never met either of the boys before, but he enjoyed himself. "All day long I have been lying on the cliff or the sands at work," he wrote in *Impressions and Comments*, "while from time to time my eyes rested on the friendly vision of a dear woman, not too far away, playing with her child. The sun and the air, mixed with that radiant vision, enter into my blood, pouring a new vigour into my veins and a new inspiration into my thoughts."

Françoise had till this time felt her life divided into separate compartments, her friendship with Havelock, her work, the care of her children, her responsibility towards her husband. She found it hard to visualise her son and Havelock together. But she found in Havelock more understanding of her problems as a mother than she had ever received from her husband.

During this holiday they discussed further plans for integrating her life. During the summer, she had spent three hours a day travelling from home to school. She must move down to the East End to be closer to the school and to Havelock. Her post as a teacher was temporary; she must work to get "established." Supplies of money from Cyon were so small and infrequent, she must augment her salary by other work such as typing. Havelock had some papers of a rather private nature which he did not want to put out to an ordinary typist.

The links became closer, but it was still an arrangement in which Cyon had his place as Françoise's husband, in Havelock's mind as someone who could share their existence in London, though Françoise felt that if she had to live with her husband again, it must be abroad, far from the temptations of Brixton.

In October 1918 Cyon announced that as he had failed to secure a visa for himself, he was sending his son Boris, who held a British passport, in advance. He added that Boris had tuberculosis and would she see he went to school.

Françoise wrote immediately that, with her own children and

school-teaching, she had too much on her hands to look after Boris even if he was in good health. It made no difference. Boris arrived, with three pounds which his father had given him for his education, in the middle of the month, "immense, as an asparagus gone to seed, and as thin." Examination proved that he was free from tuberculosis. But from that time Cyon played small part in their plans. Even Havelock realised that he was utterly irresponsible.

In accordance with the Westcliff plan, Françoise found a house in the East End. It was a terrible house, though the best she could find in that last year of the long war. Behind multiple layers of wallpaper, between cracks in floorboards and behind wainscotting, bugs hid and bred by day; and at night they issued forth in armies, bolder than bandits because confident that however depleted their ranks would soon be reinforced.

Desperately poor, Françoise made do with Tate's cube sugar boxes disguised as furniture and scarves converted into blouses. She could never have survived without the devotion of Bessie Girling, her Cornish servant and friend, who cooked, kept house and looked after the children, more like the wife of Françoise the bread-winner than her maid.

Such destitution might have broken the spirit of Françoise if Havelock had not been almost as poor. If a scholar of fifty-nine with a world-wide reputation did not mind living in such poverty, why should a junior schoolmistress with a family of five and the vigour of the early thirties complain, especially when she had the treasure of the great man's friendship? *Amor omnia vincit.*

At the end of the war Havelock's fortunes were at lowest ebb. He had been withholding publication of certain books because he thought the climate of opinion would be more favourable if they appeared immediately after rather than during the war. The war itself had wrought a change in feeling and belief. Disillusioned in traditional ideas, many people were looking round for new ideas to take their place and some found them in what Havelock Ellis had written.

A man of very fixed habits, he continued his life as far as possible as if nothing had changed. Amy still came in to supervise his household, but the intimacy of their friendship—which had never, I believe, extended beyond what Ellis called the "play-function"—had ceased on her marriage.

One day when Françoise was at Dover Mansions, Amy called and finding Havelock occupied tried to go away. Havelock insisted that his two "dear friends" should meet one another. As Amy shook Françoise by the hand to say good-bye, she leant forward and said in a whisper, "You think you'll keep him. But you won't!"

It was an idea which had not occurred to Françoise. Havelock had made plain to her that he had many women friends, though most of them had been scattered abroad by the war. They would come back and she had no right to deny to other women the joy and love which she had been granted by the Master, *le sage de Brixton*. He had taught her the rule of the Abbey of Thelema, *Fay ce que vouldras*. It seemed to her, like everything he taught her, very wise and very beautiful.

When she began to meet these brilliant men- and women-friends of Havelock's, she could not help feeling slightly envious. Compared to her, they were so rich, so well-dressed, so leisured. She raced from home to school to Brixton and back home in what seemed a pathetic rat-run compared with their commuting between Rome, Paris, London and New York. She thought she detected in their manner a certain condescension, as if she was not *une grande sérieuse*, but a mere "flapper." And she was filled with astonishment that the great man should have time to spare for his little East End schoolmistress, even if she was in a sense his own creation.

Yet there was another truer mood, in which she could say: "He was the creation of my soul as I was the creation of his." All his life women had been the dominant influence. His mother, Agnes, Minnie, May Chapman, Louie, Olive Schreiner, Edith, Amy, Margaret Sanger. To each he had given something, from each had something in return. But to no one had he given so much as to Françoise. She was his masterpiece as an artist in loving. And in return he had received the breath-taking promise, "I will have nothing but what you offer; it is the very flower of love." No woman had ever challenged him with such unconditional surrender.

With Olive and Edith there had always been an element of reserve, of criticism, even of scepticism. He had not resented this in the matter of his potency. He accepted what he regarded as his physical limitations, and that they should accept them also and still love him spiritually was the most that he asked.

Where Françoise astonished him was in her refusal to consider that he had any physical limitations. The husband who had given her the younger child she considered himself a child. But despite all Havelock's protestations, Françoise insisted on loving him as a man, as a great lover.

And so, by one of those strange but wonderful reversals, the woman whom he had healed through the employment of love within his limitations, began to heal him with the strength of the love and trust which he had released in her. She could not and would not accept that as a lover she would "find him very disappointing." And by the miracle of her faith in his virility, she dispelled that spectre of impotence which had haunted him since adolescence. He discovered to his wonder and delight that he was, at least with Françoise, a perfectly normal man. There was nothing physiologically wrong with him at all. This idea that there was any correlation between the vesical throw and sexual potency was a pseudo-scientific rationalisation. At the age of over sixty he was a full man at last; and he had been made a full man by Françoise whom he had made into a full woman.

He was still as cautious as ever. A miracle had happened. But would it last? Would this virility that had suddenly been given to him to reveal the truth he had so long denied, that physical love is the peak, the crown, the final ecstasy of spiritual love, be withdrawn with equal suddenness?

He was frightened, because the foundations of Françoise's faith appeared to him false. He was not the great philosopher, the sage, the master she thought him to be; and yet it was her belief that he was that gave him the confidence to become what she thought him.

It was an agonising situation, because he had from the first been preparing Françoise to leave him either to return to her husband or to find the lover who would really satisfy her. He had taught her

Fay ce que vouldras, thinking that this would make what they did together guiltless and the transition to the new lover easier. But that was when she was just one of many women who had come to him with sexual problems. Now suddenly she had become unique. She was the woman whom he had been looking for all his life; the woman whom he could release and who would release him. When he wrote of her, "Such is the exquisite flowering of love which some of us who may penetrate beneath the surface of life are now and then privileged to see. The sad part of it is that we see it so seldom and then often so late." The last sentence referred to himself at over sixty and not herself at over thirty.

But he could not tell her that the situation had changed without revealing so much about himself that he might destroy the confidence which made his new happiness possible. He tried to hide her away like a man who has discovered a nugget of pure gold. But already the rumour was running round his friends of this small passionate Frenchwoman whom Havelock had found, who had the most remarkable fire and intensity. And they wanted to meet her, as the friends of Pygmalion must have crowded to meet the statue which the goddess Venus brought to life for him.

Among these friends was the novelist Hugh de Selincourt, a man in his forties, with whom Ellis had been friendly for many years. De Selincourt would send him each new novel for his criticism and Ellis would write to thank him, saying that this novel was more important than the last and he didn't feel able to make any helpful criticisms. "I merely enjoy, feeling too much in sympathy to want to criticise or to be able to do so." De Selincourt would treasure these letters and also show them to his publishers. They were the publicity manager's dream. "It seems to me a fine achievement, and is certainly very beautiful and very poignant with inevitably some pain mixed with the pleasure of it."

Hugh de Selincourt was a follower of Shelley and James Hinton. He believed in Free Love and thought Havelock Ellis's work in the field of sex was of paramount importance. It is hard to say whether his ideas were due to a flaw in his marriage or the flaw in his marriage due to his ideas. His wife had fallen in love with another man

HUGH DE SELINCOURT

whom she could not marry, because he was already married to a woman who had been certified insane. De Selincourt's philosophy enabled him to accept his wife's adultery as something natural and beautiful. He continued to live with her, being in fact deeply attached to her; and at the same time he claimed for himself complete extra-marital freedom. He talked about sex in general, and the sex-lives of his friends in particular, with what he thought was perfect freedom but which perhaps betrayed a lack of sexual confidence. He said no man worth anything as a lover used contraceptives and he could satisfy any woman without himself having an orgasm. Though the statement may well have been true, this would seem to have been what Ellis would have called "an anomaly" rather than a criterion of normality. Retardation of ejaculation is less considered than prematurity, because less embarrassing, but it is equally a deviation from that simultaneity which is regarded, I think rightly, as the form of coitus mutually most satisfying. De Selincourt was in practice, as Ellis was in theory, a "Knight of the Holy Ghost." He regarded it as part of his mission in life to employ his singular endowment in selfless service of the other sex; and if he gained anything from it, rather than sensual pleasure, it was the reassurance that if his wife preferred somebody else to him, this was not because of his lack of virility.

Hearing of Françoise, de Selincourt pressed Havelock to introduce him to her. Ellis stalled for some time but at last agreed to bring Françoise to a meal at a West-end restaurant. Françoise felt embarrassed, wearing her home-made dress in a place so fashionable. But Hugh was delightful. He was deferential to Havelock and attentive to Françoise, bubbling over with high spirits and enthusiasms, a gnat of a man, thought Françoise, beside her dear old Havelock snail.

Soon afterwards Hugh wrote Françoise a note saying that he would like to visit her at her home. Françoise told Havelock that she was going to refuse. By her standards Hugh was a wealthy man. He could not help looking down on the very humble style in which she and her family lived. Besides, she had very little leisure and all she had she would prefer to spend with Havelock himself.

Havelock pooh-poohed her objections. It would do Françoise good to meet intelligent people with civilised ideas. He wrote to de Selincourt telling him to take no notice if Françoise refused his request. He wanted two such good friends of his to be good friends of one another.

So Hugh called and they talked of Havelock Ellis and his greatness and the book she wanted to write which was to be called *What Woman Owes to Havelock Ellis*. Hugh said that his admiration for Havelock was so great that he would consider it an honour to be allowed to help her with this tribute.

There began a series of letters and meetings devoted to the discussion of Havelock and what Woman—and Man—owed to him. She had hoped that it would bring her still closer to the man she adored. Yet discussing him with Hugh pushed Havelock away from her. "To write about you to no matter what Monsieur, even if so encouraging, takes too much from the time I have to think of the Faun [1] and dream of him," Françoise wrote to Havelock. But with his characteristic unawareness of emotional undercurrents, he took no notice of it. He left as usual to spend his Cornish winter at Cadgwith, feeling happy to think that his Naiad had such congenial company in his absence.

With Havelock out of the way, de Selincourt turned his attention gradually from the Master to Françoise herself. Though this is what any expert seducer would have done, it must not be thought for a moment that in his own eyes or those of Françoise de Selincourt was a seducer. Seduction is a word from the vocabulary of the philanderer; it does not occur in the language of Free Love. Seduction is ugly and a breach of trust. What de Selincourt proposed was a beautiful physical union between two souls already drawn close by their love for the great teacher who had freed men and women from the bondage of obsolete moral laws and superstitious sexual conventions.

[1] They evolved for each other a number of love-names. He was Faun and she was Naiad. He was *mon ange, le sage de Brixton*. She was *Framboise*, the Bear, *la pétroleuse, Fanchon, la Douce*, etc. I have used these as sparingly as possible, because love-names can never gather in the mind of others the snowball of tender recollections that they have for the lovers themselves.

Fay ce que vouldras. In loving one another while loving Havelock, Hugh argued, they were creating a union of special beauty. In the filthy world's eyes it might appear an infidelity, but it was really a transcendental affirmation of faith.

How far Hugh believed this it is not possible to say. But a man who could write to Margaret Sanger as he did: "The whole place breathes your sweetness . . . Every nerve of me continues in tumult . . . Ah! the glory of you!" and later: "My whole life has widened out under your touch. I'm like a drunken man—all of a rapture . . . I was aching and beaten and sore. You've given it all back to me in renewed power and loveliness," clearly lived in his own empyrean.

Françoise was carried away. It was a startling idea which would never have occurred to her before the awaking of her full erotic personality. But since then she had been initiated into a world so full of unsuspected mysteries that nothing surprised her any more; and this discipular communion in the shadow of the Master was in the tradition not merely of Hinton but of Ellis himself; and not merely the tradition, the practice also. If it was right for Havelock to have dear woman friends apart from herself, as it assuredly was, so it was right for her to have a dear man friend like Hugh. "If you could hear the way he speaks of you," she wrote to Havelock. "He knows all the wonder of you with such reality that his words thrilled me almost as deeply as your presence in the flesh, or better still, in the spirit." Her letters were full of Hugh and the help he was giving on "the baby-book" which she would present to Havelock in place of a child.

Havelock saw the glimmer of the red light. "Of course I should like de Selincourt's plans to come off, but the Naiad must not overstrain herself. Also it's all very fine to go and make a baby-book with him—and then pretend I am the father." He had known the happiness which he enjoyed was precarious and he prepared to accept the inevitable with dignity. "*Whatever* you do it will not be foolishly and hastily; *whatever* you do you will do it if it is a real part of you. . . . Your Faun is not so young and foolish as to think he must try to tie you up and pull you back."

When finally Hugh "opened his heart, he had but to open his

arms" for Françoise to fall into them. By then Hugh was so identified with Havelock, that she did not realise that she was embarking on having two lovers. Hugh *was* Havelock, and her heart imagined that "the Faun rejoiced at this prolongation of himself."

Havelock knew that something was happening between Françoise and Hugh. But he suppressed his jealousy and his sadness. He expressed only concern about her health, which he sensed was being strained by the hectic association with de Selincourt. Whatever else happened he must accept as he had accepted all the other misfortunes life had brought.

His fears were justified. Françoise and Hugh both contracted a chest infection. Hugh developed pleurisy and Françoise a double pneumonia from which she nearly died.

Havelock took Françoise to Paris to recuperate. Havelock had often said he would like to see the paintings of her brother Paul. But now the chance arose, he refused to go. They had a quarrel in which Françoise exclaimed, "I want to die. You have gone from me spiritually."

Havelock said nothing. He explained later that he thought her outburst was due to the excessive heat and the weakness left by her illness. In fact he thought that she had gone from him and he was making way for his successor.

The quarrel was made up, but the sense of impermanence haunted him. He devised a test to see if she loved him. Man Ray had taken a photograph of Françoise which he particularly liked. Of the two copies she possessed she gave one to Havelock and proposed to give the other to Hugh. Havelock said she ought to keep it because her children might like to have it, when they grew up.

Unaware that it was a test, Françoise gave it to Hugh.

That made Havelock suspect that Françoise and Hugh were lovers. He did not ask any questions, but he wrote to Françoise condemning Shelley and Hinton. "Both had beautiful visions of life, but when they tried to carry them out made a terrible mess of their lives and spread misery around them. Their ideas have always seemed fascinating to me, *but they are not my ideas.* Mine are absolutely the opposite to them."

[*Man Ray*.

FRANÇOISE

Françoise immediately went to see Havelock. But a long tortured conversation revealed only the extent of their separation, not its cause. Havelock, convinced from the start that he would never hold Françoise, was hurt only that she had never told him that she and Hugh were lovers. Françoise was utterly bewildered that he should resent her practising what he preached or had seemed to preach; and she could not see how her love for Hugh which really was a form of homage to Havelock should be wrong; while all those intimate friendships of his with other women, which were certainly no homage to her, should be harmless.

There followed a bombardment of long, passionate, explanatory letters,[1] each trying to explain the misunderstandings of the other but failing because of the basic misunderstanding under which each laboured. Françoise was writing to her sage, her master, her angel, her creator, her god. But they were read by a hypersensitive old gentleman who in his sixties had fallen deeply in love with a woman young enough to be his daughter, only to have his beloved taken away from him by his so-called friend, a sexual athlete twenty years younger than himself.

The natural and dignified thing for Havelock to do was to retire gracefully. "I have been too shy and reticent with you about many things," he confessed, "and you have been much too respectful to me, treating me as if I were as old as I seem, and possessing a wisdom I haven't a trace of." He sought only "new links to bind us together in place of those that are broken."

His assumption that her love for him had been eclipsed by her love for Hugh, its pale lunar image, filled Françoise with panic. "You have been the beloved, the lover, the friend most divine," she wrote. "You are still this, will always be, and I cannot live with you on other terms."

Such an assurance would have carried weight, if Havelock had not been convinced of his sexual inadequacy. "If you had said to me beforehand," he replied, " 'I am in love with Hugh and I intend to form a relationship of some kind with him but do not intend to tell you anything about it,' I should have felt sad, but I

[1] They are quoted in great detail in *Friendship's Odyssey*.

should have said, 'Then we will say good-bye. You are perfectly free. And I think you are quite right. I know what a poor sort of lover I am, and I want you to have everything you need. I shall soon be able to rejoice over it, and, anyhow, I shall never cease to feel, as long as I live, what wonderful lovely years we have had together.' "

The operative phrase was "what a poor lover I am," but to Françoise he was always the prince of lovers. What she seized on was his jealousy of Hugh. What right had he to be jealous when she had conquered her jealousy of his women friends?

Though the letters continued to volley back and forth, apparently without progress, Havelock and Françoise gradually began to understand one another. The six years they had known each other had been wonderful, and yet there was an element of falsity, of fancy dress. They were more Faun and Naiad than Havelock and Françoise. Now harshly and painfully they were getting to know one another as man and woman.

Just as it had been Françoise who gave him his full manhood with her love, so it was she who with her faith brought him, the great advocate of physical nudity, to bare the nakedness of his soul. He asked her to treat him not as a master but an equal. She took him at his word and into her letters entered the note of authority. She reminded him that he had always said that the physical was unimportant compared to the spiritual.

"This is not right," he answered, denying everything he had said to Olive and Edith,[1] "The physical is *immensely important*. Even if in itself it were a small thing 'God hangs the greatest weight on the smallest wire,' as Goethe said."

He was forced to acknowledge that Françoise had acted with a spiritual superiority. "The difference between us has been that my infidelities (I never so regarded them) were *sins* but very small; yours was *not* a sin, but very big. So that I was able to say in perfect good faith that there was no third person, not knowing that you were living in an entirely different world of ideas." [2]

[1] Except when he formed his friendship with Margaret Sanger.
[2] *Friendship's Odyssey*, p. 380.

Henceforward Havelock forswore his infidelities, which it was not so difficult to do because they were small and unimportant compared to the pleasures of friendship; but in return Françoise had to forswear her very big not-sin, which was far harder because in physical terms de Selincourt was a far more accomplished lover.

After a hard struggle she succeeded in doing so; but she continued to reproach herself with having estranged the two men who had been friends. She tried to effect a reconciliation, but with only a show of success. De Selincourt, whole-hearted Hintonian, did not recognise that he had done any injury to Havelock Ellis and was quite prepared to carry on as before. But Havelock never forgot what he regarded as a stab in the back. In his autobiography the gibes which occur at intervals about "sexual athletes" were directed at de Selincourt.[1]

Françoise on the other hand felt no bitterness. Through Hugh, she said, she came to grips with the bitterest ordeal of her life; and to him she owed ultimately and indirectly some of the greatest truths she was yet to discover about life. Havelock might have said the same, for without that ordeal the deep, clear-sighted happiness of his remaining life with Françoise would never have been achieved.

[1] And de Selincourt recognised them as such. For example where Ellis wrote "It must be a hard task for the sexual athlete to become a great lover," de Selincourt wrote in the margin of his copy, "Hint of sneer quite unnecessary: self-defence?"

18

> The happiest years of my life have been with you. I have never dreamed such happiness possible for me. These years still seem a miracle.
>
> Havelock Ellis to Françoise in a letter to be read after his death

AGE AND experience modify character but they do not change it. In an agony of mind he had revealed himself to Françoise and she accepted him and showed him that this was the whole physical man she knew him to be. The impotence which he had feared might set in with her knowledge of him as he really was did not return until some time later, when it might be put down to advancing age. Yet he remained the shy, the slow, the cautious person he had always been, spending a lot of his time hidden away in his shell.

The result of the ordeal was emotionally tantamount to a state of unmarried monogamy. But they continued their separate establishments and separate lives until Françoise fell ill, as the result of this long worry and the failure to mend the friendship of Havelock and Hugh. She underwent a major operation and spent the summer recuperating in a cottage which she shared with Havelock in the country. It was the first time that they had spent months on end together, living as man and wife, and they were happy and harmonious.

But when September came, Françoise had to return to her teaching. She still felt very weak. She gave up the night-classes which she had taken to supplement her meagre salary. Yet even so it was a strain to cope with the day-work. Instead of going to Cornwall for the winter, Havelock moved to a Sussex seaside town, so that she could spend week-ends with him; and Françoise reached the point where she was so near collapse that she decided that if Havelock did not ask her to give up teaching and live with him, it would show that he was blind and had never loved her.

Havelock was not blind. But he had never undertaken to live with anyone permanently. His separations from Edith were the only things that had made his periods with her tolerable. Both he and Françoise had heavy commitments. He had to contribute to the support of his sisters. Françoise had François and Paul, her two sons, to keep and educate. And, though he liked the boys at a distance, he was uncertain how he would like them in larger doses.

He had scored a success with *The Dance of Life*, especially in the United States. To his pleasure and surprise the first half-yearly royalty cheque brought him a thousand pounds. No book of his had ever approached the best-seller class before.

Yet he knew that *The Dance of Life* was not a repeatable success. It was the only book which he had planned as a whole. Whereas in *The New Spirit* he had tried to reduce every form of human activity to religion, in *The Dance of Life* he tried far more successfully to reduce all human activity to the form of art. Though he had published fragments of *The Dance of Life* before he produced it in book form, he had planned the book as a whole and worked on it for a dozen years. It was far more mature than *The New Spirit* and *Affirmations*, which contained barbed and wounding asides that betrayed the author's uncertainty and discontent. Olive Schreiner even earlier than that had complained to Havelock that when he wrote bitternesses crept in which he never showed in conversation. In *The Dance of Life* he was almost as free as in *Impressions and Comments*. There was also a delightful mellowness in his views, partly because he had reached the age when a writer, if ever, becomes good-tempered and partly because he had found happiness with Françoise. The sharp intrusive things he wrote when he was in love with Olive and Edith were often the explosions of frustration, as for example when he called St Thomas à Kempis's *Imitation* "religious pornography."

His aesthetic theory of life chimed in with the post-war mood. Religion, philosophy and politics were among the casualties of the first World War, but Art remained unwounded and was invested with the functions of the casualties. Acts, lives and beliefs were judged by whether they were beautiful or ugly, because in a world where absolutes could no longer be accepted, the relatives of artistic order were the best substitute. No book expressed the *Zeitgeist* of the first half of the 1920s so succinctly as *The Dance of Life*, and it may be said that at the moment of its publication, time caught up with its author, who had hitherto always been in advance of his time. At the age of sixty-four Havelock Ellis had become one of the great contemporaries.

I first read *The Dance of Life* about a year after it was published, when I was aged sixteen; and I shall never forget the experience, because it was the first time that I had ever read a book which I felt was specially written for me. That feeling must have been shared by a very large number of Havelock Ellis's spiritual children at that time.

But when Françoise was approaching her crisis in September 1927, that financial peak had been passed. Havelock was being loaded with an adulation which he did not feel he needed. Isaac Goldberg, an American journalist, had published *Havelock Ellis, A Biographical and Critical Essay*, which Ellis had found rather embarrassingly flattering, and Houston Peterson, an American student, had produced a far better book called *Havelock Ellis, Philosopher of Love*, which Ellis would have preferred to be called *In the Mind of Havelock Ellis*. It contained excellent research material, together with speculations about his private life the inaccuracy of which Ellis was not prepared to expose.

At the same time, everything that he had written was in great demand. The short story *Kanga Creek*, his only work of fiction, based on his experiences at Sparkes Creek and written at the request of Olive Schreiner in 1884, had been published by the Golden Cockerel Press in 1922, who issued his *Sonnets, with Folk Songs from the Spanish* in 1925. There was a magic in his name. But he knew that he was approaching the end of his life. In 1916 he had been ready to die. In 1927 he felt more alive than he had felt ten years before, thanks to Françoise, but he was only two years off his three-score years and ten and he was reluctant to take on the support of a wife, two children and a maidservant.

His hesitation is understandable. At that age, especially after a lifetime of married bachelordom, one does not lightly take on such commitments.

But when he saw Françoise at this decisive week-end, he told her to give up teaching and come to live with him.

She refused. The invitation was enough to give her the courage to carry on by herself. She could not lay this burden on him.

Some time after this, she saw Hugh de Selincourt again. He said, "Why don't you and Havelock live together as man and wife? Everybody knows about you."

Françoise said: "I earn £275 a year. And Havelock gives me something. But without what I earn, we could never live. And it isn't fair on Havelock. He is old."

"Yes, I understand," de Selincourt said.

Two months later Margaret Sanger wrote to Françoise asking if she would be Havelock's secretary at a salary equivalent to what she had earned at the school. Margaret had always wanted to pay a tribute to Havelock on his seventieth birthday. But Hugh's suggestion, though Havelock was only sixty-nine, seemed the most practical thing that could be done. She knew and loved all three of the people in this unhappy triangle and she hoped that by implementing Hugh's suggestion she might bring them all together again.[1]

At the age of sixty-nine, however young in heart and nimble-brained you are, it is hard to cope with new situations except in terms of precedents. He thought back to the days when Edith and he were getting married. "We'll each bear half the expenses," he said. "That's the best arrangement. Fifty-fifty."

Françoise pointed out that she had no private income and two children. She was being paid to be his secretary and perhaps could earn a little extra money by translation and other work. But there was no question of fifty-fifty. They all had to live on what the two of them could earn.

Though this was not a revolutionary way of running a family,

[1] In that she failed. But the money established Havelock and Françoise together. After the slump the allowance ceased. But Margaret celebrated Havelock's birthday each year in her *Birth Control Review*, and in 1938 presented them with a eheque from herself and friends which enabled them to buy a small and much needed car.

Havelock was very dubious about it. It didn't seem equal to him: That wasn't the way that Edith and he had managed it.

With a rare exercise of tact Françoise did not point out that the way he and Edith had managed it had saddled him with Woodpecker Farm against his will and a pile of debts after Edith's death.

They agreed that he should give up Dover Mansions and she her little house in the East End; and instead of his going out of London to lodgings in Cornwall or the south coast for the winter, the best thing was to have a cottage in the country where Havelock and she could work, and a house in South London where Bessie Girling could look after the boys, and they could stay when it was necessary to come up to London for business or research.

But once again the habits of a lifetime asserted themselves. He had always looked after himself. He was not sure that he could bear to be looked after. It was all right in the country. Edith had always looked after him in Cornwall, except at the end. Françoise could look after him in the cottage at Wivelsfield Green, Sussex, with its outdoor sanitation and indoor charm. But in the house in South London, on Herne Hill, it was a very different matter. At Dover Mansions he had always looked after himself, and he had looked after Edith too, when she stayed with him there, and he could do it and he liked doing it.

"And you shall go on doing it, just as long as you like," said Françoise. She arranged that he should have his own suite on the first floor of the Herne Hill house, complete with its own little kitchen, where Havelock could cook his own special breakfasts, as he had done in Sparkes Creek half a century before. And if the smell of eggs and bacon wafting up the staircase did assail his nostrils—well, his kitchen could be, and very soon was, converted into a morning-room for them both, in which they ate Bessie Girling's succulent breakfasts.

To her boys, at least in their early teens, Havelock's appearance at meals was a trifle awesome. The frightening silence of Pascal's eternal spaces was broken only by a high voice asking for the butter, marmalade or cruet.

But as the boys grew older and Havelock more used to the idea that he was not by nature an aesthetic anchorite but had chosen to be one, because Edith was so difficult in large doses, he discovered in himself a paternal pride and love in which he had thought he was totally deficient. Instead of the boys being a bore as he had feared at first, they were fascinating in their growth. He wrote to his friends about them with a warmth and pride he might have feared to show if they had been his own. And they were so obviously talented and intelligent that he had none of the eugenic reservations about their heredity which he had produced about himself and Edith. They were there, and they were good, and that was enough.

Françoise spent more time with Havelock at Wivelsfield Green than she did with her sons at Herne Hill. Sometimes she felt guilty of neglecting them. But the admirable Bessie had long been everyday mother to them and they derived more from the occasional vision of their mother's happiness than from the constant prospect of her unhappiness, which would have been the alternative. Children thrive better in a climate normally calm but fanned at times by the south wind of love, than one across which storms break and the east winds blow.

And also they were all living under the umbrella of fame. To Havelock came people from many different places seeking help and encouragement. One of the most famous of these was Radclyffe Hall. She had worked for many years establishing herself as a novelist and with the success of *Adam's Breed* she felt that she was at last in a strong enough position to write a novel pleading for the recognition of congenital sexual inversion as a psychological fact which must be recognised in society. It was her ambition that sexual inverts should be allowed to marry and live together as openly as men and their wives did.

She spent two years writing *The Well of Loneliness*, fully cognisant of the danger to her reputation as a woman and an artist. "I am only sustained in my determination to set forth for the general public the tragedy of such lives," she wrote to Havelock Ellis, on 18 April 1928, "by the knowledge of the courage with which men of science, chief among them yourself, have of recent years tried to elucidate the facts of inversion for the benefit of serious students."

Her book, she added, might create no impression at all; in which case her two years' work would have been wasted. But what she most feared was that it might create the impression she would most deeply deplore; "that of being eagerly seized upon by the undesirable elements of the public as salacious diversion."

Havelock Ellis read the novel and gave it his private blessing, though he advised that his approval should not be publicised for fear of bringing on it the same fate which had overtaken *Sexual Inversion* thirty years before.

The climate of public opinion had changed during those thirty years. Sexual discussion was no longer taboo. Indeed in some circles conversation seldom left the subject of sex; and the rising generation was as knowledgeable about transvestism, fetichism and the pleasure–pain field as the previous generation had been about fossils and pressed seaweeds. What had begun as a movement for sexual freedom looked like developing into an epidemic of sexual licence. The middle-aged and elderly looked on appalled by an outspokenness which appeared as salacious frivolity.

Jonathan Cape accepted *The Well of Loneliness* for British publication, but American publishers were frightened. Doubleday Page, Harper and Houghton Mifflin turned it down.

It was published in London in July 1928 and received sympathetic and understanding reviews from all the serious papers. Then on August 19, in the middle of the silly season, James Douglas, the editor and chief muckraker of the *Sunday Express*, came out with what Radclyffe Hall described as "a vituperative blast of filthy abuse," demanding that the Home Secretary should stop publication.

Jonathan Cape sent a copy of the book together with a sheaf of favourable reviews for the perusal of the Home Secretary, Sir William Joynson-Hicks. "Jix," as he was called, was a devout nonconformist, the English counterpart of America's Anthony Comstock, who considered that his divine mission was the hunting down of obscene literature. He answered by return of post that no more copies of *The Well of Loneliness* were to be printed, as the book was obscene by reason of its subject. What he thought of literary critics can be inferred by his retort in the House of Commons a year later, when he was being questioned by F. W. Pethick-Lawrence on the seizure of D. H. Lawrence manuscripts by Scotland Yard. He did not "seek literary advice when deciding if matter was obscene."

"I have little to tell you, dear Havelock Ellis," Radclyffe Hall wrote reporting this news, "for you above all men must know how hard this blow has hit me. But worn out in body as I am at the moment, I do want you to know that my spirit is undaunted. I have stumbled on after you and Edith, a humble but very gladly willing disciple. I well know that I have had little to give for I am only a writer of fiction, but that little all I have offered to those persecuted people whom you and your wife have so splendidly defended."

Radclyffe Hall had written her novel with the most careful avoidance of anything that could savour of coarseness. (Rose Macaulay described it as "a most gentlemanly book"). But Jonathan Cape was forced to withdraw the English edition pending prosecution for publishing an obscene libel. Meanwhile a Continental edition was prepared in Paris and a first edition of 6,000 copies was soon exhausted. As with *Sexual Inversion* the attempt to suppress the book merely gave it a publicity it would never have achieved on its own.

Ellis, remembering the Bedborough case, suggested a fund to help pay legal costs. "Many people have offered me money already," Radclyffe Hall replied, "but I do not feel that I can accept money as long as I have assets." To raise cash she sold her house in Holland Street, Kensington, and gave up her motor-car. She agreed to split costs fifty-fifty with Jonathan Cape, hoping that she would be allowed to speak on behalf of her book, though the case was brought only against Jonathan Cape and the printers.

Norman Birkett, on behalf of Cape, tried to plead that there was no reference to the physical aspects of sexual inversion in *The Well of Loneliness*, but Radclyffe Hall insisted that he withdraw the plea. The case was lost; in Radclyffe Hall's opinion, prejudged before it reached the courts.

And when it was taken to the Court of Appeal, the Director of Public Prosecutions refused permission for the Justices of the Court of Quarter Sessions to read *The Well of Loneliness* before passing judgment on it. Radclyffe Hall sent four copies of the letter refusing this permission to Havelock Ellis, with the request that he should show them around to influential people. She hoped that the pressure of public opinion would restrain the Home Secretary.

In this she was wrong. Narrow and misguided as Jix was, he was a man of principle, and he went on gaily with his obscenity-hunting until the Prime Minister rid himself of the political liability by creating him Viscount Brentford and kicking him upstairs.

In the private consolation of Radclyffe Hall and her defence in public Havelock Ellis was in his element. Jix represented the death-struggle of Mrs Grundy, Havelock's lifelong enemy. He was in at the death, along with D. H. Lawrence and many others. But the people who killed Mrs Grundy were Jix himself, with his bigotry, and the anonymous author of *Mother Goose Rhymes Censored*, one of which read

> There was a little girl
> And she had a little curl
> Right down the middle of her ——
> When she was —— she was very, very ——
> But when she was —— she was horrid.

In carrying on the defence of Radclyffe Hall, Havelock Ellis felt he was finishing off his lifework. Radclyffe Hall might write: "I take real exception to one thing in your letter—you dare to speak of 'old age' in connection with yourself. This is untrue, men like you can never grow old, and anyhow you are *not* old, and anyhow it hurts me, so don't think it or say it or write it." But all the same Havelock did feel old.

He himself had found at last the happiness which he had told Olive Schreiner was something for which neither she nor he were destined. He had found it in the most ordinary way, living with a woman who loved him so deeply that even when he became impotent she remained faithful, sublimating the desires of a more than normally passionate nature, and with two boys, whom he came to regard as his sons, though he was not their father. He who had boasted to Edith that Symons and Louie considered him, though married, as free as if he were single, became as devoted to Françoise as if they were married. He who had said that it was part of his nature not to be able to live long in close proximity with anyone, however much he loved them, found it equally part of his nature not to be long away from Françoise.

He continued with his work. He had published a seventh volume of the *Studies* on *Eonism and other Supplementary Studies*. By Eonism he meant what is more commonly called transvestism or cross-dressing. In 1933, he produced a condensed version, a Manual for Students on the *Psychology of Sex* which was published in Britain as well as the U.S.A. In 1936 Random House republished the *Studies* in four volumes, rearranged and with a new foreword. He wrote a large number of short essays for the British and American press, which were reprinted in *My Confessional* and *Questions of the Day*. Like Bertrand Russell and J. B. S. Haldane, he was a brilliant feature writer, with a capacity for generalisation both provocative and disarmingly casual. He followed *Little Essays of Love and Virtue*, which had been designed principally for the young, with a companion volume, *More Essays of Love and Virtue*, designed primarily for the middle-aged. In these two volumes he garnered the wisdom of his years, advising people on their emotional problems. They are tolerant, commonsensical, goldenly mediocre, free from that desire to shock which marred much of his early work. And he produced in 1936 his last literary collection, *From Rousseau to Proust*, which contained one of the most sympathetic of his personal reminiscences, an account of his early days in Paris.

In the course of that book he wrote of Rousseau what he might have wished to be said of himself. "There are various great and definite achievements to be placed to his credit or discredit. But, above and beyond those, there is one undesigned achievement far rarer; he has changed the spiritual and emotional atmosphere of our Western world. We feel and think a little differently because Rousseau lived. This does not mean that he was absolutely original; many others were moving in the same direction. But it was Rousseau who, by some natural personal quality, effected the general change.

"The change is so general that we have long since become unconscious of it, and that it is even possible to deny its existence. We are not trained to take tracings of the spiritual respiration, or even to apply a sensitive finger to the pulse of life.

"The rare men who at the interval of centuries exert this miraculous effect on the respiratory activities of the spirit are by no means necessarily the kind of men whom we like to count 'great.' That is why their influence is often denied, and they themselves vituperated. They are not the men whom, like Shakespeare, we easily venerate, men who, if not at every point approved, are regarded as splendid and well balanced humans, supreme examples of the possibilities of our species. But, even on that very account, we bow before them; they have heightened humanity but remained normally human. They have not added any new peculiarity to the human reaction to life and the universe.

"That can only be done by an abnormal man who is, almost inevitably, an imperfect man, under-developed on one side if over-developed on another. It is only such a man who is forced to approach life from a new angle. There may possibly be millions so forced. But when it happens that a man thus made comes along in an age peculiarly fitted to respond to the vision from this new angle, and uniquely gifted with the power to express it, he will win for himself a place among those immortals who create the world."

19

It is essential to the human dignity of a truly civilised society that it should hold in its hands not only the Key of Birth but the Key of Death.

Impressions and Comments, 27 November 1913

DURING THE winter of 1931–32 Havelock found that he had difficulty in swallowing. It felt as if there was a growth in his throat. When it did not go away, Havelock decided that he probably had a cancer.

After a time he told Françoise about it as gently as he could. She was a dramatic and excitable woman and she urged him to be X-rayed immediately. But Havelock refused. It might not be cancer and if it were, it would be impossible to operate. He applied the therapy of acceptance. If he found things difficult to swallow, the best way was to eat things easy to swallow. He was not alarmed. "There can be no ideal conception of Life and no true conception of Nature if we seek to shut out Death and Pain," he had written nearly twenty years before. "It is the feeble shrinking from Death and the flabby horror of Pain that mark the final stage of decay in any civilisation."

Françoise might have argued that if the X-ray revealed that he was not suffering from cancer of the throat but something else, treatment might be possible. But Havelock was a doctor and she trusted his judgment. "Ecstasy and anguish are the life-blood of the world," he had written. "It is only because one has drunk deep, if but once only of that mingled cup that at last, and only at last, one becomes the Master of Life and the Master of Death, unable in the end even to see them apart, or to find any blemish in the face of either. So, unmoved in spirit, we can depart from Life to Death, satisfied and serene, swathed in the benediction of 'the Peace of God which passeth all understanding,' as in the old days they called it."

When it became plain that it was not growing fast enough to be a cancer or non-malignant growth, Françoise consulted two doctors who had examined him to find what they thought was wrong. One said it was merely a nervous spasm and an X-ray would at least prove nothing was organically wrong. Havelock consented to be examined by Dr Abrams's Reflexophone, which revealed some slight growth; but there was no need for alarm.

So it went on for four years without lowering his vitality or deteriorating his general health. When visitors came for a meal he ate sparingly so that they would not notice that anything was wrong.

In December 1935 he went down with influenza, which brought on bronchitis and other complications. He grew so weak that Françoise saw death about the place.

Havelock would not let her sleep with him for fear that his coughing would keep her awake. She was nursing him all alone in a primitive cottage as Havelock had nursed Edith during her depression at Carbis, and she lay awake, as he had, fearful that he might need her and she be asleep.

The strain of nursing him was too great. By the time he had passed the crisis, she was crippled with sciatica and neuritis. While Havelock recovered with resilience, she did not pick up. She had known that while she was living with Havelock he was dying with her. During his illness she had been afraid that he would die; after it, she was more afraid of what a long time he might take to die. She had no courage left for a long struggle.

She went to Aix-les-Bains for an eight-weeks' cure for her neuritis. By the time she returned she had regained her strength to face the future.

She found Havelock recovered, except for his throat, which was worse. He found it hard to keep food down. Sometimes he had time to leave the room, at others he regurgitated in front of her. "When life and strength seem to be ebbing away, the idea of actively courting Death grows absurd," he had written. "Let Death do the courting! We may not be so hard to win, but let the chief responsibility be hers." She found him glorified by the fact that he took his difficulties so lightly.

Havelock devoted more and more of his time to his autobiography. He knew that he could not do justice to the final period with Françoise and he laid this task on her. This was to be, in the form of her autobiography, that book *What Havelock Ellis means to Woman*, which she had never written despite or because of Hugh de Selincourt's aid. His own work on *My Life* was a pottering perfectionism, the addition of glosses which when incorporated in the text made it read in such a misleadingly equivocal way.

They worked together on their respective books until the end of 1936. Then suddenly in January 1937 Bessie Girling fell ill. She had been carrying on the house at Herne Hill, though Paul had married and left home and François was at Oxford. It was always ready for Havelock or Françoise, if they needed to come to London.

They had noticed that more and more of the work of the house had devolved on the maid; which was natural, because Bessie was sixty-two and feeling her years. Now the maid revealed that for some time Bessie had had a pain in her breast, but had said nothing because Havelock and Françoise had been so ill. The maid had said that in that case she would tell Françoise, but Bessie had turned on her and threatened her with dismissal if she did.

Bessie Girling was taken into hospital, where they diagnosed cancer of the breast so near to the heart that it was impossible to operate. Françoise begged the doctor to tell Bessie that her condition was incurable; and then if Bessie wished, to help her out of this world. The doctor refused to do either of these things.

Françoise did not tell Bessie that nothing could be done for her, because she considered that given such knowledge a patient should also be offered the chance of euthanasia. She allowed Bessie to continue under the illusion that the changing of the dressings was effecting a cure.

By the door of the ward was a bed to which patients were moved when they were approaching death. This made it easier to remove the corpse without upsetting other patients. One day when Bessie had been lying in the ward for over six months, she was moved to the bed by the door. Then she realised that Françoise, for whom she had worked for nearly twenty years with utter devotion and trust, had deceived her. She felt that she ought to have been told and she became bitter towards Françoise.

Within a month of knowing that she was incurable, Bessie Girling had made her end. She had no feeble shrinking from Death and no flabby horror of Pain.

But Havelock wrote an article for the *News Chronicle*, based on the suffering of Bessie Girling, and putting the case for euthanasia. He was in fact pleading not for her but for himself. Bessie Girling, once she knew that she was going to die, didn't ask to be killed. She set about dying as singlemindedly as she had looked after Françoise, her children and Havelock Ellis.

In February 1937 the lump in Havelock's throat grew so bad that he could scarcely finish a meal without regurgitating. He fell ill with pleurisy but he was not ready to die. Françoise was puzzled. If she had been in his condition, she felt, she would have longed to die. But once again he pulled through, nursed by Françoise in the little cottage which had originally seemed so charming but which was so primitive that she resolved boldly to make a complete break with the past. The house at Herne Hill and the cottage at Wivelsfield Green must both be abandoned. In their place she found a small house at Hintlesham in Havelock's beloved East Anglia. Cherry Ground was in the parish of Washbrook, where one of Havelock's ancestors had been vicar three hundred years before. It stood in two acres of ground, mostly orchard, and as soon as Havelock saw it, he fell in love with it. It was where he wanted to die. He knew he would never leave this place alive and he stood with Françoise, his hand upon her shoulder for support, looking up into the September sky watching stars shoot and burn to nothing, wondering if by that time next year he too would be burnt to nothing. "Death, in his casual tentative indifferent way," he had written sixteen years before, "just gave me a torturing prick with his scythe as he passed by, leaving me alive but bleeding. Ever since I lie on my back invalid, for the first time in my active life, and whether he is likely to come again soon there is none to tell me.

"Yet, I find, I remain serene, even continuously cheerful. For some years past I have accommodated my arrangements to Death and guided my activities accordingly, even though I may not yet have completed everything I had planned as the minimum—for I am content the maximum should go—of my Day's Work—my Day's Play—in the world. Without rest yet without haste—it is the law of my nature which I have no intention of changing now. My faith has carried me through so far and will accompany me to the end. Death is the final Master and Lord. But Death must await my good pleasure. I command Death because I have no fear of Death, but only love."

There was little more of the Day's Work or Play. He had discovered what was wrong with his throat, though the doctors still thought he was a *malade imaginaire.* He had developed a condition far commoner in the very young than the very old, a pouch in the oesophagus the mouth of which was turned upwards. Food gathered in this pouch and obstructed the passage to the stomach.[1] But having discovered what was wrong, neither he nor any doctor could do anything about it.

At Cherry Ground Havelock prepared himself serenely to meet Death. He went out and worked in his sun-hut in the garden, adding little bits to the autobiography which he considered his masterpiece and which became a bit worse with each addition he made. He became more and more withdrawn from the world outside.

But Françoise worried about the situation in Europe. She foresaw the slaughter of 1914–18 being repeated for different slogans but with the same carnage, the same proliferation of evil. In Françoise there burned twin flames, the love of love and the hatred of war. She took herself off and wrote a denunciation of war at any price. Then she brought it to Havelock and showed it to him.

As he read it, it must have reminded him of the lecture which that young woman to whom his wife owed thirty pounds had enclosed in her first letter to him.

[1] He thought this dated back to his childhood and was responsible for his adolescent stomach-pains. But Françoise seems right to date it from a fall which he had had in Cadgwith in 1928. If he had been examined then, the later trouble might have been avoided. But it would have been out of character; he lived and died by accepting his physical limitations.

"I see," he said.

"You don't see," she said. "You must put your name to this."

He looked at it again. He had never been a pacifist, though he had always hated wars. "I didn't write it," he said. "You must publish it under your own name."

"Under my name no one will print it," she answered. "Who am I? My name is nothing. You must give it your name, if you love me."

He had asked Françoise if he could give her his name and she had refused, because she did not know whether Cyon was still alive. He had given her nothing of his own in all these years. He could give her his name. He took the article and signed it. It could do no harm, and even if it did little good, it would make his beloved Françoise happy.

On the strength of the name she sold the article to the *News Chronicle* and it was later reprinted in *Peace News*.

The obstruction in the oesophagus grew worse. He could no longer swallow egg and milk. He was reduced to things like junkets and because there are few things like junkets, he grew weaker every day.

Yet he persisted in independence. He was not supposed to walk without someone to help him. But one day he struggled from his study towards his sun-hut. On the way there he fell and could not rise till the gardener picked him up.

He grew so thin that Françoise cursed herself for having put a mirror in the bathroom. Havelock stood in front of it mocking the emaciated stranger who mocked back at him.

He was so weak by the end of February 1939 that he ran a slight fever all day. He had stopped working. He spent his time either in bed or sitting in the armchair by his bedroom window. He seemed to Françoise already to have passed out of her life. What he was looking at was not the garden, but gardens beyond the garden. "As, absorbed in my own occupation, my eye chanced to sweep across my window just now, it caught in passing the sensation of a small tree opposite, on the upper reflecting surface of whose leaves a pale London sun was shining, and that sensation appeared to mental perception as it were the lovely image of a pear tree in blossom, such as had joyously flashed on me a few months ago at Saffron Walden. At once and with no sense of transition that perception passed on into the thought: Why do we say that the dead die?"[1]

He was in almost continuous pain from his throat. He could keep down little except milk, into which Françoise ground vitamin tablets in the hope that these might fortify him. But his spirit had passed beyond the world of pain; it was serene, at rest.

In so far as he thought of anything, it was how he could make his death valuable, as his life had been. He had taken what had been given him, weakness as well as strength, and moulded it as a modeller his clay. He knew that he was dying slowly in a way that was stripped of dignity. "It is essential to the human dignity of a truly civilised society," he thought, "that it should hold in its hands not only the Key of Birth but the Key of Death." He did not believe that God took a life when He judged the soul ready to depart. Soul and body and sentience were resolved into the elements and became new life entering into the leaves of grass and the flesh of animals cropping it and the bodies of carnivores. Medical science, dedicated superstitiously to the perpetuation of life at all costs, instead of assuaging pain, perpetuated useless agony. Not because he was afraid of bearing pain, but because he believed that man should hold the Key of Death, he decided to make his own end. It should be a blow struck for euthanasia.

He told Françoise of his decision at Easter and asked her to help him. She was not surprised. She had expected and dreaded this because she knew his views on euthanasia. She was filled with fear, because though she believed in mercy-killing she did not think he could ask her to commit what was legally murder. Though she and Havelock regarded themselves as married, she was legally another man's wife. She could visualise the headlines in the yellow press. OCTOGENARIAN SEXOLOGIST MURDERED. MISTRESS PLEADS MERCY-KILLING. She thought of François and Paul, the smirch on their lives.

Yet she meant what she had said so many years ago. She would

[1] *Impressions and Comments*, 25 July 1922.

take only what he offered, it was the very flower of love. "I will do what you want," she said, "if you will let me go too."

Havelock would hear nothing of this. Françoise was young. Her time had not come. There was still work for her to do. She had duties to others. In the dream-world to which he had retired he did not seem to realise that what he asked of her might curtail her usefulness as effectively as the suicide she proposed. She wondered whether his brain was going; yet at the very moment that this suspicion came to her, she found herself agreeing to what he wanted; she would kill him but not herself.

The assurance made him happy and Françoise promised to see a friend who might help; Françoise foresaw that it would be she and not Havelock who would be called on to be the martyr of the fight for death-control. What Havelock was asking from her was far more harrowing than suicide, and something which she feared it might not be possible to perform successfully. Would Havelock who could not even swallow eggs in milk be able to keep down a sufficient quantity of oral poison to kill him? And how, when neither of them had ever used a hypodermic syringe, could they administer an intravenous injection?

Her mind could find no solution to these problems, but her body found one. She was laid low with acute neuritis.

But by May she had recovered. She hoped that in the meantime Havelock had been able to see what he was demanding from her point of view. But Françoise's collapse had only strengthened his determination. He loathed the body that made him a burden on Françoise, and the sooner they made an end the better.

Françoise called in a new doctor, hoping that he would be prepared to kill Havelock. But the new doctor did not take any interest in this idea. He was far more interested in Havelock's theory of the oesophageal pouch. Examination by X-ray confirmed the diagnosis and Françoise called in a throat specialist. It was possible to operate, but the specialist said that if he were Dr Ellis, he would never consent to it. It involved by-passing the oesophagus and feeding direct to the stomach. It might prolong life, but could not cure him.

So she was back with the slowly dying man, who begged her to make an end. If one of his friends produced a poison, she would be driven to use it.

At the end of June the doctor told Françoise she would have to take a holiday. In his opinion Ellis would last into the winter and the strain on her health might be too great unless she had a thorough rest for a fortnight. He arranged that Edith and Laura, Havelock's two sisters, should come to Cherry Ground to look after him, and the district nurse should call every day.

Havelock urged her to go. He at last had a promise of help from a friend. The material had not yet arrived. But he wanted to say good-bye to Edith and Laura, and by the time she returned everything would be ready.

So it had come at last.

Françoise agreed to go away to Matlock in the Derbyshire peak where fifty-five years ago Olive had gone to be "close to God." She had some qualms about leaving Havelock to his sisters. Edith was sixty-eight and Laura seventy-two, but with the help of the district nurse they could not go far wong. She gave Edith strict instructions about grinding up the pills, which were at the right hand of a drawer in his chest, and adding them to his milk.

For a week and five days she walked the hills of Matlock wrestling with the problem Havelock had posed her. In human terms it appeared insoluble. She did not believe that God intended the incurable to linger on in suffering, when they wanted to die. If she helped Havelock out of life, it would be an act of love and so good in the eyes of God. Yet she would be committing murder and she did not know whether Havelock perceived what the act might involve her in. He had seemed so abstracted as he sat by his bedroom window that it was possible he did not think of her but of other things.

The problem could not be solved by thought; it demanded an act of faith and love. She reflected how often through obeying the dictate of love she had invited disaster, and how disaster was miraculously averted, because she had acted in good faith. She had usually realised the peril in which she had been only after it was over. This time it was apparent beforehand. On the last day but one of her holiday she saw that this made no difference. If Havelock wanted her to kill him, she would do so whatever the consequences. It was the final act of love and no harm would come of it. Perhaps what was necessary was a *cause célèbre* which would change the law to allow mercy killing. She did not know what the outcome would be, but her difficulty was resolved.

She went back to her hotel, sent a telegram to Cherry Ground to say that she would spend the night at a certain hotel in London and return in the late afternoon of Saturday after doing some shopping. Then she caught a train to London.

At breakfast next morning, 8 July 1939, she was called to the telephone. One of the sisters—Françoise could not tell which, as she was growing rather deaf—said that Havelock was asking for her urgently and she must come at once.

She arrived at Cherry Ground at eleven and went straight up to Havelock's bedroom, followed by the two sisters. Havelock was lying in bed. The change in his condition over the past fortnight shocked Françoise. She could see by his face that he was dying.

He smiled and in a weak voice he said, "I took the pills every day."

"Yes," said Edith proudly. "He was very good. Look what a lot he has taken." She went to the chest and took out of the drawer not the box of vitamin tablets but a bottle of proprietary pills which Françoise had forgotten was there. Françoise had used these on two previous occasions when Havelock had been suffering from oedema in his legs. On each occasion one pill a day for two days had been enough to reduce the swelling and she had been careful to give no more because Havelock suffered from low blood pressure, and she had found from personal experience that the pills gave her a "sinking feeling" in her heart.

For two weeks instead of vitamin tablets Edith had been plying Havelock, who was suffering from dehydration, with pills to reduce oedema. In that Françoise found the explanation of Havelock's deterioration.

But her first instinct was merely to clear the room of the sisters.

The collective ages of the three Ellises was two hundred and twenty years. They made her feel like a babe in arms and she was relieved when Havelock told Laura and Edith to leave.

When they had gone, she found that she could not hear what Havelock was saying. His voice was so weak and anxiety increased her natural deafness. She brought him a writing pad and a pencil and he wrote that he had been sent the stuff he had asked for. She told him that she would do what he wanted.

"When?" he wrote.

She said that they must wait until his sisters had left. It seemed madness to kill him when he was so obviously dying quickly.

When would they go? he asked. Would they go to-morrow?

To-morrow was a Sunday. It might be awkward for them to travel on a Sunday. Havelock's face shone with the radiance of a man on the edge of death and unafraid. But he was determined to turn the Key of Death himself, to make his ending significant. "Would Françoise see when they were going?"

She found Laura and Edith in their bedroom. She asked them if they thought Havelock was dying and they said "No." One of them had been a nurse and should have known the signs of approaching death. Françoise wondered if she was cheating herself into thinking he was worse than he was. She was glad to hear they did not want to leave until Monday.

She went back to Havelock and sat with him through the day. Sometimes he used the pad. He wrote, "I liked the nurse much from the first, very prompt and business-like and not a bit prudish." Dying, he disliked the prudish as much as ever. Most of the time he was silent, resting his hand on hers and occasionally pressing it. She watched his face and eyes. He was happy and unafraid. At nine o'clock in the evening he had what she thought was a heart attack.

She telephoned the doctor. "Dr Ellis is dying," she said. "I want you to come round and give him an injection." She was speaking under deep emotion and the doctor thought she had panicked. He told her he had given Dr Ellis an injection that morning and he would give him another early next day.

"I tell you Dr Ellis is dying," she said, not certain whether the injection she wanted for Havelock was one to revive him or put him out of his pain.

"If you're still worried later," said the doctor, "give me a ring."

She told the sisters that she was sure Havelock was dying and asked if they wanted to say good-bye. They went in and said a few words to Havelock and then they went out into the corridor. "Am I not right?" Françoise asked.

One of the sisters took her on one side. "My sister has never seen anyone die," she said. The sisters went back to their bedroom and Françoise returned to Havelock. At about eleven he had what she thought was a second heart attack, but he wouldn't let her call the doctor. "He can do no more for me," he said. He was in less pain and there was little change in his breathing. It was as if his heart faltered and then went on.

"You are so tired," he said, "and I feel better. You go to bed. Perhaps I may sleep a little."

She wanted to stay, but he said the light bothered him. She switched off the light and went downstairs to boil a kettle for hot water with which to wash.

When she came up ten minutes later, she saw from the line of light under his door that he had turned on his lamp again. She went in, knowing that he could not be asleep.

She was right. He was lying back on his pillow dead.

What had happened in this final struggle for the Key of Death? Françoise had a sense of the "uncanny" at first. When she had been at Matlock, she had prayed in her heart that the cup would pass from her; that having resolved to kill the man she loved, she would not have to do so when the time came. The death of Havelock appeared like a direct answer to this prayer.

But then she reflected on Edith's mistake with the pills and she decided that the deterioration of his condition was due to the discontinuing of the vitamin tablets and the administration of pills which to a person already suffering from low blood pressure might be fatal. It was just another of those natural miracles which Havelock had experienced throughout his life.

I have consulted chemists about the action these pills might have had in such a case and they assure me that the dosage which is in homeopathic quantities would be unlikely to have any effect on the heart taken at the rate of two a day over a fortnight. Even a whole bottle taken at one go would probably have little effect.

This however would be true only if the formula of the pills in 1939 (when it was unnecessary to state the formulae of medicines) was the same as it is to-day.

Havelock's death, therefore, might be merely the answer to Françoise's prayer, or it might be merely the consequence of taking the wrong pills. It might also be both. God does not disdain His natural means; nor does He prove to the intellect that He answers prayers. Prayer is an act of faith, and the acknowledgment that the prayer is answered a further act of faith.

This is a matter on which the reader must make his own judgment; as also on whether or not Havelock was successful in his determination to make his death significant. He wanted to prove that it was essential to the human dignity that it should hold in its hands the Key of Death. But he proved that even when he held the Key of Death in his hands, it was turned in the lock for him without any loss of dignity.

When Edith died, Havelock received a letter to be read only after her death, which restored the love and faith which had been torn and tattered during the years of decline.

Still dazed by the manner of his death, Françoise found a similar letter from Havelock:

My darling Naiad,

This is the last letter you will ever receive from me, so I want to say over again—though I have said it so often before—with what deep love in my heart I shall leave you. I want to say again, too, that you must not feel I am dead. Those whom we love go on living in our hearts as long as we live. I like to feel I shall still be alive in your heart and not really dead until you die, which I hope will not be just yet. Do not think me selfish if I want you still to live. There are things to be done for me that no one can do as well as you.

When I first met you I thought my life was over. In one sense perhaps it was. But the happiest years of my life have been with you. I have never dreamed such happiness possible for me. These years still seem a miracle. And even troubles in our life still left love untouched. That love has never been disturbed for one moment. The chief love of my life was naturally for Edith, because its most active period was passed by her side. . . . But my life with her was often stormy, and our love was mixed with pain and trouble, even though that may have made it deeper. It could not clash with my love for you with whom I have known such heavenly oy and peace.

My everlasting love to my darling Naiad,

Faun.

Havelock Ellis anticipated no survival after his death except in the hearts of those who loved him. This was not because he disliked the idea of life after death, but because he found it scientifically inconceivable. On discovering that his soul could exist apart from his body, his first impulse would have been to communicate this delightful discovery to Françoise if that were possible.

The Saturday after he died, Françoise was sitting in Havelock's study, when he came in, absorbed as usual in his inner world. He looked along the shelves at his books, and then went out through the French windows, walking across the grass towards his sun-hut until he was hidden by the trees.

It was not the last time that Françoise saw him.

List of Books by Havelock Ellis

This list is confined to original works by Ellis published in book form. A very complete bibliography of his writings up to the year 1928, including periodical contributions, introductions, prefaces and translations, will be found in *Havelock Ellis, Philosopher of Love*, by Houston Peterson (London, George Allen & Unwin, Ltd., 1928).

Sexual Inversion, by Havelock Ellis and J. A. Symonds. London: Wilson Macmillan, 1897. (Withdrawn before publication at the request of Symonds' executors. A German translation of this work by Hans Kurella, under the title *Das konträre Geschlechtsgefühl*, was published at Leipzig, George H. Wigands Verlag, in 1896.)

Sexual Inversion, by Havelock Ellis. (*Studies in the Psychology of Sex*, Vol. I.) Watford: The University Press, 1897. (Reprinted from the above, omitting Symonds's contributions and allusions to Symonds in the preface.) 2nd edition, revised. Philadelphia: F. A. Davis Co., 1901. (Renumbered as *Studies in the Psychology of Sex*, Vol. II). 3rd edition, revised and enlarged, 1915.

The Evolution of Modesty, The Phenomena of Sexual Periodicity, Auto-Erotism. (*Studies in the Psychology of Sex*, Vol. II) Leipzig: The University Press, Limited, 1899. (Despite the imprint this book was not printed in Leipzig, but in England.) 2nd edition, revised and renumbered as Studies in the Psychology of Sex, Vol. I. Philadelphia: F. A. Davis Co., 1900. 3rd edition, 1910.

The Analysis of the Sexual Impulse, Love and Pain, The Sexual Impulse in Women. (*Studies in the Psychology of Sex*, Vol. III.) Philadelphia; F. A. Davis Co. 1903. 2nd edition, revised and enlarged, 1913.

Sexual Selection in Man. I. Touch. II. Smell. III. Hearing. IV. Vision. (*Studies in the Psychology of Sex*, Vol. IV.) Philadelphia: F. A. Davis Co., 1905.

Erotic Symbolism, The Mechanism of Detumescence, The Psychic State in Pregnancy. (*Studies in the Psychology of Sex*, Vol. V.) Philadelphia: F. A. Davis Co., 1906.

Sex in Relation to Society. (*Studies in the Psychology of Sex*, Vol. VI.) Philadelphia: F. A. Davis Co., 1910. Revised and abridged edition, London: Heinemann, 1937.

Eonism and other Supplementary Studies. (*Studies in the Psychology of Sex*, Vol. VII.) Philadelphia: F. A. Davis Co., 1928.

Psychology of Sex: The Biology of Sex—The Sexual Impulse in Youth—Sexual Deviation—The Erotic Symbolisms—Homosexuality—The Art of Love. A Manual for Students. London: William Heinemann (Medical Books) Ltd, 1933.

Studies in the Psychology of Sex. 4 Vols. New York: Random House, 1936. (Rearranged, and with a new foreword.)

The New Spirit. London: George Bell, 1890. 2nd edition, 1891; 3rd edition, 1892 (W. Scott); 4th edition, 1926 (Constable).

The Criminal. London: Walter Scott, 1890. 2nd edition, 1895; 3rd edition, revised and enlarged, 1900; 4th edition, 1910.

The Nationalisation of Health. London: Fisher Unwin, 1892.

Man and Woman: A Study of Human Secondary Sexual Characters. London: Walter Scott, 1894. 4th edition, revised, 1904; 5th edition, revised, 1914; 6th edition, 1926 (Black); 7th edition, 1929 (Boston, Houghton Mifflin); 8th edition, 1934 (Heinemann).

Affirmations. London: Walter Scott, 1898. 2nd edition, 1915 (Constable); 3rd edition, 1926 (Constable).

A Note on the Bedborough Trial. The University Press, Watford, London, 1898. (A privately printed pamphlet of 23 pages.)

The Nineteenth Century: A Dialogue in Utopia. London; Grant Richards, 1900.

A Study of British Genius. London: Hurst & Blackett, 1904. 2nd edition, revised and enlarged, 1927 (Constable).

The Soul of Spain. London: Constable, 1908. New edition, 1937 (with a new preface on the Spanish Civil War).

The World of Dreams. London: Constable, 1911.

The Problem of Race Degeneration. London: Cassell, 1911.

The Task of Social Hygiene. London: Constable, 1912. New edition, 1927.

Impressions and Comments. First Series. London: Constable, 1914.

Essays in War-time. London: Constable, 1916.

The Erotic Rights of Women, and The Objects of Marriage. Two Essays. London: British Society for the Study of Sex Psychology, Publication No. 5, 1918.

The Philosophy of Conflict and Other Fssays in War Time. 2nd series. London: Constable, 1919.

Impressions and Comments. Second Series 1914–1920. London: Constable, 1921.

The Play-Function of Sex. London: British Society for the Study of Sex Psychology, Publication No. 9, 1921.

Kanga Creek: An Australian Idyll. Waltham St Lawrence: Golden Cockerel Press, 1922. New editions, New York, Black Hawk Press, 1935; The Oriole Press, Berkeley Heights, N.J., 1938.

Little Essays of Love and Virtue. London: Black, 1922.

The Dance of Life. London: Constable, 1923. New edition, New York, Modern Library, 1929.

Impressions and Comments. Third (and Final) Series, 1920–23. London: Constable, 1924.

Sonnets, with Folk Songs from the Spanish. Waltham St Lawrence: Golden Cockerel Press, 1925.

The Art of Life: Gleanings from the Works of Havelock Ellis. Collected by Mrs S. Herbert. (Constable's Miscellany.) London: Constable, 1929.

Marriage To-day and To-morrow. San Francisco: Westgate Press, 1929.

Fountain of Life: Being the Impressions and Comments of Havelock Ellis. Boston: Houghton Mifflin, 1930. (The 3 series in 1, with a new preface.)

The Colour-Sense in Literature. London: Ulysses Book Shop, 1931.

Concerning Jude the Obscure. London: Ulysses Book Shop, 1931.

The Revaluation of Obscenity. Paris, The Hours Press, 1931.

More Essays of Love and Virtue. London: Constable, 1931.

Song of Songs: A drama by Ernest Renan. Translated by Havelock Ellis. The Oriole Press, Berkeley Heights, N.J., 1932. Also edition by City of Birmingham School of Painting College of Arts and Crafts, 1937.

Views and Reviews: A Selection of Uncollected Articles 1884–1932. 1st and 2nd series. 2 Vols. London: Desmond Harmsworth, 1932.

George Chapman: With Illustrative Passages. London: Nonesuch Press, 1934.

My Confessional: Questions of Our Day. London: John Lane, 1934.

From Rousseau to Proust. London: Constable, 1936.

Questions of Our Day. London: John Lane, 1936.

Selected Essays (Everyman's Library.) London: Dent, 1936.

On Life and Sex: Essays of Love and Virtue. 2 Vols. in one. Garden City, Long Island, N.Y., Garden City Publishing Co., 1937. New and enlarged edition (containing three additional essays), London, Heinemann, 1945, N.Y., New American Library, 1951.

Poems. Selected by John Gawsworth. London: Richards Press, 1937.

Morals, Manners and Men. (Thinker's Library.) London: Watts, 1939.

My Life. London: Heinemann, 1940.

The Genius of Europe. London, Williams & Norgate, 1950.

From Marlowe to Shaw. London, Williams & Norgate, 1950.

Sex and Marriage. London, Ernest Benn, and N.Y., Random House, 1951.

Books about Havelock Ellis

Havelock Ellis, A Biographical and Critical Survey, by Isaac Goldberg, (Constable & Co., 1926), containing also a chapter on the writings of Mrs Havelock Ellis, and an Ellis Miscellany of early poems, poetic translations and notes made during the Australian period.

Havelock Ellis, Philosopher of Love, by Houston Peterson (London, George Allen & Unwin, 1928).

Essays by Mrs Havelock Ellis (Free Spirit Press, N.J., 1924) contains an essay "Havelock Ellis".

Fragments of an analysis with Freud, Joseph Wortis, M.D. (N.Y., Simon & Shuster, 1954). Dr Wortis was given a grant to study homosexuality, by a foundation of which Ellis was an advisory member. He elected to have a short training analysis under Freud, and his account of this shows the private views of Ellis on Freud and Freud on Ellis.

Friendship's Odyssey by Françoise Delisle [Françoise Lafitte Cyon] (Heinemann, 1946). This autobiography is really two volumes in one. The first is the story of Madame Cyon's life up to the time that she met Ellis; the second is a continuation of Ellis's life from the death of Edith Ellis in 1916 to Ellis's own death in 1939. It was written at Ellis's request and is essential as a supplement to Havelock Ellis's *My Life*.

INDEX

"Abnormal in Eugenics, The," 196
Adam's Breed, 263
Adult, 162–4, 166–7
Affirmations, 112, 117, 180, 232, 259
Agnes (H.E.'s first love), 41–3, 46, 47, 54, 248
Agnes, Sister, 25
Allen, Grant, 164
Amy, *see* Smith, Amy Barker
Anatomy of Melancholy, The, 114
Ancoats, 139
Apothecaries, Society of, 106
Apuleius, 116
Arnold, Matthew, 70
Ashford, Mr, 64–6
Asquith, H. H., 160
At Scotland Yard, 171
Aubrey, John, 108
Australian journal, H.E.'s, 47–9, 52–63, 92–3
Aveling, Dr Edward, 94
Aveling, Eleanor Marx, 94, 107
Avory, Horace, 164–6

Bancroft, Mary Laetitia (later Mrs Lees), 122–3
Barwick Brothers, 65–6
Baudelaire, Charles, 151
Bax, Belfort, 81, 164
Bax, Clifford, 14
Bechstein Hall, 222
Bedborough, George, 162–7, 174
Bedborough Trial, 163–8, 173; *see also*, *Note on the Bedborough Trial, A*
Bertillon, Dr, 118
Bessie, Françoise Delisle's maid, 236, 247, 262, 271–2
Bethlem Hospital, 126, 212, 215–18
Bevill, Frederick, 50, 52, 53, 59
"Bladder as a Dynamometer, The," 39
Birkett, Norman, 265
Bloch, Iwan, 145, 154
Bonar, Dr, 119
Booley, Mrs, 78
Bowdlerisation, 199 n.
Brantôme, Pierre de, 68
British Museum, 183, 222
Brooke, Evelyn, 130
Brooke, Honor, 125
Brooke, Rev. Stopford, 119, 125, 193, 208
Brooke, Sybil, 130
Brown, Horatio, 156, 160–1
Brücke, 53
Buchanan-Gould, Vera, 103 n., 104
Burns, John, 81, 116
Burton, Robert, 114

Camelot Classics, 106, 134
Carbis, 126, 129, 134, 136, 176–81, 185, 210–4, 220
Carlyle, Thomas, 43
Carpenter, Dr Alfred, 17
Carpenter, Edward, 87, 93, 95, 97, 98, 100, 102, 122, 132, 135, 138, 139, 146, 147, 152–3, 156, 157, 164, 174, 189, 214, 223, 239
Catholic Church, 158
Chapman, Berta, 58, 59, 60
Chapman, May, 57, 58–60, 93
Chapman, Mr, 57, 59, 248
Charcot, 118
Chastelain, de, 31, 41, 43
Cherry Ground, 272–82
Chicago, 191, 195, 199
Christ, Jesus, 112
Chubb, Percival, 83–4, 86–7, 119
Claire, Edith's "friend," 136–9, 142, 146–7, 175, 229
Cobb, Mrs, 97
Cobbledick, 122
Coleridge, Samuel Taylor, 108
Colour-blindness, 147, 148–51
Coloured hearing, 148–51
Collis, J. S., 14
Comstock Act, 197

Comstock, Anthony, 198
Congreve, William, 108
Contemporary Science Series, 110, 146
Corelli, Marie, 223
Cort Theatre, 195
Corthorn, Dr Alice, 189 n.
Court Theatre, 181
Craik, Mrs, 27
Crane, Walter, 164
Criminal, The, 28, 110–1, 118, 157
Cronwright, S. C., 101–4
Croydon, 17
Cyclothymic or manic depression, 125, 133, 208–18

Daily Chronicle, 168
Dames Galantes, 68
Dance of Life, The, 68, 117, 180, 232, 259–60
Daniel Deronda, 69
Darwin, Charles, 48
Dawson, Oswald, 166
Daudet, Alphonse, 141
Davidson, Thomas, 84–6, 114
De Matrimonio, 158
Democracy in the Kitchen, 133
Diabetes, 189, 192
Dickens, Charles, 108
"Diderot," 45, 107, 110, 111
Dogmen of Dafur, 115
Dolcino, Fra, 112
Donkin, Dr, 96, 104
Dostoievski, 111
Douglas, James, 264
Dover Mansions, 182, 188, 197, 206, 218, 219, 220, 221, 236, 242, 248, 260
Doyle, Father, 25
Drake, Mrs, 125
Drysdale, Dr and Mrs C. V., 197
Drysdale, George, 46, 48

Eliot, George, 69
Ellis, Capt. (H.E.'s father), 17–9, 30, 41, 45–7, 49, 50, 66
Ellis, Mrs E. P. (H.E.'s mother), 17–22, 24, 30, 39, 41, 42, 45–7, 98–100, 248
Ellis, Edith (H.E.'s sister), 277, 279–80
Ellis, Mrs Havelock (Edith Mary Oldham Lees), 33, 58, 119 *et passim*
Ellis, Laura, 277, 279–80
Ellis, Louie, 19, 21, 23, 47, 77, 121, 129, 134, 248
Empress, s.s., 25, 27
Endell Street Hospital 89, 92
English Literature, 62
Eonism and other Supplementary Studies, 267
Erck, Rev. John, 34–6, 45, 46, 48, 56, 70
Euthanasia, 14, 271, 272, 275–82
Everyman's Library, 134
Evolution of Sex, 110
Evolution of Sexual Modesty, 241
Exchange and Mart, 32

Faber, Beryl (Mrs Cosmo Hamilton), 182
Fabian Society, 87
Fay ce que vouldras, 100–1, 248, 253
Fellowship of the New Life, 86–7, 89, 119, 133, 196
Fellowship House, 130
Fielding, Henry, 108
Flaubert, 118
Florentine Nights, 106
Fontlands, 51, 52, 66
Ford, John, 107
Fort School, Sydney, 63
Foulger, John C., 80–3
French and German College, 30–1, 41
Free Press Defence Committee, 164, 167
Freud, Sigmund, 24, 38, 53, 55, 119, 147, 173–4, 238, 241
Friendship's Odyssey, 235, 243, 255, 256
From Man to Man, 103 n.
From Rousseau to Proust, 267–8

Gau (alias Zaar) Julius, 91, 103 n.
Gawsworth, John, 158 n.
Geddes, Prof. Patrick, 110
Girling, Bessie, 236, 247, 262, 271–2
Girton House, 125, 193
Gladstone, W. E., 96
Goethe, 96, 57, 111, 256
Goldberg, Isaac, 260
Goncourt, brothers, 111
Goongerwarrie, 53, 66, 67
Grafton Grammar School, 56–60, 61, 66, 67, 93

Greenslet, Ferris, 231
Grigsby, Miss Emily, 187–8
Grundy, 107, 108, 109, 266

Haddon, Caroline, 77, 78–81, 89, 92, 97, 127
Haldane, J. B. S., 267
Hall, Radclyffe, 263–6
Hamilton, Dr, 214–8
Hardy, Thomas, 44, 89
"Hardy, The Novels of Thomas," 107
Harman, Lilian, 162–4
Haslemere, 135, 141–2
Havelock Ellis, a Biographical and Critical Essay, 260
Havelock Ellis: Philosopher of Love, 167
Havelock, Gen. Sir Henry, 18
Hayle Convent Nursing Home, 214–8
Heine, 106, 111
Herne Hill, 262, 271, 272
Hinton, Howard, 78, 81, 97, 100
Hinton, James, 70–3, 78–81, 82, 84, 85, 89, 100, 126, 189, 288, 250, 253, 254
Hinton, Mrs James, 78, 80, 82, 89, 126, 223
Hinton, Margaret, 126, 212
Holmes, Oliver Wendell, 70
Hopkins, Ellice, 75, 77
Horder, Lord, 106
Hotel d'Oxford et Cambridge, 100, 130, 194
Huysmans, J. K., 111, 119, 151
Hyndman, H. M., 81, 164
Hypnotism, 157

Ibsen, Henrik, 111
Imitation of Christ, 213–4, 259
Impressions and Comments, 231–4, 259; First Series, 180, 226; Second Series, 193, 198, 246, 269; Third Series, 269
Inayat Khan, 222
Indian Review, 107
Inge, Dean, 153
"Integrity of Havelock Ellis, The", 153
Iron, Ralph, *see* Schreiner, Olive

James Hinton: a Sketch, 207, 231
Jenoure, Aida, 124
Johnston, Miss (H.E.'s music teacher), 46, 69, 77
Jones, Agnes, 78, 80, 92, 119–21, 129
Jonson, Ben, 108
Joubert, 70
Journal of Medical Science, 157
Joynson-Hicks, Sir William (Viscount Brentford), 264–6
Junction Creek, 63–76

Kanga Creek: an Australian Idyll, 260
Keats, John, 42
Keisker, Dr Laura, 203
Kennerley, Mitchell, 194–5, 206–7
Kingsley, Charles, 43
Kinsey standards, 138, 140
Kit's Woman, 143, 160, 188, 223, 237
Krafft-Ebing, 157
Kurella, Dr Hans, 157, 165
Kyllman, Otto, 231

Lamb, Charles, 107–8
Lamorna Cove, 119, 129, 132, 135, 192
Lancet, 168, 171
Landor, Walter Savage, 106
La Terre, 109, 110
Law-Breaker, The, 80, 106
Lawrence, D. H., 265–6
Lectures on Art, 62
Lecture Tours (Edith's) in U.S.A., First, 190–2; Second, 193–204; Third (Projected), 209–10
Lees, Edith, *see* Mrs Havelock Ellis
Lees, Samuel Oldham, 122–4
Legitimation League, 162–3
Legnani, Signorina, 134
Leipzig University Press, 169
Lily, 176–9, 189, 190, 195, 229
Life and Letters of James Hinton, The, 75, 78
Letters of Olive Schreiner, The, 101–4
Life of Olive Schreiner, The, 101–4
Life in Nature, 71, 75
Little Essays of Love and Virtue, 154, 244–5, 267
Little Theatre, Chicago, 223
Liverpool, 204–6
Lombroso, Cesare, 110
Lover's Calendar, The, 178–9
Love's Coming of Age, 157

"Loves of To-morrow, The," 196
Lusitania, s.s., 205
Luther, Martin, 111
Lyceum Club, 185–6, 190, 211, 217

Mackay, Angus, 43–5, 46, 48, 56, 81
Maclean, Dr, 190
Madame Bovary, 107
Mallarmé, 119, 151
Man and Woman, 145, 157
Man of Genius, The, 110
Manceine, Marie de, 110
Marlowe, Christopher, 107, 109, 138
Marshall, F. H., 145
Marx, Eleanor, *see* Aveling, Eleanor Marx
"Masculinism and Feminism," 192, 196
Masefield, John, 186
Massingham, H. W., 168
Masterman Ready, 26
Maurice, F. D., 43
Mediterranean Race, 110
Melville, Chief Inspector, 163
Melville, Herman, 111
"Mental Havoc Wrought by the War, The," 235
Mermaid Series, 107–10, 159
Merton Old Church, 30–1
Michelangelo, 62, 138
Middleton, Thomas, 107
Millie (Edith's servant), 211–12
Minneapolis, s.s., 190
Minnetonka, 193
Mill, John Stewart, 62
Modern Thought, 80–1
Moore, George, 96, 164
More Essays of Love and Virtue, 154, 267
Morley, John, 62
Morocco, 175
Morris, Alfred, 51–3, 56, 59, 62
My Confessional, 267
My Cornish Neighbours, 223
My Life, 20, 23, 25, 28, 35, 36–8, 40, 42, 44, 45, 48, 52, 81, 84, 88, 127, 131, 135, 136, 137, 157, 168, 172, 173, 190, 198, 200, 203, 227–30, 257, 271

Nakedness, 95
Nana, 110, 111
Nationalisation of Health, 180
Natural Law, an Essay on Ethics, 73–4
Neo-Malthusian Society, 197
New Spirit, The, 111–2, 118, 120, 180, 226, 232, 259
New York, 190, 192, 194–5, 197
News Chronicle, 274
Nietzsche, 223
Nineteenth Century, The: A Dialogue in Utopia, 180
Noble Life, A, 27
Note on the Bedborough Trial, A, 168, 169
Not Without Honour, 103 n.
Novitiate for Marriage, A, 133

Olive, Pierre d', 112
Open Letter to Biographers, An, 7, 17, 29, 41, 52, 77, 106, 118, 145, 180
Ouida, 58
"Outcome of Legitimation, The," 166

Paddington Registry Office, 129
Parme, Jean de, 112
Pascal, 201
Pearson, Prof. Karl, 97–8, 102, 104, 115
Pease, Edward, 86
Peer Gynt, 99
Penta, Dr Pasquale, 165
Perrycoste, F. H., 159, 164
Peterson, Houston, 167
Philadelphia, s.s., 205
Pillars of Society and Other Plays, 106
Piping Hot!, 110
Platt, Minnie, 53–4, 56, 248
Plowman, Max, 113
Podmore, Frank, 87, 164
Poore, Prof., 160–1
Poplars, The (private school attended by H.E.), 43–5, 48
Porter, Henry, 107
Precious Stones of the Bible, The, 82–3, 152
Priscilla (Edith's maid), 184–5
Problem of Race-Degeneration, The, 180
Progressive Association, 82–3, 89, 90
Psychic experiences (Havelock), 30, (Edith), 178–9, (Françoise), 282
Psychoanalysis in relation to Sex, 241
Psychopathia Sexualis, 186

Questions of the Day, 267

Rabelais, 46
Ray, Man, 254
Renan, Ernest, 48
Rhys, Ernest, 106, 134
Robertson, J. M., 159
Rodin, Auguste, 119
Roland, Dr Sinclair, *see* Villiers, Dr Roland, de
Rousseau, Jean Jacques, 35, 62, 111, 267–8
Ruskin, John, 43, 62
Russell, Bertrand, 267
Russell, Hon. Rollo, 135, 141

St Francis of Assisi, 112–13
St Mary's Terrace, Paddington, 121, 130, 133
St Paul, 79
St Paul's Cathedral, 111–12
St Thomas à Kempis, 213–14
St Thomas's Hospital, 82, 106, 141
Salpêtrière, 118
Sanchez, 158
Sanger, Margaret, 154, 196–210, 230, 235, 248, 253, 261
Sanger, Margaret, An Autobiography, 154 n., 198 n.
Sappho, 138, 153
Sayer, Dr Ettie, 218, 220
Schjelderup, 150
Schreiner, Ellie, 93
Schreiner, 58, Olive, 88–105, 121, 126, 127–8, 135, 189, 198, 248, 266
Scotland Yard, 162, 167
Seaweed, see Kit's Woman
Selincourt, Hugh de, 250–7, 261, 271
Sergi, 110
Sex and Marriage, 158, 159 n.
Sex in relation to Society, 155
Sexual impotence, 39, 180, 249
Sexual inversion (Edith's), 122, 136–9
Sexual Inversion, 140, 142, 143, 146–56, 157, 159–72, 174, 180
Sexual Life of our Time, 154
Seymour, Henry, 164
Shakespeare, William, 62, 124, 138, 153, 268
Shamrock Press, 223
Sharp, William, 164
Shaw, George Bernard, 87, 164
Shelley, Percy Bysshe, 46, 250, 254
Simcox, Edith J., 73–4, 113
Singer, J. Astor, 159–61
Singer, Mrs, 160
Sleep, 110
Smethwick, 80
Smith, Amy Barker, 141–4, 175, 198, 207, 229, 248
Smith, Dr Barker, 141, 219, 225
Socrates, 138, 153
Sonnets, with Folk Songs from the Spanish, 260
Soul of Spain, The, 180
Spain, 26, 175
Sparkes Creek, 63–76, 77, 82, 88, 116–7, 260
Speen, 207–10
Spencer, Herbert, 48
Spenser, Edmund, 46
Stanley-Jones, Dr, 216 n.
Stanwell, 192
Stead, W. T., 100
Stevens, Joseph, 43
Story of an African Farm, The, 88, 89, 91, 102
Strindberg, 111
Studies in the Psychology of Sex, 39, 101, 142, 153–5, 158, 161, 169, 171, 180, 190, 197, 227, 231, 239
Study of British Genius, 180
Subjection of Kezia, The, 181, 183, 223
Suicide (Edith's attempts), 207, 209, 216–7
Surrey, s.s., 47, 48
Swedenborg, Emanuel, 222
Sweeney, John, 163–4, 165, 166 171 n.
Swinburne, Algernon Charles, 46, 62, 107, 109
Symonds, John Addington, 107, 140, 146, 156, 160–1
Symons, Arthur, 107, 118–9, 130, 134, 138, 151
Synaesthesia, 151

Taine, 62
Tangier, 175
Task of Social Hygiene, The, 35, 180
Taylor, Ellen, 119–21
Tennyson, Alfred, 44

Thackeray, W. M., 108
Thesma, Madame, 124
Three Modern Seers, 223, 234, 237
To-day, 81
Tolstoy, Leo, 111
Trobriand islanders, 115
Tuke, Dr Hack, 157–9, 163
Tyndall, 124

Ulrichs, K. H., 146, 151, 157
Undine, 103 n.
Undinism, 20, 24, 55
Urnings, 146
Urolagnia, 21, 24, 39, 128, 138

Vere, Edward de, 108
Verlaine, Paul, 119, 151
Victoria, Queen, 108
Villiers, Dr Roland de, 159–64, 169–72
Vizetelly, Henry, 107–10, 159

"W" (Lily's friend), 184, 190, 219
Walter Scott Publishing Co., 106, 110, 159
Watford University Press, 161, 162, 167, 169
Weissenfeld, George Ferdinand Springmühl von, *see* Villiers Dr Roland de
Weldon, Maude, 97
Well of Loneliness, The, 263–6
Wells, Sir Spencer, 165
West, Algernon (Edith's solicitor), 122, 220, 221
Westcliff-on-Sea, 246–7
Westminster Review, 89, 107
"What is Pureness?", 81
What Woman Owes to Havelock Ellis, 252
White, Henry Kirke, 54–5
Whitman, Walt, 111, 138
Wide, Wide World, The, 42
Wilde, Oscar, 96, 156, 157, 237
Winckelmann, 152
Wirksworth, Derbyshire, 94
Wivelsfield Green, Sussex, 262, 272
Woburn, Beds., 94
Wolfenden Committee, 146
"Women,The Changing Status of," 107
Woodpecker Farm, 182–7, 262
Wordsworth, William, 44, 108
World of Dreams, The, 180
Wycherley, William, 108

Yeats, W. B., 96
Yvonne, 209, 210, 216–7, 224

Zola, 107, 109, 110